BEARING FALSE WITNESS

Bearing False Witness

DEBUNKING
CENTURIES OF
ANTI-CATHOLIC
HISTORY

Rodney Stark

TEMPLETON PRESS

Templeton Press
300 Conshohocken State Road, Suite 500
West Conshohocken, PA 19428
www.templetonpress.org

Designed and typeset by Gopa & Ted2, Inc.

Library of Congress Cataloging-in-Publication Data

Names: Stark, Rodney, author.
Title: Bearing false witness : debunking centuries of anti-Catholic history /
    Rodney Stark.
Description: West Conshohocken, PA : Templeton Press, 2016. | Includes
    bibliographical references and index.
Identifiers: LCCN 2016008676 | ISBN 9781599474991 (hardback)
Subjects: LCSH: Catholic Church--Apologetic works. | Catholic
    Church--Controversial literature--History and criticism. | Catholic
    Church--Doctrines. | Church history. | BISAC: RELIGION / Christianity /
    Catholic. | RELIGION / Biblical Studies / History & Culture. | RELIGION
    / Christianity / History.
Classification: LCC BX1752 .S76 2016 | DDC 282.09--dc23 LC record available
    at http://lccn.loc.gov/2016008676

Printed in the United States of America

16 17 18 19 20   10 9 8 7 6 5 4 3 2 1

Contents

The myth of Catholic barbarity: This 1598 engraving, published in Holland, shows a Spanish don feeding Indian children to his dogs. It was typical of the anti-Spanish, anti-Catholic propaganda of the time.

Confronting Distinguished Bigots

W HILE GROWING UP as an American Protestant with intellectual pretensions, I always wondered why Catholics made such a fuss over Columbus Day. Didn't they see the irony in the fact that although Columbus was a Catholic, his voyage of discovery was accomplished against unyielding opposition from Roman Catholic prelates who cited biblical proof that the earth was flat and that any attempt to reach Asia by sailing West would result in the ships falling off the edge of the world?

Everybody knew that about the Catholics and Columbus. We not only learned it in school, the story of Columbus proving the world to be round also was told in movies, Broadway plays,[1] and even in popular songs.[2] Yet, there they were every October 12: throngs of Knights of Columbus members accompanied by priests, marching in celebration of the arrival of the "Great Navigator" in the New World. How absurd.

And how astonishing to discover many years later that the whole story about why Catholic advisors opposed Columbus was a lie.[3]

By the fifteenth century (and for many centuries before) every educated European, including Roman Catholic prelates, knew the earth was round. The opposition Columbus encountered was not about the shape of the earth, but about the fact that he was wildly wrong about the circumference of the globe. He estimated it was about 2,800 miles from the Canary Islands to Japan. In reality it is about 14,000 miles. His clerical opponents knew about how far it really was and opposed his voyage on grounds that Columbus and his men would all die at sea. Had the Western Hemisphere not been there, and no one knew it existed, the *Niña, Pinta,* and *Santa Maria* might as well have fallen off the earth, for everyone aboard would have died of thirst and starvation.

Amazingly enough, there was no hint about Columbus having to prove that the earth was round in his own journal or in his son's book, *History of the Admiral.* The story was unknown until more than three hundred years later when it appeared in a biography of Columbus published in 1828. The author, Washington Irving (1783–1859), best known for his fiction—in *The Legend of Sleepy Hollow* he introduced the Headless Horseman.[4] Although the tale about Columbus and the flat earth was equally fictional, Irving presented it as fact. Almost at once the story was eagerly embraced by historians who were so certain of the wickedness and stupidity of the Roman Catholic Church that they felt no need to seek any additional confirmation, although some of them must have realized that the story had appeared out of nowhere. Anyway, that's how the tradition that Columbus proved the world was round got into all the textbooks.

By Washington Irving's day, this was a well-worn pattern, as many vicious distortions and lies had entered the historical canon with the seal of distinguished scholarly approval, so long as they reflected badly on the Catholic Church (keep in mind that Catholics were refused admission to Oxford and Cambridge until 1871, and some American colleges did not admit them in those days either). Unfortunately, unlike the Columbus story, many of these equally spurious anti-Catholic accusations remain an accepted part of the Western historical heritage. Indeed, a survey of Austrian and German textbooks conducted in 2009 found that the falsehood about Columbus and the flat earth was still being taught in those nations![5]

It all began with the European wars stemming from the Reformation that pitted Protestants versus Catholics and took millions of lives, during which Spain emerged as the major Catholic power. In response, Britain and Holland fostered intense propaganda campaigns that depicted the Spanish as bloodthirsty and fanatical barbarians. The distinguished medieval historian Jeffrey Burton Russell explained, "Innumerable books and pamphlets poured from northern presses accusing the Spanish Empire of inhuman depravity and horrible atrocities. . . . Spain was cast as a place of darkness, ignorance, and evil."[6] Informed modern scholars not only reject this malicious image, they even have given it a name: the "Black Legend."[7] Nevertheless, this impression of Spain and of Spanish Catholics remains very much alive in our culture—mere mention of the "Spanish Inquisition" evokes disgust and outrage.

But it wasn't only angry Protestants who invented and embraced these tales. Many of the falsehoods considered in subsequent chapters were sponsored by antireligious writers, especially during the so-called Enlightenment, whose work was condoned only because it was seen as anti-Catholic rather than as what it truly was—although more recently such scholars have paraded their irreligion as well as their contempt for Catholicism.[8] In his day, however, Edward Gibbon (1737–94) would surely have been in deep trouble had the bitterly antireligious views he expressed in *The History of the Decline and Fall of the Roman Empire* not been incorrectly seen as applying only to Roman Catholicism. But, because in the days of the Roman Empire Catholicism was the only Christian church, Gibbon's readers assumed his attacks were specific to Catholicism and not aimed at religion in general.

Although Gibbon was one of the very first "distinguished bigots," he is in excellent company—the list of celebrated, anti-Catholic scholars (some of them still living) is long indeed. We will meet scores of them in subsequent chapters, some of them many times. Worse yet, in recent years some of the most malignant contributions to anti-Catholic history have been made by alienated Catholics, many of whom are seminary dropouts, former priests, or ex-nuns, such as John Cornwell, James Carroll, and Karen Armstrong. Normally, attacks originating with defectors from a particular group are treated with some circumspection. But, attacks on the Church made by "lapsed" Catholics are widely regarded as thereby of special reliability!

In any event, should you doubt that your knowledge of Western history is distorted by the work of these distinguished bigots, consider whether you believe any of the following statements:

- The Catholic Church motivated and actively participated in nearly two millennia of anti-Semitic violence, justifying it on grounds that the Jews were responsible for the Crucifixion, until the Vatican II Council was shamed into retracting that doctrine in 1965. But, the Church still has not made amends for the fact that Pope Pius XII is rightfully known as "Hitler's Pope."

- Only recently have we become aware of remarkably enlightened Christian gospels, long ago suppressed by narrow-minded Catholic prelates.

- Once in power as the official church of Rome, Christians quickly and brutally persecuted paganism out of existence.

- The fall of Rome and the ascendancy of the Church precipitated Europe's decline into a millennium of ignorance and backwardness. These Dark Ages lasted until the Renaissance/Enlightenment, when secular scholars burst through the centuries of Catholic barriers against reason.

- Initiated by the pope, the Crusades were but the first bloody chapter in the history of unprovoked and brutal European colonialism.

- The Spanish Inquisition tortured and murdered huge numbers of innocent people for "imaginary" crimes, such as witchcraft and blasphemy.

- The Catholic Church feared and persecuted scientists, as the case of Galileo makes clear. Therefore, the Scientific "Revolution" occurred mainly in Protestant societies because only there could the Catholic Church not suppress independent thought.

► Being entirely comfortable with slavery, the Catholic Church did nothing to oppose its introduction in the New World nor to make it more humane.

► Until very recently, the Catholic view of the ideal state was summed up in the phrase, "The divine right of kings." Consequently, the Church has bitterly resisted all efforts to establish more liberal governments, eagerly supporting dictators.

► It was the Protestant Reformation that broke the repressive Catholic grip on progress and ushered in capitalism, religious freedom, and the modern world.

Each of these statements is part of the common culture, widely accepted and frequently repeated. But, each is false and many are the exact opposite of the truth! A chapter will be devoted to summarizing recent repetitions of each of these statements and to demonstrating that each is most certainly false.

It seems pertinent to point out that I did not set out to write this book from scratch. Rather, in the course of writing several other books on medieval history[9] as well as on early Christianity,[10] I kept encountering serious distortions rooted in obvious anti-Catholicism—the authors often explicitly expressed their hatred of the Church. Having written asides in these earlier books on many of the examples listed above, I finally decided that the issue of distinguished anti-Catholic history is too important and its consequences too pervasive to be left to these scattered refutations. So I gathered, revised, and substantially extended my previous discussions while adding new ones. In doing so, I have not attempted to "whitewash" Church history. In these same earlier books, I wrote at some length on such matters as corrupt clergy, brutal attacks on "heretics," and on more recent misdeeds and shortcomings of the Church, such as covering up for pedophile priests and the misguided advocacy of liberation theology. But no matter how much importance one places on these negative aspects of Church history, it does not justify the extreme exaggerations, false accusations, and patent frauds addressed in the chapters that follow. Faced with this enormous literature of lies, I have heeded the words of Columbia University's Garrett Mattingly (1900–62), "Nor does it matter at all to the dead whether they receive justice at the hands of succeeding generations. But to the living, to do justice, however belatedly, should matter."[11]

You may be wondering, if these are notorious falsehoods, why do they persist? In part because they are so mutually reinforcing and deeply embedded in our common culture that it seems impossible for them not to be true. One easily assumes that in our "enlightened" times, surely these claims would have been rejected long ago if they were false. I confess that when I first encountered the claim that not only did the Spanish Inquisition spill very little blood but that it mainly was a major force in support of moderation and justice, I dismissed it as another exercise in outlandish, attention-seeking revisionism. Upon further investigation, I was stunned to discover that in fact, among other things, it was the Inquisition that prevented the murderous witchcraft craze, which flourished in most of Europe during the sixteenth and seventeenth centuries, from spreading to Spain and Italy. Instead of burning witches, the inquisitors sent a few people to be hanged because they had burned witches.

Be assured that you will not be asked to take my word on these refutations. Sometimes I have done basic research needed to overturn one of these spurious anti-Catholic claims, and in those cases I document my findings so fully that anyone can check them. But, in most instances, I am simply reporting the prevailing view among qualified experts. Unfortunately, even though they often grumble because a particular anti-Catholic fabrication lives on, most of these experts continue to write only for one another and do not undertake to share their knowledge with the general reading public—the Columbus myth remained in the textbooks and popular culture for decades after scholars had traced it back to its fraudulent origins.[12] I have undertaken to make the work of these fine scholars widely available, taking care to cite and fully acknowledge their work—short biographies of major contributors will be presented in each chapter.

Finally, I am not a Roman Catholic, and I did not write this book in defense of the Church. I wrote it in defense of history.

The myth of the Church as condoning anti-Semitic violence: Found throughout the Internet, this image is almost always identified as a photograph of Pope Pius XII greeting Adolf Hitler—despite the fact that the Catholic prelate shown here is lacking the pope's very distinctive nose. It is, in fact, a photograph of Archbishop Cesare Orsenigo, the Vatican's ambassador to Germany.

Sins of Anti-Semitism 1

"FOR CENTURIES, persecution of the Jews was justified in the name of God. The inspiration for the medieval ghettos and for the bloody pogroms of history was provided by the doctrine that the Jews had murdered Christ and thereby provoked God's eternal wrath and punishment."[1]

That is the first paragraph of a book I published many years ago. It seems appropriate to begin this chapter by explaining how I came to write it.

During my first year of graduate school at Berkeley, I was recruited by the director of the Survey Research Center to work on a major research project devoted to studying anti-Semitism, funded by the Anti-Defamation League of B'nai B'rith. I was soon assigned to that portion of the research devoted to the effects of Christian teachings on negative beliefs and feelings about Jews. Although I had not yet even earned my master's degree, I soon took primary responsibility for designing and executing major public opinion surveys devoted to this topic, analyzing the results, and writing the book *Christian Beliefs and Anti-Semitism*.

Not surprisingly, the data showed that there was a significant link between belief and prejudice—those American Christians who blamed "the Jews" for the Crucifixion were also more likely to accept standard anti-Semitic stereotypes of the Jews as avaricious, cheap, clannish, unethical, and unpatriotic. Consequently, before I had completed a draft of the book, I was asked to prepare a brief summary of the findings to be distributed to the bishops attending Vatican II—the remarkable

Ecumenical Council convened by Pope John XXIII in 1962. According to Cardinal Augustin Bea, as quoted in the *New York Times*,[2] that summary of mine played a significant role in producing the council's statement on the Jews (*Nostra Aetate*), which read:

> True, the Jewish authorities and those who followed their lead pressed for the death of Christ; still, what happened in His passion cannot be charged against all the Jews, without distinction, then alive, nor against the Jews of today. Although the Church is the new people of God, the Jews should not be presented as rejected or accursed by God, as if this followed from the Holy Scriptures. All should see to it, then, that in catechetical work or in the preaching of the word of God they do not teach anything that does not conform to the truth of the Gospel and the spirit of Christ. Furthermore, in her rejection of every persecution against any man, the Church, mindful of the patrimony she shares with the Jews and moved not by political reasons but by the Gospel's spiritual love, decries hatred, persecutions, displays of anti-Semitism, directed against Jews at any time and by anyone.

I was very pleased that the council had acted, and was proud to have played any part in bringing it about. However, at that time I was far too unsophisticated to appreciate the many subtleties in the council's text, and I lacked sufficient historical background to realize that there really wasn't anything new here—that the Church never had taught that the Jews were outside God's love. And it was many years before I became aware of the extent to which the Catholic Church has stood as a consistent barrier against anti-Semitic violence, albeit Christians who attacked the Jews often justified their actions on religious grounds. My awareness of these matters grew as I worked on different aspects of ancient and medieval history—in one instance writing a long analysis of all known outbursts of anti-Semitic violence in both Europe and Islam, spanning the period 500 through 1600.[3] Eventually, this work forced me to reconsider the entire link between Christianity and anti-Semitism.

Keep in mind that through the many centuries there have been a huge number of Roman Catholic clergy—some of them saints, some of them opportunists, some of them devout, some of them corrupt, many of them ignorant, a few of them atheists, and even an occasional howling lunatic. Not surprisingly, some of these clergy did believe that God hated all the Jews, and even a few may have gotten involved in outbursts of anti-Semitic violence. But, as will be seen, such views and actions did not have official standing and did not reflect the normal behavior of Catholic clergy toward Jews. To the contrary, the clergy often defended local Jews from attacks, sometimes risking their own lives by doing so.

Inventing Anti-Semitism

Let's begin at the start: many contemporary scholars charge that the Church originated anti-Semitism.[4] The celebrated feminist theologian Rosemary Ruether has even claimed that "the church must bear a substantial responsibility for a tragic history of the Jew in Christendom which was the foundation upon which political anti-Semitism and the Nazi use of it was erected."[5] Jules Isaac struck the same chord: "without centuries of Christian catechism, propaganda, and vituperation, the Hilterian teachings, propaganda, and vituperation would not have been possible."[6] And, according to Robert T. Osborn, "Christians have been anti-Jewish and anti-Semitic, apparently from the beginning."[7]

These charges are based on passages in the New Testament that attack the Jews for rejecting Christ and for persecuting Christians, although all of the scholars who believe that the Christians invented anti-Semitism know that deep hostility toward Jews existed long before the birth of Jesus. Perhaps because of their antagonism toward the early Church, scholars dismissed what the ancients sometimes felt toward the Jews as merely "antipathy."[8] It did not amount to anything lasting and basic, such as what might be called anti-Semitism, but was momentary, arising entirely from political conflicts such as the Maccabean Revolt. In fact, these negative feelings toward Jews were only "sporadic," mere "isolated pockets of distemper."[9] In contrast, they claimed real anti-Semitism was deep and abiding, something entirely new introduced by Christianity and born of Christian arrogance and ambition. If this were so, then many leading Roman intellectuals must have been secret Christians!

It was the great Roman philosopher and statesman Lucius Annaeus Seneca (4 BCE–65 CE) who denounced Jews as an "accursed race"[10] and condemned their influence. It was Marcus Tullius Cicero (106–43 BCE), regarded as the greatest Roman orator, who complained that Jewish rites and observances were "at variance with the glory of our empire, [and] the dignity of our name."[11] It was the esteemed Roman historian Cornelius Tacitus (56–117 CE) who railed against the Jews because they "despise the gods" and called their religious practices "sinister and revolting." Not only that, according to Tacitus, the Jews had "entrenched themselves by their very wickedness" and they sought "increasing wealth" through "their stubborn loyalty" to one another. He remarked: "But the rest of the world they confront with hatred reserved for enemies."[12] I am unable to detect how Tacitus's complaints differ from standard modern anti-Semitism as it usually is defined and measured.

Nor was it only a matter of words. The Jews were expelled from Rome in 139 BCE by an edict that charged them with attempting "to introduce their own rites" to the Romans and thereby "to infect Roman morals."[13] Then, in 19 CE, Emperor Tiberius ordered the Jews in Rome to burn all their religious vestments and assigned all Jewish males of military age to serve in Sardinia to suppress brigandage, where, according to Tacitus, "if they succumbed to the pestilential climate, it was a cheap loss."[14] In addition, all other Jews were banished not only from the city, but from Italy "on pain of slavery for life if they did not obey," as told by Paulinus Suetonius (c. 71–135 CE).[15] In 70 CE, Emperor Vespasian imposed a special tax on all Jews in the empire, thereby impounding their contributions that had been made annually to the temple in Jerusalem. And in 95 CE, Emperor Domitian executed his cousin Flavius Clemens and "many others" for having "drifted into Jewish ways," as Cassius Dio (163–229 CE) put it.[16]

Even so, the Romans did not invent anti-Semitism. There are several surviving versions of an account of an expulsion of lepers and undesirable foreigners from Egypt that parallel the Exodus. These accounts have been interpreted by some scholars as the first appearance of anti-Semitism. There also are quite hostile treatments of the Jews as godless misanthropes, written in the first century BCE by Greeks, including Didorus Siculus (c. 90 BCE–30 BCE), Strabo (c. 63 BCE–24 CE), and Apion (20 BCE–45 CE), who even accused the Jews of ritual cannibalism.[17]

Clearly, then, anti-Semitism did not arise from the conflict between Christians and Jews as to the divinity of Jesus. Rather, it stemmed from the intense commitment that exclusive religions invariably generate among their adherents and the hostile responses this commitment provokes among outsiders. As the distinguished E. Mary Smallwood put it, Jewish "[e]xclusiveness bred unpopularity, which in turn bred anti-Semitism,"[18] just as Christian exclusiveness subsequently bred Roman antagonism toward them too. In fact, not only were Jews and Christians persecuted by Rome, but so were some exclusive pagan faiths, including congregations devoted to Isis and to Cybele (Magna Mater).[19]

With the demise of these pagan faiths and the rise of Christianity, anti-Semitism was the only one of these ancient prejudices to survive. But unless one believes that the Church was the only channel of cultural transmission, there is no reason to suppose this legacy of pre-Christian anti-Semitism did not live on in Western Civilization—probably often linked to definitions of Jews as religious outsiders, but not dependent on that linkage. That is, antagonism toward Jews probably had a life of its own, rooted in classical times and sensitive to continuing Jewish exclusiveness. For example, the New Testament does not portray Jews as wealthy misers, but this image was as central to the medieval hatred of Jews as it was to Tacitus and his fellow Romans. In addition, of course, is the anti-Semitism inherent in the theological conflict between the two faiths.

Early Religious Conflict

There are a number of harsh, fearful, and hostile references to Jews scattered throughout the New Testament. One of the most incendiary and most frequently cited of these is the passage in Matthew 27:24–26: "So when Pilate saw that he could do nothing, but rather that a riot was beginning, he took water and washed his hands before the crowd, saying, 'I am innocent of this man's blood; see to it yourselves.' Then the people as a whole answered, 'His blood be on us and on our children.' So he released Barabbas for them; and after flogging Jesus, he handed him over to be crucified."[20]

Other examples include:

- ▸ Matthew 23:37: "Jerusalem, Jerusalem, the city that kills the prophets and stones those who are sent to it."
- ▸ John 5:16–18: "Therefore the Jews started persecuting Jesus, because he was doing such things [curing a sick man] on the sabbath. But Jesus answered them, 'My father is still working, and I also am working.' For this reason the Jews were seeking all the more to kill him, because he was not only breaking the sabbath, but was also calling God his own Father."

Understandably, passages such as these have caused many modern Christians a great deal of anguish as well as provoked bitterness among many Jews. Unfortunately, in condemning these and similar New Testament passages, Christian apologists and Jewish critics far too often interpret them out of context and in wholly noncomparative ways. As for context, these lines were written by men who still regarded themselves as Jews, albeit of a more enlightened kind, and were addressed to Jews who had failed, or who refused, to recognize "progress." Thus, harsh Christian critics, such as J. T. Sanders,[21] should not focus entirely on the New Testament but also should compare its statements about the Jews with Old Testament polemics against other Jews who failed to meet a particular prophet's standards of proper faith. For example, Jeremiah (18:23) asked the Lord: "Do not forgive their iniquity, do not blot out their sin from your sight. Let them be tripped up before you: deal with them while you are angry." Then, warming to his theme, Jeremiah (19:7–9) quoted the Lord's response: "And in this place I will make void the plans of Judah and Jerusalem, and will make them fall by the sword before their enemies, and by the hand of those who seek their life. I will give their dead bodies for food to the birds of the air and to the wild animals of the earth. . . . And I will make them eat the flesh of their sons and the flesh of their daughters."

Dozens of similar verses can be found in the Old Testament and provide a context within which the New Testament polemics can be seen as typical of "in-house prophetic criticism."[22]

In similar fashion, much anguish about anti-Jewish statements in the New Testament arises because they are anachronistically taken to be the statements of a nasty and abusive Christian majority. No account is taken of the fact that when these passages were written, Christians were a tiny, persecuted minority, not only amid the huge Greco-Roman empire, but vis-à-vis the large populations of Jews, including those in Palestine and those making up the many substantial diasporan communities of Jews scattered in the various larger Greco-Roman cities. For it was within these Jewish communities that the early Christians concentrated their efforts to convert.[23] As late as the year 100 CE, by which time the Gospels already were in circulation, there probably were slightly fewer than 8,000 Christians on earth, and even a century later, there still were only about 200,000 Christians.[24] In contrast, there were about 7 million Jews—only a million of them in Palestine.[25] In early days, it was not the Romans, but the surrounding Jewish populations who were the most serious source of danger to Christians.

The evidence of Jewish persecution of Christians is scattered and obviously very incomplete, but there are compelling reasons to believe that persecution was common and that it continued for several centuries.[26] For one thing, Christianity was an intolerable abomination in the eyes of observant Jews. Unlike pagans whose sins could be dismissed as those of ignorant outsiders, Christian disregard of the Law was a lapse by those, many of whom had been raised as Jews, who claimed to be the rightful heirs to the entire Jewish tradition. Worse yet, the Christians were asserting an outrageous heresy, not only by claiming that Jesus was the promised messiah, but by proclaiming him the Son of God, they seemed to dispense with monotheism.[27] In the eyes of religious Jews, these were terrible offenses that required violent responses.[28]

As for evidence of actual Jewish attempts to punish these crimes, we do know that in Acts 22:4–5 Paul confessed that prior to his conversion in about the year 35 CE, he delivered Christians to the "high priest and council of elders" for punishment, and Acts reports several instances during which "apostles" were flogged. The deacon Stephen was stoned to death by order of the Sanhedrin in about the year 37 CE. Then, after Paul had shifted his mission efforts to the West, he received a number of beatings and an unsuccessful stoning by local Jewish leaders in various cities. Next, according to the great Jewish historian Josephus (37–101 CE), and confirmed by Christian historian Eusebius (263–339 CE), James, the brother of Jesus and head of the church, was publicly mocked and executed by Jewish leaders in Jerusalem in 61 or 62 CE. The Jewish threat was real.

Consequently, a number of scholars have pointed out that the anti-Jewish passages found in the New Testament should be interpreted as only *one* side of a very angry religious conflict. But what has been missing is firm evidence of the *other* side, of contemptuous anti-Christian expressions in Jewish sources, such as the Talmud, the collection of writings by learned rabbis that began in the first century. Some viciously anti-Christian passages alleged to come from the Talmud were published by a Spanish Dominican friar in the thirteenth century (said to have been leaked to him by Jewish converts to Christianity) and were later quoted by Martin Luther.[29] A similar two-volume work was published in Germany in 1700. Both publications attracted attention from anti-Semites who cited them in angry pamphlets, but their authenticity was disavowed by both Jews and Christians—complaints by the Jewish community in Frankfurt caused the German volumes to be confiscated by the government.[30] Thus, it has long been the general scholarly belief that there were no authentic references to Jesus in the Talmud,[31] and that aside from several isolated incidents, there was no significant Jewish persecution of Christians.[32] Hence, James Everett Seaver confidently reported that Jewish hatred of the early Christians "has no existence in historical fact."[33]

This view has now been completely refuted by Peter Schäfer's superb study. Having impeccable credentials as director of Judaic Studies at Princeton, Schäfer worked with both the Jerusalem and Babylonian Talmuds—the former having been written by rabbis in the first and second centuries while the latter probably dating from the third through sixth centuries. Scattered through these enormous compendia, there are in fact many remarks about Jesus. As Schäfer characterized them:

> They are counternarratives that parody the New Testament stories, most notably the story of Jesus' birth and death. They ridicule Jesus' birth from a virgin. . . . Most remarkably, they counter the New Testament Passion story with its message of Jews' guilt and shame as Christ killers. Instead, they reverse it completely: Yes, they maintain, we accept responsibility for it, but there is no reason to feel ashamed because we rightfully executed a blasphemer and idolater. Jesus deserved death, and got what he deserved. Accordingly, they subvert the Christian idea of Jesus' resurrection by having him punished forever in hell and making clear that this fate awaits his followers as well, who believe in this impostor.[34]

Schäfer continued more specifically:

▶ Although she was married to Joseph, Mary conceived during an adulterous interlude with a Roman soldier named Pandera (the name perhaps being a play on the word *parthenos*, or virgin). According to Jewish Law, both should have been stoned to death.

▶ Jesus was a *mamzer* (a bastard) and would have thereby been excluded from any participation in Jewish religious life—in some interpretations of the Law, mamzers were themselves to be stoned.

- Jesus engaged in sexual promiscuity with Mary Magdalene among others.
- Jesus was convicted of sorcery.
- Jesus was not crucified, but instead was stoned by Jews who then hanged his body upon a tree.
- Jesus is spending eternity in hell, boiling in excrement.

So there we have it. New Testament antagonism toward the Jews is fully balanced by Talmudic antagonism toward the Christians—and keep in mind that most of this exchange took place when Christians were the tiny minority. Of course, when Christians became the overwhelming majority, their attitudes toward Jews became of far greater social significance than whatever anti-Christianism Jews sustained in that era. But misleading or misled historians to the contrary, the Church did not translate the antagonisms of the New Testament into a warrant for anti-Semitic attacks.

The Church and Anti-Semitic Attacks

In preparation for writing a book on the historical consequences of monotheism,[35] I undertook to assemble data on every fatal anti-Semitic attack by groups of western European Christians from the year 500 through 1600. I began with the year 500 because reported conflicts prior to that are very poorly documented and of dubious historicity. In any event, as I assembled reliably documented instances, I discovered something quite remarkable: there appears to have been only one such event between the years 500 and 1096—a mob killed several Jews at Clermont in Southern Gaul (now France) in 554 and forced a number of others to accept Christian baptism. That there were no other such incidents reflects the fact that the Church condemned this act, stressing that forced conversions were invalid and that Jews should be let alone,[36] a position that was asserted again and again by the Church through the centuries; the prohibition on forced baptism was even applied to Muslims during the Crusades.[37]

My inability to find any other attacks during this long period has been confirmed by distinguished Jewish historians. The Israeli historian Nachum T. Gidal referred to this era as the "Halcyon Days"[38] of Christian-Jewish relations, and the prize-winning scholar of Jewish history, Robert Chazan, described the period as "tranquil."[39] Léon Poliakov (1910–97), one of the most respected contemporary historians of anti-Semitism, wrote of the "favorable status of Jews" during this era: "Kings, nobles and bishops granted Jews a broad autonomy: thus they administered their own communities and lived according to their own laws. Talmudic scholarship flowered again on the banks of the Rhine and the Seine at the very period when it was falling into decay in Babylonia. . . . [The Jews] continued to mix freely with the Christian populations and to live on excellent terms with them. . . . Until the eleventh century, no chronicles mention outbursts of popular hatred of the Jews."[40] Thus, it was that for more than five centuries, hostile New Testament statements about Jews had no violent consequences.

A number of medieval historians have pointed out that during this same era the Church took virtually no interest in heresy. Not that there were no heretics, but that the Church chose to ignore them.[41] In my judgment, the two phenomena are linked—the tolerant policies toward both Jews and heretics were a function of the fact that neither posed any institutional threat to the Church. Stated more formally: where a relatively secure religious monopoly exists, a substantial amount of religious nonconformity will be tolerated to the extent that the dissenters are perceived as posing no threat to the power of the religious elite.[42] The Church felt secure and tranquility prevailed.

This era of toleration ended in the eleventh century because the conflict with Islam that boiled over into the Crusades changed perceptions of religious threats. Major religious conflicts will generate a general climate of religious intolerance, causing toleration to be withheld or withdrawn even from nonthreatening, but nonconforming, religious groups.[43] This need not even be the policy of the leaders of the monopoly Church—conflict may generate a climate of opinion that prompts members of the laity to action on behalf of perceived religious threats. This explains the eleventh-century explosion of fatal anti-Semitic outbursts in parts of Christendom as well as the initiation of bloody campaigns against heresy. It also is consistent with the fact that as serious conflict with Christianity broke out, similar anti-Semitic attacks and heresy-hunting began within Islam![44]

Catholic clergy initiated the violent repression of heresies that began in the eleventh century, many of which escalated into bloody campaigns, such as those against the Cathars (Albigensians). But the clergy did not initiate or lead the outbursts of anti-Semitism that began then too. These were led by laymen, and it was churchmen who stood up against them and usually managed to prevent further attacks.

Some historians believe that there were anti-Jewish attacks in the wake of the "People's Crusade,"[45] that "ramshackle horde"[46] of men, women, and children who followed Peter the Hermit all the way to Turkey in 1096, only to be massacred. Other historians report no such attacks.[47] It is agreed, however, that Peter's followers looted and extorted their way east and that both Christians and Jews were victimized.

However, it is well documented that more than five centuries of tranquility in Jewish-Christian relations ended on May 3, 1096, when a minor Rhineland count, Emich of Leisingen, led an attack on the Jewish population of Speyer (Spier).[48] Emich had been left in charge when his duke marched off to the Holy Land in the force raised by Henry IV, the holy Roman emperor, to fight the First Crusade. Emich was supposed to organize a company of reinforcements and then bring them east to join the campaign. Because a false rumor had been circulating that before he marched east Henry IV planned to murder all the Jews in the Rhineland to avenge the death of Christ, Henry had written to all his vassals denouncing this story and commanding them to see to the safety of all Jews. But Emich still believed that it made no sense to march off to fight

God's enemies in the East while leaving behind the enemies of Christ. So he led his men to Speyer.

However, the bishop of Speyer took the local Jews under his protection, and Emich's forces could only lay their hands on a dozen Jews who had somehow failed to heed the bishop's alarm. All twelve were killed. Then Emich led his forces to Worms. Here, too, the bishop took the local Jews into his palace for protection. But this time Emich would have none of that, and his forces broke down the bishop's gates and killed about five hundred Jews. The same pattern was repeated the following week in Mainz. Just as before, the bishop attempted to shield the Jews, but he was attacked and forced to flee for his life. The same actions occurred again in Cologne and then in Metz. As Léon Poliakov summed up: "It is important to note that almost everywhere . . . bishops attempted, sometimes even at the peril of their own lives, to protect the Jews."[49] At this point, a portion of Emich's forces broke away and set out to purge the Moselle Valley of Jews. Being careful only to attack towns *without a resident bishop*, they managed to kill several thousand Jews.

Meanwhile, two other leaders of reinforcements also attacked Jews. Volkmar overwhelmed the opposition of the local bishop and massacred Jews in Prague. Gottschalk led a murderous attack on the Jews of Ratisbon (Regensberg). The pope "harshly condemned" all these attacks, "but there was little more he could do."[50] However, it turned out that there was a lot that the knights of Hungary could do. When Volkmar and his forces reached Hungary and attempted to continue their attacks on Jews, they were wiped out by Hungarian knights who rode in support of their bishop. The same fate befell Gottschalk. And when Emich and his forces reached Hungary, they too were denied passage because of their bloody attacks on Jews. When they tried to force their way through, they also were dispatched by Hungarian knights.

According to the revered historian of the Crusades Sir Steven Runciman (1903–2000), these defeats struck "most good Christians" as "punishments meted out from on high to the murderers of Jews."[51] This was consistent with the efforts of local bishops to preserve the Jews and with the fact that other armies gathered for the First Crusade did not molest Jews—with the exception of several hundred Jews who died in Jerusalem when the entire city was massacred subsequent to its fall to Crusaders.

Unfortunately, while the attacks on the Rhineland Jews were the work of a few, they set a pattern by directing attention to the issue of continuing to permit Jews to reject Jesus in a context where religious conformity was of growing concern. Even a few churchmen succumbed to this temptation. By the time of the Second Crusade (1146–49), Abbé Pierre of the French monastery at Cluny pointed out, "What good is the good of going to the end of the world at great loss of men and money, to fight Saracens, when we permit among us other infidels who are a thousand times more guilty toward Christ than are the Mohammedans?"[52]

Nevertheless, it was not in France, but only in the Rhine Valley that massacres of Jews took place during the Second Crusade—once again in Cologne, Mainz, Metz, Worms, and Speyer.[53] In this instance, a monk named Radulph helped stir up the anti-Semitic outbursts. But the death toll would have been far higher had it not been for Saint Bernard of Clairvaux, who rode to the Rhine Valley and ordered an end to the killings. This intervention was reported by Ephraim of Bonn, a Jewish chronicler:

> Then the Lord heard our sigh. . . . He sent after the evil priest a decent priest, a great man. . . . His name was Abbot Bernard, from the city of Clairvaux . . . [who] said to them "It is fitting that you go forth against Muslims. However, anyone who attacks a Jew and tries to kill him is as though he attacks Jesus himself. My pupil Radulph who advised destroying them did not advise properly. For in the book of Psalms is written concerning the Jews, "Kill them not, lest my people forget." Everyone esteemed this priest as one of their saints. . . . Were it not for the mercies of our Creator Who sent the aforesaid abbot

. . . there would not have been a remnant or survivor among the Jews.[54]

Soon the Crusades petered out, but the outbursts of violence against the Jews continued in the Rhineland. The earlier incidents had penetrated deeply into the popular culture; additionally, this was an area markedly lacking in political authority. Instead, it was a "politically fractured area"[55] where a variety of heretical movements arose and prospered because neither Church nor government could suppress them, and it was here that mobs continued to attack Jews. Thus, in 1270, local rabble-rousers who claimed to be descendants of the *Judenbreter* (Jews-roasters) of the Crusade era, killed Jews all along the Rhine. Similar attacks occurred again in 1283, 1285, 1286, and 1298.[56]

When the Black Death (1347–50) broke out in Europe, it was once again only in the Rhine Valley that the Church was unable to protect the Jews against charges that they had brought on the plague by secretly poisoning the wells. This story began in Spain, where initially it was claimed to have been Muslims who poisoned the wells. Then the story changed, and the Spanish Jews were accused of spreading the plague and so that is where the initial anti-Semitic attacks began. But they were quickly stopped cold by the local bishops, armed with a bull issued by Pope Clement IV, who directed the clergy to protect the Jews, denounced all claims about poisoned wells, and ordered that those who spread that rumor, as well as anyone who harmed Jews, be excommunicated.[57]

But even papal authority failed in the Rhineland. So, once again, a wave of Jewish massacres swept along the Rhine, through the familiar list of cities: Speyer, Mainz, Metz, Worms, and Cologne. Why did rabid anti-Semitism persist only here and not in other German areas? As noted, probably because elsewhere local elites were sufficiently powerful to have prevented a tradition of Jew-killing from getting started. As to why lethal attacks on local Jews ceased in the Rhineland early in the fifteenth century, there were no Jews there anymore. First came a massive migration of Jews from the Rhine Valley to Eastern Europe.

At the same time, many of these notoriously anti-Semitic communities evicted their Jews—Cologne did so in 1424 and most of the rest soon after. No Jews were permitted to reside in these areas again until the middle of the nineteenth century! The eviction of the Rhineland Jews was not the doing of the Church as is evident in the fact that large Jewish communities remained scattered across the rest of Germany. Keep in mind, too, that when Jews were expelled elsewhere, as from England (1290), France (1306), and Spain (1492), this was done as the work of secular authorities, not at the urging of the Church.

But if the Church stood as a barrier to attacks on the Jews of Europe, it did collaborate in many forms of discrimination against them. In most places, the construction of synagogues required permission, there were disputes as to when Passover could be celebrated, and conversion from Christianity to Judaism was strictly forbidden. Many prohibitions were placed on social contacts between Christians and Jews: intermarriage was illegal and so were sexual relations, and Jews could not have Christian servants. Eventually, in most parts of Europe, Jews were required to wear a badge or some other identifying mark. Often, too, Jews were required to live in a special part of town, which came to be known as the ghetto (a corruption of the Italian *borghetto*, or "little borough").

Muslims and Jews

For generations, historians have identified the situation of the Jews in Muslim Spain as a "Golden Age," in contrast with the brutal anti-Semitism of Christendom.[58] No one disagreed with Stanley Lane-Poole when in 1897 he claimed that "the history of Spain offers us a melancholy contrast. For nearly eight centuries under her Mohammedan rulers, Spain set all Europe a shining example of a civilised and enlightened state. . . . Whatever makes a kingdom great and prosperous, whatsoever tends to refinement and civilization was found in Moslem Spain."[59]

He went on to contrast this shining example with the cruel and fanatical Spain that expelled the Jews following the final defeat of the Moors by Ferdinand and Isabella in 1492.

Nor did anyone challenge the celebrated Jewish historian Heinrich Hirsh Graetz when he asserted, "Judaism ever strove towards the light, whilst monastic Christianity remained in darkness. Thus in the tenth century there was only one country that offered suitable soil for the development of Judaism, where it could blossom and flourish—it was Mahometan Spain."[60] And most intellectuals nodded in agreement when Albert Einstein's son-in-law Rudolf Kayer exulted, "It is like a historical miracle that in the very same era of history" in which "orgies of persecution" against Jews occurred in Christina Europe, the Jews of Moorish Spain "enjoyed a golden age, the like of which they had not known since the days of the Bible."[61] Not to be outdone, Anthony Burgess wrote that after the fall of Granada, "The magnificent Emirate of Córdoba, where beauty, tolerance, learning and order prevailed, was only a memory."[62] Indeed, in a volume commemorating the five hundredth anniversary of the expulsion of the Jews from Christian Spain, it was noted that the "Golden Age of Spanish Jewry . . . was personified above all by Maimonides."[63]

It is difficult to know how anyone, even the most bitter anti-Catholic, could truly have believed any of this! By itself, the biography of Moses Maimonides (1135–1204) makes a travesty of all these claims. In 1148, the Maimonides family pretended to convert to Islam when the Jews of Córdoba were told to become Muslims or leave, upon pain of death. Note that when most historians mention that in 1492 Ferdinand and Isabella ordered the Jews of Spain to convert to Christianity or leave, they forget to mention that the Muslims had imposed the same demand in the twelfth century. Nor do they mention that many Jews who opted to leave Moorish Spain rather than pretend to convert settled in the Christian areas of northern Spain. In any event, after eleven years of posing as converts, the Maimonides family became so fearful of discovery that they fled to Morocco where they continued their deception. Thus, throughout his adult life, the most celebrated medieval Jewish thinker posed as a Muslim.[64] His story clearly reveals that, as Richard Fletcher has put it so well, "Moorish Spain was not a tolerant and enlightened society even in its most cultivated epoch."[65]

In fact, just as Jews lived as a suppressed minority in Christendom, even during the "tranquil" period both Jews and Christians were always placed under severe restrictions and were highly stigmatized in Muslim societies. As the remarkable historian of Islam Marshall G. S. Hodgson (1922–68) pointed out, from very early times Muslim authorities often went to great lengths to humiliate and punish *dhimmis*—those being Jews and Christians who refused to convert to Islam. It was official policy that *dhimmis* should "feel inferior and to know 'their place' . . . [imposing laws such as] that Christians and Jews should not ride horses, for instance, but at most mules, or even that they should wear certain marks of their religion on their costume when among Muslims."[66] In some places, non-Muslims were prohibited from wearing clothing similar to that of Muslims, nor could they be armed.[67] In addition, non-Muslims were invariably severely taxed compared with Muslims.[68]

That Christians imposed equally disgraceful humiliations upon Jews is beside the point, which is that the claim about Islam's greater tolerance is an absurd fiction. Historians have managed to get away with such spurious nonsense not only by carefully ignoring *dhimmitude*, but also by twisting the fact that in both Christian and Muslim areas there was a long tranquil period in relations with Jews and by choosing to compare the tranquil era in Islam with the later era of anti-Semitic violence in Christendom. But just as Christian intolerance was greatly heightened by the conflicts with Islam involving the Crusades, so, too, did these conflicts result in similar outbursts in Islam. In Grenada alone, thousands of Jews were massacred late in the eleventh century,[69] a fact that goes unmentioned in the many historical accounts of "glorious" Grenada. In similar fashion, Western biographers of Muhammad have been reluctant to acknowledge (or quick to justify) that the first Muslim massacre of Jews occurred in Medina when Muhammad had all the local adult Jewish males (about seven hundred of them) beheaded after forcing them to dig their own graves.[70]

The Eleventh Commandment

When all is said and done, the most compelling question about the Church and anti-Semitism may not be why Christians sometimes attacked the Jews, but why they tolerated them at all. Unlike Christian heretics such as the Cathars, Waldensians, Fraticelli, and similar groups, the Jews were the only sizeable, openly nonconformist religious group that survived in Europe until the Lutherans did so by force of arms. As Robert Chazan observed, despite being the objects of suspicion and enduring many forms of discrimination, the "essential fact remained . . . that Jews were to be permitted to exist within Christian society and to fulfill their religious obligations as Jews."[71]

Christians made this exception for the Jews because of the theological doctrine that the Second Coming would be ushered in by the conversion of the Jews, which was interpreted to mean that Jewish nonconformity was part of God's plan and that their eventual conversion was in God's hands as well. Consequently, no pope in the Middle Ages ever undertook a campaign to convert the Jews,[72] and Saint Augustine (354–430) taught that anyone who killed Jews would "suffer [God's] sevenfold vengeance."[73] As for those who would dismiss these as mere words, it seems appropriate here to quote at length the highly respected historian Steven T. Katz, director of the Elie Wiesel Center for Judaic Studies at Boston University. Identifying "Thou Shalt Not Annihilate the Jews" as the "Eleventh Christian Commandment," Katz wrote:

> Though Christendom possessed the power, over the course of nearly fifteen hundred years, to destroy that segment of the Jewish people it dominated, it chose not to do so . . . because the physical extirpation of Jewry was never, at any time, the

Box 1.1. Some leading historians whose work informed this chapter. Specific studies by each can be found in the bibliography.

Robert Chazan is professor of Hebrew and Judaic Studies at New York University. He studied to become a rabbi at Jewish Theological Seminary (graduated in 1962) and then earned his PhD from Columbia University in 1967. He has published a dozen books, all of them well received.

David G. Dalin is an American Conservative rabbi and historian. He received his PhD in history from Brandeis University and has held distinguished visiting appointments at various universities and institutes, including Princeton and the Hoover Institution at Stanford University. He has written a number of books on Judaism, but none more important to this chapter than his exposé of the false charges that Pope Pius XII supported the Nazis.

Nachum T. Gidal (1909–96) was born in Germany and, being a Jew, left for Switzerland in 1933 and then settled in Jerusalem. He spent World War II working as a photojournalist for a British army publication. After the war, he came to the United States and, after a stint with *LIFE* magazine, joined the faculty of the New School for Social Research in New York City.

Léon Poliakov (1910–97) was a French historian, born in Russia to a Jewish family that moved to Italy. After World War II, he cofounded the Center of Contemporary Jewish Documentation and assisted at the Nuremberg Trials of Nazi war criminals. He is best known for a four-volume study of anti-Semitism.

Peter Schäfer is professor of Jewish Studies at Princeton University. After studying at Hebrew University in Jerusalem, he received his DPhil from the University of Freiberg. In 1994, he was awarded the Leibniz Prize, the most prestigious research prize in Germany. The author of several dozen books, in 1998 he accepted an appointment at Princeton.

official policy of any church or of any Christian state. Rather than actively seeking to eliminate Judaism, the ultimate luminescent irony . . . is that Christian dogmatics entailed protecting Jews and Judaism from extinction. Although Christian civilization demeaned and debased Jews . . . the church, paradoxically, was committed to Jewish survival—until, that is, the collective repentance of the "Israel of the flesh" would usher in the Second Coming.[74]

Thus it is that the statement on the Jews issued by Vatican II in 1965 was nothing more (or less) than a forceful restatement of the traditional church teachings in language appropriate for the time.

Unfortunately, this particular manifestation of anti-Catholic history lives on with renewed venom in recent indictments of Pope Pius XII as Hitler's collaborator in the Holocaust, which also is said to be quite in keeping with the pope's support of Franco and the Spanish fascists. Ironically, this historical libel has mainly been propagated by alienated Catholics, while the most compelling support for the pope has come from Jews.

"Hitler's Pope"

It seems to have been mostly forgotten that the campaign to link the pope to Hitler was initiated by the Soviet Union, presumably in hopes of neutralizing the Vatican in post–World War II affairs. Early in 1944, *Izvestia* (the official party daily published in Moscow) claimed that Pope Pius XII had supported the Nazi regime. The next day, the *New York Times* condemned the article as malicious propaganda and vigorously asserted the pope's opposition to all forms of tyranny. But the Soviets continued, and one of their agents soon published a book claiming that the Vatican had signed a secret pact with Hitler.[75] It was an obvious fake, embraced only by party-liners and by "professional" anti-Catholic writers—of whom there were a surprising number in that era. Fortunately, the Soviet disinformation campaign was drowned out by a remarkable chorus of praise for the pope coming from Jewish sources in the immediate aftermath of World War II. As they noted, Hitler had bitterly attacked the Catholic Church, had closed all the Catholic schools, and had arrested thousands of priests and nuns and sent them to Dachau and other death camps.[76]

As the world learned of the horrors of the Nazi death camps, Pope Pius XII was widely praised for his vigorous and devoted efforts to saving Jewish lives during the war. In 1943, Chaim Weizmann, who would become the first president of Israel, wrote: "the Holy See is lending its powerful help wherever it can, to mitigate the fate of my persecuted co-religionists."[77] Moshe Sharett, soon to be Israel's first foreign minister and second prime minister, met with the pope during the last days of the war: "I told him that my first duty was to thank him, and through him the Catholic Church, on behalf of the Jewish public for all they had done in various countries to rescue Jews."[78] Upon the pope's death in 1958, Golda Meir, a future prime minister of Israel, noted his efforts on behalf of the Jews of Europe, calling him "a great servant of peace,"[79] for it was well-known among that generation of Israelis that Pope Pius XII had made many personal efforts to protect and shelter Jews from the Nazis.

But then the anti-Catholic revisionism began. First came a play, *The Deputy*, written by a very left-wing German, Rolf Hochhuth. In it, Pope Pius XII was portrayed as an anti-Semite who was entirely indifferent to the Holocaust. Having opened to critical acclaim in Berlin in 1963, *The Deputy* opened in London later that year and had its Broadway debut in February 1964. Eventually it was translated into more than twenty languages, was made into a movie in 2002 (titled *Amen*), and had a London revival in 2006. The theatrical reviewers for the major daily papers in both Britain and the United States hailed the play,[80] and Susan Sontag led the way for New York intellectuals: "*The Deputy* also stresses, and this is the controversial part of the play, a strong case for the complicity of the German Catholic Church and of Pope Pius XII. This case I am convinced is true, and well taken. . . . And the importance, historical and moral, of this difficult truth at the present time cannot be overestimated."[81]

Nevertheless, qualified historians rejected *The Deputy*. Writing from Cambridge, Eamon Duffy testified that an examination of all pertinent documents "decisively established the falsehood of Hochhuth's specific allegations."[82] Prominent Jews agreed. Joseph L. Lichten of the Anti-Defamation League published a withering refutation of *The Deputy* and its admirers. So did the Israeli diplomat Pinchas Lapide, who testified that Pope Pius XII "was instrumental in saving at least 700,000, but probably as many as 860,000 Jews from certain death at Nazi hands."[83] These claims and others reporting the pope's efforts to save Jews were confirmed by many others with deep knowledge of the Holocaust.

At this point, attacks on the pope as a Nazi accomplice seemed to have been put to rest, although an occasional rumble still occurred in extreme left-wing circles. But several years ago, it started all over again with a spate of new books. Even though these books display remarkable ignorance as well as self-indulgence, they mostly received very positive reviews in the popular press and sold very well, thus stimulating and justifying a great deal of "informed" anti-Catholicism. As so often happens, many qualified historians have written scathing reviews that reveal the extreme biases and scholarly incompetence of these authors,[84] but these reviews have not been widely circulated.

The first major blast in this new assault was *Hitler's Pope: The Secret History of Pius XII* (1999) by John Cornwell. The primary thesis was that Pope Pius XII negotiated a deal that helped the Nazis take over Germany, thus condemning Europe's Jews to the death camps. In keeping with that thesis, the photograph on book's dust jacket would seem to show the soon-to-be Pope Pius XII visiting Nazi headquarters. What it actually shows is him leaving a reception for the president of the Weimar Republic in 1927.[85] The pope never met Hitler and left Germany in 1929, well before the Nazis' rise to power. The rest of the book consists mainly of similar distortions and misstatements.

Hitler's Pope sold very well, rising to fourteenth on the *New York Times'*

list of nonfiction bestsellers, and it received extended, favorable coverage on the TV show *60 Minutes.* That the author is a dropout from
a Catholic seminary has been taken as evidence that he is not motivated by anti-Catholicism. But that ignores the fact that Cornwell has
described himself as a "lapsed Catholic."[86] It also ignores subsequent
evidence that Cornwell's claims to having examined secret and incrimi-
nating documents in the Vatican Library were fraudulent.[87] Finally, and
most importantly, like most of the new attempts to link the pope to Hitler, Cornwell's book is part of an effort by alienated Catholics to push
the Church in very liberal directions. As explained by Rabbi David G.
Dalin, "The Holocaust is simply the biggest club available for liberal
Catholics to use against traditional Catholics in their attempt to bash the
papacy and thereby to smash traditional Catholic teaching. . . . [These]
polemics . . . of lapsed or angry liberal Catholics exploit the tragedy
of the Jewish people during the Holocaust to foster their own political
agenda."[88]

This description applies equally well to James Carroll, author of *Constantine's Sword: The Church and the Jews—A History* (2001). Carroll is a
novelist and an ex-priest, and both identities have shaped his book,
which claims that the Christ story itself is the basis for unrelenting
Christian anti-Semitism. As he put it, "Auschwitz is the climax of the
story that begins at Golgotha. . . . Auschwitz, when seen in the links of
causality, reveals that the hatred of Jews has been no incidental anomaly
but a central action of Christian history. . . . Because the hatred of Jews
had been made holy, it became lethal."[89] Carroll then devoted hundreds
of pages to a distorted review of medieval materials already covered in
this chapter and to excursions in theology: he dismisses the resurrection as harmful nonsense made up long after the fact and proposes that
Christians can overcome their anti-Semitism only by rejecting the idea
that Jesus was divine. The book also is crammed with Carroll's obses-
sive reflections on his own private life (how his mother made him a
priest) and his preferences (he likes Bob Dylan). Finally, after 495 pages,

Carroll's book arrives at a discussion of Pius XII and Hitler, only to settle for an uninspired rehash of Cornwall's *Hitler's Pope*.

Carroll's book also sold very well, was very positively reviewed in the popular press, and was highly praised by Garry Wills and Karen Armstrong. But the book was disdained by real scholars. Thus, the celebrated Protestant historian Robert Louis Wilken noted that although Carroll's subtitle claims his book is a work of history, it is nothing of the sort, being "driven by theological animus" and based "almost wholly on the works of others."[90]

In similar fashion, books by Gary Wills, Daniel Jonah Goldhagen, Michael Phayer, and David Kertzer are angry rehashes of the same material in the same unscholarly ways. Finally, there is *Under His Very Windows: The Vatican and the Holocaust in Italy* (2002) by Susan Zuccotti. The author admits that when the Nazis attempted to round up and transport the Jews of Italy, at least 85 percent survived, most of them having been hidden in convents, monasteries, churches, and other Roman Catholic buildings, where many of them stayed until Allied troops arrived. But, according to Zuccotti, this was done without any encouragement from Pius XII, who remained unmoved by the plight of the Jews. She advanced this view against the testimony of scores of clergy, monks, and nuns that their actions were prompted by the pope; Zuccotti dismissed them as attempting to place the pope in a favorable light. She also dismissed the testimony of many Jews in favor of the pope as based on nothing but "benevolent ignorance,"[91] and she chose to ignore well-known facts, such as that the pope himself used his summer home, Castel Gandolfo, to shelter thousands of Jews during the war, providing them with kosher food and turning his private apartment into an obstetrical ward.

But the whole truth is that Eugenio Pacelli spoke out against Hitler and racism during the 1930s, even before he became Pope Pius XII, and he continued to do so all through the war. In March 1935, he sent an "open letter" to the bishop of Cologne in which he called the Nazis "false prophets with the pride of Lucifer." In 1937, during a sermon at Notre Dame in Paris, he identified Germany as "that noble and powerful nation whom bad shepherds would lead astray into an ideology of race."[92] Consider these headlines in the *New York Times*:

- ▶ October 28, 1939: "Pope Condemns Dictators, Treaty Violators, Racism."
- ▶ August 6, 1942: "Pope Is Said to Plead for Jews Listed for Removal from France."
- ▶ August 27, 1942: "Vichy Seizes Jews; Pope Pius Ignored."

And, on December 26, 1941, the *New York Times* editorialized: "The voice of Pius XII is a lonely voice in the silence and darkness enveloping Europe this Christmas. . . . In calling for a 'real new order' based on 'liberty, justice, and love,' . . . the pope put himself squarely against Hitlerism."

If more evidence is needed, dozens of prominent Jews have spoken out to thank the pope for his vigorous efforts to avert the Holocaust and for his personal and relatively successful efforts to save the Jews of Italy. Although it goes unmentioned in the new attacks on the pope, Hitler was so angered that in 1942 the German Ministry of Propaganda put out ten million copies of a pamphlet identifying Pius XII as the "pro-Jewish pope,"[93] and the next year Hitler tried to have the pope kidnapped.[94] Finally, a radio message from Nazi headquarters in Rome to Berlin, sent ten days after the attempted roundup of the Italian Jews, and intercepted by the Allies on October 26, 1943, reads: "Vatican has apparently for a long time been assisting many Jews to escape."[95]

Conclusion

It is quite true that for centuries the Catholic Church condoned an ugly array of anti-Semitic beliefs and participated in various forms of discrimination against Jews (as did the Protestants when they arrived upon the scene). This unpleasant fact gives plausibility to the charges that the Church also was deeply implicated in the pogroms that began in medieval times and culminated in the Holocaust. However, much that is plausible is not true, and in this instance it is not. The Roman Catholic Church has a long and honorable record of stout opposition to attacks upon Jews. And Pope Pius XII fully lived up to that tradition.

The myth of suppressed gospels: This image is a page from the *Gospel of Thomas*, one of the many lost Gnostic gospels recovered during the twentieth century. Many experts claim that these works were suppressed because they disagreed with official Catholic doctrines.

The Suppressed Gospels 2

B OOKSTORES ARE BURSTING with newly discovered Christian gospels that were excluded from the New Testament and
suppressed for nearly two thousand years by the narrow-
minded men who imposed their rule on the early Church—even today
these scriptures are condemned by the Roman Catholic hierarchy.[1]
Among the bestsellers are: *The Secret Gospel of Thomas*, *The Gospel of Mary*,
The Secret Book of John, and *The Gospel of Judas*. These gospels were only
"lost," not unknown, because they were discussed and often quoted at
great length in writings by early church fathers, all of whom discredited
their authors as "vile heretics."[2] It seems likely that these "lost" gospels aroused such militant antagonism because they so clearly reveal
that Roman Catholicism is a "perversion of authentic Christianity."[3]

Attacks on these dissenting Christian scriptures began with *Against
Heresies* by Irenaeus, bishop of Lyon, published late in the second century. Judging from the quotations presented by Irenaeus and others,
these heretical writings were strange to the point of absurdity and of
no great loss. However, during the past century, actual copies of most
of these lost gospels have been discovered, prompting a great deal of
excitement and controversy because these suppressed texts depict both
Jesus and early Christianity as "remarkably different"[4] from the traditional teachings. They present a far more complex cosmology than that
in the authorized New Testament, as well as a far more human, sub-
versive, and very mystical Jesus. According to the prominent scholar
Marvin Meyer, these newly recovered gospels are "just as precious,

and perhaps even more precious" than the texts in the New Testament.[5] No wonder these gospels are promoting major revisions of traditional Christian teachings, especially among leading Bible scholars at the more sophisticated divinity schools.

As Princeton's Elaine Pagels explained: "All the old questions—the original questions, sharply debated at the beginning of Christianity— are being reopened. How is one to understand the resurrection? What about women's participation in priestly and episcopal office? Who was Christ, and how does he relate to the believer? What are the similarities between Christianity and other world religions?"[6] Rosemary Radford Reuther of the Claremont School of Theology in California believes that the lost gospels reconnect us with a wrongly suppressed and more enlightened Christianity, allowing us to "glimpse a time when a great variety of Christianities, some experimenting boldly with the personal and social changes and theological interpretations of redemption, not only competed as equals with emerging clerical and patriarchal forms, but in many places were the predominant form of Christianity. These, just as much as those who won as the 'orthodox,' saw themselves as building on ancient traditions going back to Jesus."[7] As for Burton Mack, recently retired from the Claremont School of Theology and author of *The Lost Gospel* (1993), these discoveries reveal that conventional Christianity is a complete hoax: "It's over. We've had enough apocalypses. We've had enough martyrs. Christianity has had a two-thousand-year run, and it's over."[8] And the late Robert Funk, founder of the highly publicized Jesus Seminar, agreed with Mack that in light of the lost gospels, "it is no longer credible to think of Jesus as divine . . . [that belief] is sub-rational and sub-ethical. . . . Jesus did not rise from the dead except perhaps in some metaphorical sense."[9]

Lost gospels began to turn up at the end of the nineteenth century; a *Gospel of Mary* was purchased from a Cairo dealer in 1896. But the major discovery was made at the village of Nag Hammadi in Egypt in 1945. Thirteen volumes bound in red leather, containing more than forty lost gospels, were found carefully buried in a large earthenware jar. These volumes dated from the fourth century and were written in Coptic, all of them having been translated from earlier originals, probably written in Greek. Since these lost gospels became available, they have inspired a great deal of publicity and many claims, including "fact-based" novels. Attention has been focused on alleged plots to suppress these revelations, especially those asserting that Jesus married and raised a family. In addition to fiction and make-believe history,[10] many more respectable scholarly books have been written to celebrate the alternative Christianity revealed by these gospels.[11] For example, Elaine Pagels has devoted considerable effort to demonstrating why she finds the suppressed gospels to be more satisfying than those contained in the New Testament, especially *The Secret Gospel of Thomas*, to which she has recently devoted an entire book.

Unlike most other newly found gospels and those included in the New Testament, *Thomas* has no narrative and consists only of 114 sayings attributed to Jesus, beginning: "1) These are the obscure (or hidden) sayings that the living Jesus uttered and which Didymus Jude Thomas [his twin] wrote down. And he said, 'Whoever finds meaning in these sayings will not taste death.'"[12]

While some of the 114 sayings also appear in the New Testament, many do not. For example: "7) JESUS said: 'Blessed is the lion that the human being will devour so that the lion becomes human. And cursed is the human being that the lion devours; and the lion will become human'" and "56) JESUS said: 'Whoever has become acquainted with the world has found a corpse, and the world is not worthy of the one who found the corpse.'"

Like most of the other lost gospels, *Thomas* does not encourage the followers of Jesus to spread their faith to the world. Instead, Christianity is presented as a set of "hidden" teachings reserved for a small, initiated elite, which is why most of these lost gospels are referred to collectively as *Gnostic*; the term "refers to 'revealed knowledge' available only to those who have received secret teachings from a heavenly revealer."[13] As *Thomas* put it: "49) Blessed are those who are solitary and superior" and "62) It is to those [worthy] of [my] secrets that I am telling my secrets."

Pagels is hardly alone in her admiration for *Thomas*. The group known as the Jesus Seminar considers *Thomas* to be a more authentic source of Jesus's sayings than are the "official" four gospels of the New Testament. Funk, chairman and founder of the seminar, was given to referring to Matthew, Mark, Luke, John, and *Thomas* as the "five gospels." He elaborated: "The Jesus of the Gospels is an imaginative theological construct, into which has been woven traces of that enigmatic sage from Nazareth—traces that cry out for recognition and liberation from the firm grip of those whose faith overpowered their memories. The search for the authentic Jesus is a search for the forgotten Jesus."[14] As depicted in most of the lost gospels, this forgotten Jesus was "not so much a historical personage as a reality within the believer."[15] This is consistent with Funk's view, noted earlier, that even if Jesus existed he was merely a mortal wisdom teacher.

Two of the most publicized of the recently recovered gospels were not part of the cache discovered at Nag Hammadi. As noted, *The Gospel of Mary* was discovered in Cairo in 1896. The claimed author of this gospel is not the mother of Jesus, but Mary Magdalene, the follower of Jesus who is said to have been the first to discover his resurrection. The first six or so pages of this gospel have been lost, and what remains are several tiny fragments and a papyrus manuscript about eight pages long. Ignored for nearly a century, *Mary* has been published several times recently, accompanied by a media drumbeat of "new" discovery.

The best known of these publications is *The Gospel of Mary of Magdala: Jesus and the First Woman Apostle* (2003) by Karen King of Harvard's Divinity School. Although the translation of *Mary* takes up only five pages in her book, King is able to devote more than two hundred pages to the various implications and hidden meanings she detects in these few lines. According to King, *Mary* reveals "a radical interpretation of Jesus' teachings as a path to inner spiritual knowledge; it rejects his suffering and death as the path to eternal life; it exposes the erroneous view that Mary of Magdala was a prostitute for what it is—a piece of theological fiction; it presents the most straightforward and convincing argument in any early Christian writing for the legitimacy of women's leadership . . . and it asks us to rethink the basis for church authority."[16] The need to rethink the issue of female leadership follows from the fact that this gospel claims that Mary was the most important apostle, in whom Jesus confided secrets he did not tell the others. But King does not mention that on the gender issue, *Mary* not only differs from the conventional church but also is at variance with other lost gospels as well. Consider this saying from *Thomas*: "114) Simon Peter said to them, 'Mary should leave us, for females are not worthy of life.' Jesus said, 'See, I am going to attract her to make her male so that she too might become a living spirit that resembles you males. For every female (element) that makes itself male will enter the kingdom of heavens.'"[17]

Perhaps the most controversial of the teachings in *Mary*, one that in addition to feminism appeals so strongly to many modern scholars, is that there really is no such thing as sin—it is an illusion generated in humans because of their mistaken belief that material reality exists:

> 3) Then Peter said to him, "You have been explaining every topic to us; tell us one other thing. What is the sin of the world?"
>
> The Savior replied, "There is no such thing as sin; rather you yourselves are what produces sin. . . . This is why you get sick and die: because [you love] what deceives you."[18]

The tiny *Mary* manuscript also inspired book-length treatment by Jean-Yves Leloup in *The Gospel of Mary Magdalene* (2002). Leloup used it, in part, to argue that for theological reasons Jesus must have experienced "his sexuality, [otherwise] sexuality would be unredeemed. In that case, he could not be Savior in the full sense of the word. . . . The Gospel of Mary . . . reminds us that [Jesus] was capable of intimacy with women."[19] That Jesus may have been sexually involved with, or even married to, Mary Magdalene has become a common theme in new interpretations of Jesus.

More recently, immense press coverage was given to *The Gospel of Judas*, released by *National Geographic* in April 2006. Despite the media hype, this gospel was not newly discovered, having been found in a cave in Egypt in 1978. It circulated among antiquities dealers for many years before being purchased for the National Geographic Society for a reported one million dollars. This manuscript consists of thirteen sheets of papyrus, written on front and back in Coptic, and dates from about the fourth century.[20] Although the gospel claims to have been written by Judas, it was by a much later author—the original was not written until sometime in the second century. What made this such a media event is the claim that Judas was not the betrayer of Christ, as long portrayed by the New Testament, but the most trusted of the apostles, the one in whom Jesus confided many "mysteries of the kingdom" unknown to the others. Judas did tell the authorities where to arrest Jesus, but he did so only because Jesus instructed him to—so Jesus could fulfill his mission to be crucified.

Some scholars quickly embraced this as the true version. Most others have skirted that issue and stressed that, as Bart D. Ehrman put it, this gospel may not give "us more reliable information about what happened in the life of Jesus, but . . . it gives us more reliable information about what was happening in the lives of his followers in the decades after his death."[21] As could be expected, both Elaine Pagels and Karen King rushed to praise this new gospel as a major addition to the body of "proof" that early Christianity was very diverse and theologically more sophisticated than the faith that became dominant.[22] Indeed, the two quickly coauthored a book-length commentary: *Reading Judas: The Gospel of Judas and the Shaping of Christianity* (2007).

To sum up their book: the narrow, creedal faith reflected in the New Testament fails to represent some very major traditions of early Christian thought. And probably because they were so liberating and undogmatic, the gospels circulated among these other Christianities were vilified and suppressed by the Catholic Church.

Not so!

For one thing, these gospels were not so much suppressed as they were discarded as obvious forgeries and nonsense. The complaint that Irenaeus and others misquoted these "lost" gospels in order to make it easier to discredit them may have seemed a reasonable assumption while the actual texts were lost, but since they have been found it is clear that the early church fathers quoted the original texts essentially word for word, perhaps believing that they "were so contorted and ludicrous that the heretics were best condemned out of their own mouths."[23] Even so, many modern advocates of Gnosticism continue to pretend that the church fathers grossly misrepresented these writings. As Marvin Meyer put it, the accounts offered by the early churchmen "are biased and apparently distort many features of gnostic religion."[24] And Pagels has continued to condemn Irenaeus for identifying the authors of these gospels as "heretics, which means people who make choices about what to think. Irenaeus didn't want people making choices. He wanted them to think what the bishop told them to think."[25] Although she avoids the topic, presumably Pagels is willing to accept the doctrine that God is the epitome of evil and the gleeful cause of human suffering, as merely a choice, not a heresy—for *that* is the most fundamental message of the lost gospels!

Which brings us to the greatest distortion of them all: to present these as *Christian* gospels. Any honest reading of the primary Gnostic gospels reveals that, despite some Christian content, these are fundamentally *pagan scriptures* and thus are precisely the bizarre heresies that the early church fathers said they were!

It is revealing that so much is written about these texts by modern scholars who somehow never get around to quoting the central doctrines of the Gnostic gospels. Although Elaine Pagels wrote a whole book celebrating *The Secret Gospel of Thomas*, she was unable to find the space needed to print the brief 114 sayings that make it up—which would have required very few pages. But even had she done so, *Thomas* is so

Box 2.1. Some leading historians whose work informed this chapter. Specific studies by each can be found in the bibliography.

PHILIP JENKINS is distinguished professor of history and codirector of the Program on Historical Studies of Religion at the Institute for Studies of Religion at Baylor University. He was born in Wales and was educated at Cambridge, where he took a rare double first-class honours and then continued to earn a PhD. Before coming to Baylor, he was for many years professor of humanities at Pennsylvania State University. Author of more than twenty books, his *Hidden Gospels: How the Search for Jesus Lost Its Way* (2001) was an instant classic.

BENTLEY LAYTON is professor of religious studies and of Near Eastern languages at Yale University. He received his PhD from Harvard and is not only famous for his studies of Gnosticism but also for his authoritative translations of the Gnostic gospels. In addition, his Coptic grammar is the standard text.

PHEME PERKINS is professor of theology at Boston College. She was born in Louisville, Kentucky, and received her PhD from Harvard University in 1971. She is widely respected for her distinguished books, particularly *Gnosticism and the New Testament* (1993), and her role as associate editor of *The New Oxford Annotated Bible* (3rd ed.).

MICHAEL WILLIAMS is professor of comparative religion at the University of Washington. Born in Texas, he received his PhD at Harvard. His book *Rethinking "Gnosticism": An Argument for Dismantling a Dubious Category* (1996) shook up the field. I was privileged to be his colleague for many years at Washington.

cryptic that few readers would have detected the fundamental premises of the Gnostic gospels, the underlying themes of books such as *Thomas, Mary,* and *Judas.* These themes are:

1. The world and everything in it is totally corrupt because it was created by an inferior and utterly evil, renegade Godling!

2. The Creation was but the bizarre plaything of this Satanic rebel, a depraved spiritual power who is without any redeeming virtues.

3. This evil "God" is worshipped by the Jews, who are thereby an accursed people, and conventional Christians have been falling into the same trap.

4. Jesus is not the son of this evil creature, but is a teacher, or a sage, or (sometimes) a spiritual being having the mystical powers needed to penetrate this dreadful fraud. His teachings can free an enlightened few.

5. Because the material world is utterly corrupt, extreme asceticism, including celibacy, is the only option.

The best introduction to these fundamentals of Gnosticism is to consult *The Secret Book* of *John* (or *The Apocryphon of John*). To the extent that there is a core Gnostic work, this is it—Michel Tardieu has called it "the gnostic Bible *par excellence.*"[26] It too was found in the earthen jar at Nag Hammadi, and it too was denounced by Irenaeus (who is thought to have had a slightly different version).[27] The manuscript identifies its author as the Apostle John and reports an appearance by Jesus, who instructed him about *"the mysteries which are hidden in silence"*[28] (this and the following italicized quotes are from the gospel itself).

The revelation begins with the supreme mystery, the nature of God, who is identified as the *"invisible spirit,"* so *"superior to deity"* that it *"is not fitting to think of it as divine."* Eventually, when God thought about his own perfection, that resulted in the existence of an independent entity known as *First Thought* or *Barbelo.* Barbelo also is the "Mother," and hence the consort of God the "Father," and this resulted in a self-generated Child. This trinity then produced a whole entourage of divine entities known as "aeons." For some immense time all went well, "the scene portrayed in this divine realm is one of complete order, peace, and reverence."[29] But, it didn't last. One of the divine entities went bad—the one named Wisdom. Without permission from God, Wisdom did her own creative imagining, bringing forth a child. It was a grotesque monster: "serpentine, with a lion's face, and with its eyes gleaming like flashes of lightning." To hide her folly, Wisdom "surrounded it with a luminous cloud. And she put a throne in the midst of the cloud, so that no being might see it except for the holy spirit . . . and she called its name Ialtabaōth."

Now things get interesting. Ialtabaōth doesn't merely look like a monster, he is one. "Completely self-willed, he steals spiritual power from his mother and runs off and sets about creating a world he can control as he pleases."[30] He is none other than the God of Genesis who creates "a gang of angelic henchmen, rulers ('archons') who are to help him control the realm of darkness, and he goes about setting up his rule in the classic style of a petty tyrant," as Michael Williams so aptly summarized.[31] Having created the earth and given it inhabitants, Ialtabaōth began to assert, "For my part, I am a jealous God. And there is no other god apart from me." The book now relates a revised version of the whole Adam and Eve, Garden of Eden saga. Having thrown Adam and Eve out of the Garden, Ialtabaōth instilled a desire for sexual intercourse in humans and then seduced Eve to produce Cain and Abel, the former with the face of a bear and the latter with that of a cat. Adam then fathered Seth who, unlike Cain and Abel, possessed the spirit of God. Seth and his descendants were regarded as an affront by Ialtabaōth and his henchmen, so he tried to kill them all with the flood. Having been thwarted by Noah, next Ialtabaōth sent evil angels disguised as men who took women for their brides and generated a polluted humankind.

At this point, the secret book offers a "poem of deliverance," wherein Jesus explains that he came to free humanity from the chains of Ialtabaōth. However, Jesus does not end his revelations by encouraging John to go forth and convert the world. Not at all: "For my part, I have told you all things, so that you might write them down and transmit them secretly to those who are like you in spirit."

Thus, the core message of *The Secret Book of John* and of most other lost Gnostic teachings is that the earth is held in thrall by an evil God. According to many Gnostic texts, the evil God is the God of the Jews, and his Chosen People were so designated for good reason—in that they worship and proselytize on behalf of this evil creature. Most of the lost gospels display considerable anti-Semitism. They "portray the Old Testament God as vain, ignorant, envious, and jealous—a malicious Creator who uses every means at his disposal to keep humanity from attaining true perfection."[32]

In *The Testimony of Truth*, another of the manuscripts recovered at Nag Hammadi, a section begins by recounting the story of Adam and Eve eating from the tree of knowledge as told in Genesis. Having reached the point where God has found out that Adam and Eve have eaten of the tree, God says:

"Behold, Adam has become like one of us, knowing evil from good." Then he said, "Let us cast him out of Paradise lest he take from the tree of life and eat and live forever." But of what sort is this God? First (he) maliciously refused Adam from eating of the tree of knowledge. And secondly he said, "Adam, where are you?" [This] God does not have foreknowledge; (otherwise) would he not know from the beginning? (And) afterwards he said, "Let us cast him (out) of this place, lest he eat of the tree of life and live forever." Surely he has shown himself to be a malicious grudger.

At this point, the *Testimony* shifts from an exclusive focus on the God of the Old Testament to those who worship him:

For great is the blindness of those who read, and they do not know him [for what he is]. And he said, "I am a jealous God; I will bring the sins of the fathers upon the children until three (and) four generations." And he said, "I will make their heart thick, and I will cause their mind to become blind, that they might not know nor comprehend the things that are said." But these things he said to those who believe in him (and) serve him!

These passages are not exceptional. Many Gnostic texts abound in antagonism toward the God of the Jews.

Christianity may be somewhat ambivalent about sexual expression but, being very pronatal, marital sexuality is valued. Not only did Paul admit in 1 Corinthians 7 that "it is better to marry than to burn," but he also counseled married couples not to practice chastity, but to fully extend to one another their "conjugal rights." In contrast with many "Gnostic" texts, Paul seems a virtual libertine.[33] Most lost gospels warn that sexual intercourse is to be absolutely avoided because it provides the wicked angels (archons) with the means to continue to mislead and torment humans in that sex is an act of utter defilement. In *The Sophia* [or *Wisdom*] *of Jesus Christ* (found at Nag Hammadi), following his resurrection, the Savior appears to "his twelve disciples and seven women [who] continued to be his followers" and informed them that, among other things, they can be released from the grip of forgetfulness concerning wisdom if they do not engage in "the unclean rubbing" of sexual intercourse.[34] *The Paraphrase of Shem* condemns intercourse as "defiled rubbing." *The Gospel of Philip*, another work recovered at Nag Hammadi, gets right to the point: "There are two trees growing in paradise. One bears animals, the other bears men. Adam ate from the tree which bore animals. He became an animal and he brought forth animals." Many lost gospels advocate absolute celibacy and rate it as especially virtuous to not bring children into the world. As the *Gospel of Thomas* put it: "79) Blessed are the womb that has not conceived and the breasts that have not given milk."

This persistent element in "Gnostic" writings may have been a major factor in their failure to gain supporters. Although it accorded special sanctity to those who observed celibacy, the conventional Church fully embraced those who lived in marital bliss. Nock put this well: "Christianity did indeed go a long way with those in whose eyes sexual life was unclean; it gave satisfaction to the many who were fascinated by asceticism, but it repressed those elements within itself which overstressed that point of view, and it never set its face against the compatibility of normal life with the full practice of religion."[35]

If the strange doctrines proclaimed in the Gnostic gospels were not sufficient to justify the judgment of the early church fathers that these writings had no place in the Bible, there are other substantial grounds for dismissing them. First of all, they are forgeries. Not in the sense that they are of recent manufacture, but in the sense that they were not written when they claim to have been written or by the persons to whom they are attributed. There is no reason to accept that Jesus had a twin brother, but that is who Didymus Jude Thomas, alleged author of *The Secret Gospel of Thomas*, claims to be. Indeed, since this lost gospel is believed to have been written no sooner than the middle of the second century, obviously had there been such a twin he would have been long dead before taking quill in hand. The same must be said of the gospels attributed to Mary Magdalene, John, Judas, Pilate, and the rest. The authorship is a lie as is the claim that these are eyewitness accounts of New Testament times.

In addition, the lost gospels are utterly unlike those included in the New Testament or the books making up the Old Testament in that they lack historical context and exist in an unworldly setting. The Bible abounds in correct historical and geographical details, and nearly everything takes place on this earth and involves people who probably existed. In contrast, the typical Gnostic work, like *The Secret Book of John*, gives its origins as the author's visions and mystical revelations, which are set in another reality and include almost no historical or geographical content. As Pheme Perkins explained, "Gnostics reject gods and religious traditions that are tied to this cosmos in any way at all! Thus, Gnostic mythology often seems devoid of ties to place or time."[36] In this way, Gnostic scriptures far more resemble pagan mythology than the New Testament, in that "events" so often occur in an immaterial, otherworldly, and "enchanted" setting. This is no surprise when it is recognized that these authors were attempting to assimilate Christianity into paganism.

The lost gospels were not so much associated with alternative Christian movements, as with Gnostic schools, patterned after the classical philosophical schools such as the Academy at Athens. An excellent example is the school founded by Valentius in Alexandria early in the second century. Although Valentius participated in the official church until he was expelled for heresy in about 140, his school was not devoted to training Christian intellectuals or leaders. The "truths" that concerned Valentius and his students were intuited rather than reasoned from central Christian assumptions. Moreover, they were not to be shared with the general public, but were only to be transmitted as secret doctrines to a small elite.[37] As for their efforts to fit Christianity into paganism, the Valentinians took their starting assumption directly from Plato, who postulated the existence of a lower divine being he called the Demiurge. Plato proposed that it was the Demiurge, not God, who constructed the world. In addition, Plato viewed the Demiurge as a being having only limited powers, who could only construct the world from already available materials and in accord with an already-given set of ideas. In the hands of Gnostic visionaries such as Valentius, the Demiurge became Ialtabaōth.

The lost gospels were not excluded from the Bible because the early church fathers were malicious dogmatists, but because they were fully aware that the Gnostic scriptures were not Christian.[38] And the Roman authorities agreed! As Kurt Rudolph noted, the "Gnostic sects" enjoyed "complete immunity" from the Roman persecution of Christians.[39] They did so because they were entirely willing to perform required sacrifices to the Gods of Rome. According to Eusebius, Basilides, an especially prominent Gnostic teacher, "taught that there was no harm in eating things offered to idols, or in lightheartedly denying the faith in time of persecution."[40]

Unfortunately, despite the obvious fact that the Gnostic gospels are of pagan origin, they continue to get extensive coverage in the popular media. In April 2012, the above-mentioned Karen King achieved world-wide press coverage when she revealed via a Harvard University press release that she had obtained a tiny fragment of a papyrus bearing the words "Jesus said to them, my wife." Here was certain proof that Jesus was married! This claim should have been dismissed out of hand since Gnostic texts make many outrageous claims, as noted above, and there is no reason to suppose that whoever had written this papyrus had any trustworthy source for this claim. But, for the press and for many eager Gnostic admirers, this was not a matter of concern. Presumably, because it was written on an old piece of papyrus it had to be true. Then it was discovered that this wasn't even an ancient Gnostic text—King had been fooled by a modern forgery. As the headline in the *Wall Street Journal* (May 1, 2014) proclaimed: "How the Jesus' Wife Hoax Fell Apart."

Conclusion

No doubt more manuscripts will continue to turn up—even some that are not forgeries—and the press will continue to hail each as a major find and claim that it overthrows conventional Christian doctrines. Granted that many Gnostic gospels, such as the *Gospel of Judas*, would cause major theological revisions *if* they were accepted as part of the New Testament. But that will never happen because they will bear all the disqualifying marks of their Gnostic origins, which is why Irenaeus dismissed the *Gospel of Judas* and others as fiction nearly two thousand years ago. He wrote: "They declare that Judas the traitor was thoroughly acquainted with these things, and that he alone, knowing the truth as no others did, accomplished the mystery of betrayal; by him all things, both earthly and heavenly, were thus thrown into confusion. They produce a fictitious history of this kind, which they style the Gospel of Judas."[41]

Today, the modern counterpart to Gnostic gospels is fiction meant to be taken as disguised fact, such as *The Da Vinci Code*—a bitter indictment of a Roman Catholic conspiracy to suppress the truth about Jesus.

The myth of pagan oppression: This painting shows early Christians destroying pagan shrines. It has long been believed that once in power as the official Church of Rome, Christians persecuted pagans and quickly shut down their temples.

Persecuting the Tolerant Pagans 3

WHEN CONSTANTINE BECAME emperor of Rome in 312, there were about nine million Christians, making up approximately 15 percent of the empire's population.[1] When he died in 337, more than a third were Christians, and very soon after that, Christians had become the majority.[2] How was this extraordinary growth possible?

For centuries, many Christians explained this remarkable feat as a miracle. But during the so-called Enlightenment, a purely worldly explanation was required, and one was easily found. As explained by Edward Gibbon, and then embraced by generations of equally anti-Catholic scholars, the Christian victory was produced by "intolerant zeal,"[3] aided and abetted by Constantine who connived at the brutal persecution of paganism by the Church.

The pagans were unable to survive this militant Christian onslaught because they were, in Gibbon's oft-quoted phrase, imbued with "the mild spirit of antiquity."[4] Should anyone object to this claim by citing pagan persecutions of Christians, Voltaire confided that the persecution of Christians had never amounted to much,[5] and Gibbon agreed, charging that Christian "writers of the fourth and fifth centuries" exaggerated the extent of the persecutions because they "ascribed to the magistrates of Rome the same degree of implacable and unrelenting zeal which filled their own breasts against heretics." In truth, Gibbon continued, the Roman magistrates "behaved like men of polished manners . . . [and] respected the rules of justice."[6]

For several centuries this has summed up the scholarly consensus. If anything, nostalgia for paganism has become increasingly intense. Consider Jonathan Kirsch, a regular on National Public Radio. Having begun his 2004 book, *God Against the Gods*, with a brief catalogue of lurid episodes of religious intolerance, Kirsch proceeded to regret that Emperor Julian was unable to undo Constantine's boost of Christianity and restore the empire to paganism: "It is tantalizing to consider how close he [Julian] came to bringing the spirit of respect and tolerance back into Roman government and thus back into the roots of Western civilization, and even more tantalizing to consider how different our benighted world might have been if he had succeeded."[7] Similarly, in his prize-winning study of Hellenism, Glen Bowersock wrote that "polytheism is by definition tolerant and accommodating."[8]

Even many generations of Christian writers, going as far back as Eusebius (275–339), proudly claimed that, once armed with the authority of the state, the Church had quickly smashed all the pagan temples and crushed all opposition. These writers were motivated by a spirit of triumphalism to claim that it was inevitable that the Church quickly became powerful. Thus, no one objected to Gibbon's conclusion that the Christianization of Rome was due to "the irresistible power of the Roman emperors"[9] in concert with the repressive nature of the Roman Catholic Church. As the very distinguished historian Peter Brown summed up: "From Gibbon and Burckhardt to the present day, it has been assumed that the end of paganism was inevitable, once confronted by the resolute intolerance of Christianity; that the interventions of the Christian emperors in its suppression were decisive."[10]

But it isn't true.

As Peter Brown continued, large, active pagan communities "continued to enjoy, for many generations, [a] relatively peaceable . . . existence." All that really happened is that they "slipped out of history."[11]

During the past generation, many distinguished historians[12] not only have reaffirmed the reality of the pagan persecutions of Christians, but they also have greatly qualified and minimized claims concerning the Christian coercion of pagans. To this has been added renewed interest in the political aspects of Constantine's rule, especially the remarkable studies by H. A. Drake. Consequently, we now know that a period of relative tolerance and tranquility prevailed between Christians and pagans during Constantine's reign. The Christians were, of course, growing rapidly in this era, but without substantial recourse to coercive methods. Enter Julian the Apostate. An examination of Emperor Julian's anti-Christian efforts reveals how it fully rekindled Christian fears of renewed persecutions and thereby empowered the most militant elements in the early Church. Even so, post-Julian efforts by this Christian faction to settle "old scores" with pagans resulted in only sporadic efforts at coercion and reprisal—far less extensive, much less severe, and not nearly as effective as had been thought. Nor was coercion of pagans backed by the state. Consider this clause from the Code of Justinian (529–34): "We especially command those persons who are truly Christians, or who are said to be so, that they should not abuse the authority of religion and dare to lay violent hands on Jews and pagans, who are living quietly and attempting nothing disorderly or contrary to law."[13] As this suggests, there had been some attacks by Christians on pagans, but the overall record shows that in this same era pagan mobs also had attacked Christians from time to time. Far more surprising is how few attacks of either kind seem to have occurred.[14]

Consequently, and despite the prevailing historical view that was begun by Christian writers, paganism wasn't quickly obliterated. Instead, it seeped away very slowly. The Academy at Athens did not close until 529 and "even in most Christian Eddessa . . . organized communities of pagans were still sacrificing to Zeus-Hadad in the last quarter of the sixth century."[15] When early Muslim forces threatened Carrhae (Harran) in 639, pagans still so outnumbered Christians in the city that all members of the delegation sent to negotiate with the Arabs were pagans.[16] Moreover, for a considerable time in many parts of the empire, including some major cities, the prevailing religious perspectives and practices consisted of a remarkable amalgam of paganism and Christianity. Finally, paganism never fully died out in Europe; it was assimilated by Christianity. For example, many pagan festivals continued to be celebrated, and many of the Gods lingered under very thin Christian overlays. Although the medieval church went to extreme lengths to stamp out various Christian heresies, such as the Cathars, it essentially ignored the persistence of paganism.

But if there was little effective coercion, why did so many people convert to Christianity so quickly? I have dealt with this phenomenon at great length in *The Rise of Christianity* (1996) and also in my later, more extensive work, *The Triumph of Christianity* (2011). Two general factors were involved: social and doctrinal. Socially, Christianity generated an intense congregational life—people *belonged* to a Christian congregation, while they merely frequented pagan temples. High levels of commitment and social relations not only were directly rewarding, additionally they empowered Christian groups to provide substantial "social services." Doctrinally, in contrast to paganism's limited, unreliable, and often immoral Gods, Christianity presented an image of God as moral, concerned, dependable, and omnipotent. Christianity also provided a clear method for the forgiveness of sins and offered the prospect of an attractive eternal life.

It also should be recognized that once a wave of conversions to a new faith has begun, as it had well before Constantine came along, for many people conversion is simply a matter of aligning their religious life with that of their family, friends, and neighbors who already have joined—thus creating a self-sustaining network of growth. Finally, for many people of privilege and ambition, their abandonment of paganism was a matter of opportunism—many people professed Christianity or were discreet about their paganism in order to gain social and political advantages.

Constantine Reconsidered

Constantine was not responsible for the triumph of Christianity. By the time he gained the throne, Christian growth already had become a tidal wave of exponential increase.[17] If anything, Christianity played a leading role in the triumph of Constantine, providing him with substantial and well-organized urban support. And, although historians long reported bitter outcries by pagans against Constantine's support of Christianity, the best recent scholars now agree that there is no evidence of such protests[18] and propose that even those pagans most directly involved regarded the emperor's favors to the Church as a "bearable evil."[19] Well they might have, for Constantine neither outlawed paganism nor did he condone persecution of non-Christians. In fact, although Constantine subsidized and gave official standing to the Christian Church, he continued some funding of pagan temples.[20] As for charges that he encouraged Christian mobs to destroy pagan temples, a claim that originated with the early Christian historian Eusebius, who used it to show how "the whole rotten edifice of paganism" rapidly came crashing down as part of God's plan, "it is very likely that Eusebius report[ed] everything he knew of temple destruction," yet he could offer only four instances[21] and only one of these seems a legitimate case. The other three involved Temples of Aphrodite that featured ritual prostitution.

More significant even than his toleration of pagan temples, Constantine continued to appoint pagans to the very highest positions, including those of consul and prefect. Reading across the top line in Table 3.1, we see that 56 percent of the men appointed by Constantine were Christians, 18 percent were pagans, and the religion of 26 percent is unknown. It probably is safe to assume that most, if not all, of those whose religious affiliation is unknown were, in fact, pagans.

In addition, pagan philosophers played a prominent role in his court[22] and depictions of the sun god appeared on his coins. Indeed, "Constantine directed his most ferocious rhetoric," not against pagans, but

TABLE 3.1. Religious Affiliations of Men Appointed as Consuls and Prefects, 317–455

REIGN	CHRISTIANS	PAGANS	UNKNOWN	NUMBER
Constantine (317–37)*	56%	18%	26%	55
Constantinus & Constans (337–50)*	26%	46%	28%	43
Constantius (351–61)*	63%	22%	15%	27
Julian (361–63)**	18%	82%	0%	17
Valentinian (364–75)**	31%	38%	31%	32
Valens (364–78)**	39%	25%	36%	36
Gratian (375–83)**	50%	11%	39%	44
Valentinian II (383–92)**	32%	32%	36%	19
Theodosius (379–95)	27%	19%	54%	83
Arcadius & Honorius (395–423)**	34%	12%	54%	161
Theodosius II & Valentinian III (408–55)**	48%	4%	48%	157

* Computed from Barnes, 1995.
** Computed by Raban von Haehling in Barnes, 1995.

against Christian heretics: Valentinians, Marcionites, and the "Gnostic" schools.[23] Partly for these reasons, ever since Gibbon's time, leading historians have dismissed Constantine's conversion as an insincere political gambit. But, the most recent historians[24] now regard Constantine's conversion as genuine and cite the persistence of pagan elements in his reign as examples of his commitment to religious harmony.

Amazingly, Gibbon and subsequent historians who dismissed Constantine's conversion as insincere all claimed that he was utterly sincere in brutally suppressing paganism, although it clearly was not in his best political interests to do so. These historians have offered no credible reason for this remarkable inconsistency, ignoring the fact that Constantine not only failed to suppress paganism but also repeatedly reasoned and commanded against all such efforts. Of critical importance are two edicts issued by Constantine soon after he defeated Licinius to reunite the empire. Both stressed peaceful pluralism.

The *Edict to the Palestinians* is notable for the pluralism of its language. In it, Constantine repeatedly referred to God but never mentioned Christ, using "phrases common to Christians and pagans alike [which] is consistent with the search for a common denominator that was the hallmark of his religious policy."[25] But, it is the *Edict to the Eastern Provincials* that fully expressed Constantine's commitment to accommodation and his rejection of coercive forms of conversion. He began with a prayer, invoking "the most mighty God" on behalf of "the common benefit of the world and all mankind, I long for your people to be at peace and to remain free from strife." He went on: "Let those who delight in error alike with those who believe partake of the advantages of peace and quiet. . . . Let no one disturb another, let each man hold fast to that which his soul wishes, let him make full use of this." He continued, "What each man has adopted as his persuasion, let him do no harm with this to another. . . . For it is one thing to undertake the contest for immortality voluntarily, another to compel it with punishment." Finally, Constantine condemned "the violent opposition to wicked error . . .

immoderately embedded in some souls, to the detriment to our common salvation."[26]

In both word and deed, Constantine supported religious pluralism, even while making his own commitment to Christianity explicit. Thus, during Constantine's reign, "friendships between Christian bishops and pagan grandees" were well known and many examples of the "peaceful intermingling of pagan and Christian thought may . . . be thought of as proof of the success of [Constantine's] . . . policy" of consensus and pluralism.[27] This policy was continued by "the refusal of his successors for almost fifty years to take any but token steps against pagan practices."[28] And a public culture emerged that mixed Christian and pagan elements in ways that seem remarkable, given the traditional accounts of unrelenting repression. A newly famous example is a calendar prepared in 354 for an upper-class Roman.[29]

The calendar was created by a prominent artist who later fulfilled commissions for Pope Damasus, and it is likely that many such calendars were circulated. As with Catholic calendars ever after, this one noted all of the festivals of the Church and commemorated the burial dates of important popes. But it also included illustrated sections consisting of "representations of those rites of the Roman public cult associated with each month." Careful examination of the calendar confirms that the Christian and pagan elements are not discordant elements, but they, as Peter Brown put it, "form a coherent whole; they sidle up to each other."[30] Indeed, a sort of Christo-paganism was prevalent well into the fifth century, and probably later. In Ravenna during the 440s, the bishop expressed his dismay that "the new birth of the year is blessed by outworn sacrilege" in reaction to the participation of "the most Catholic princes" of the city in pagan rites involving their dressing as "the gods of Rome" and comporting themselves before a huge audience in the Hippodrome.[31] In similar fashion, not even Saint Augustine could convince his flock in Hippo that such matters as bountiful crops and good health were not, in effect, subcontracted to pagan gods by the One True God,[32] as Christians in Hippo continued to regard it as it both legitimate and valuable to perform pagan rites. In many parts of Europe, the use of paganism as magic has continued into the modern era.[33]

Unfortunately, the era of toleration that existed under Constantine was misrepresented by early Christian writers, particularly Eusebius, who wanted to show that the emperor was the chosen instrument to achieve God's will that all traces of paganism be quickly stamped out and the One True Faith established as the Church Triumphant. It may have been an effective polemic, but it was spurious history and, worst of all, it was avidly seized upon by eighteenth- and nineteenth-century Protestant historians who were eager to place the Church in the worst possible light. In truth, it was not Constantine who reinstituted religious persecution, but Julian, the last pagan emperor.

Julian's Folly

Flavius Claudius Julianus, now known as Julian the Apostate, had only a brief (361–63) and quite disastrous rule as emperor. Despite that, he has become a virtual saint among anti-Catholic and anti-Christian intellectuals. Edward Gibbon complained[34] that Julian's many virtues have been "clouded" by the "irreconcilable hostility" of his Christian enemies who despised him for his "devout and sincere attachments to the gods of Athens and Rome."[35] Two centuries later, Gore Vidal turned Julian's life into a heroic novel. Throughout, the central theme has been that while Julian did seek to revive the vigor of paganism, he did so in a tolerant spirit. The truth is quite different.

Julian was ostensibly raised as a Christian, but some of his prominent tutors were pagans, and they steeped him in the Greek classics.[36] Under their tutelage, Julian became a puritanical, ascetic, and fanatical[37] pagan, who had been initiated into several of the mystery cults, including the Eleusinian mysteries[38] and probably Mithraism[39] as well. Julian was careful to comport "himself publicly as a Christian while worshiping the pagan gods"[40] until he took the throne. Once installed as emperor, Julian loudly revealed his contempt for those he reviled as

Box 3.1. Some leading historians whose work informed this chapter. Specific studies by each can be found in the bibliography.

TIMOTHY BARNES was for thirty-one years professor of classics at the University of Toronto, and he now holds an honorary fellowship at Edinburgh's School of Divinity. He was born in England and received his DPhil in 1970 from Oxford. In 1982, he was awarded the Philip Schaff Prize by the American Society of Church History for his book *Constantine and Eusebius*.

PETER BROWN is Rollins Professor of History Emeritus at Princeton University. He was born in Dublin, Ireland, and was educated at Oxford. Upon graduation, he was awarded a seven-year Prize Fellowship and thus began his distinguished academic career at Oxford without bothering to earn a doctorate. He soon published what became a classic work, *Augustine of Hippo: A Biography* (1967), and that made an advanced degree unnecessary. He was elected a fellow of the British Academy in 1971 and then left Britain to become professor of classics and history at the University of California, Berkeley. He moved to Princeton in 1986.

H. A. DRAKE is research professor of history at the University of California, Santa Barbara, where he has spent his entire professional career, after having received his PhD from the University of Wisconsin in 1970. His studies of Constantine challenged and subsequently changed the prevailing view that Constantine's conversion to Christianity was bogus and that he savagely imposed the church on a pagan-dominated world.

RAMSAY MACMULLEN is emeritus professor of history at Yale University. In 2001, the American Historical Association cited him as "the greatest historian of the Roman Empire alive today." I have learned more from his sixteen books than from any others on that period, especially *Paganism in the Roman Empire* (1984) and *Christianizing the Roman Empire, AD 100–400* (1989).

"Galileans" whose "haughty ministers," according to Gibbon, "neither understood nor believed their religion"[41] and at once set about trying to restore paganism as the state-supported, dominant faith.

Not wanting to create new martyrs, Julian did not initiate the bloody persecution of Christians, à la Nero or Diocletian, but he condoned the torture of several bishops, exiled others, and ignored the "summary executions that seem to have taken place in large numbers in central and southern Syria during [his] reign."[42] Thus, there was no imperial response when the "holy virgins [in Heliopolis] were rent limb from limb and their remains thrown to the pigs."[43] When knowledge that a pagan emperor now ruled prompted pagans in Alexandria to torture the city's Christian bishop, to tear him limb from limb, and to then crucify "many Christians," Julian's main concern was to obtain the dead bishop's library for himself.[44]

In a gesture that the distinguished H. A. Drake compared to "a schoolboy thumbing his nose at his teachers,"[45] Julian revived the widespread celebration of blood sacrifices, sometimes involving a hundred cattle at a time, a practice that had long been outlawed in response to Christian influence. In addition, Julian cut off state funding of the churches and subsidized the temples. He replaced Christians with pagans in high imperial offices (see Table 3.1). In an action that was far more significant than it might appear to modern readers, Julian made it illegal for Christians to teach the classics. This meant that upper-class parents had to choose between sending their offspring to be instructed by pagans or deny them the opportunity to acquire "the language, the looks, the innumerable coded signals that were absorbed unconsciously with classical *paideia* [or education, without which] Christian children would not have been able to compete in the elite culture of classical antiquity, as Julian knew full well."[46]

But, as Drake noted, the deepest of all the "wounds [Julian] was able to inflict, despite a relatively short tenure," was to revive Christian anxieties that another era of vicious persecution lay ahead: "Christians at the time . . . had no assurance that another Julian was not in the offing, and they could plausibly fear that worse was yet to come."[47] Consequently, "Julian was a blessing" for those Christians who opposed pluralism. As Drake summed up: "The effect of Julian's efforts was to polarize Christians and pagans, to remove the middle ground that traditional culture had previously provided, while at the same time lending credence to militant fears of a revival of persecution."[48] Julian's friend and admirer Liabius agreed that Julian "refused the use of force, but still the threat of fear hung over [the Christians], for they expected to be blinded or beheaded: rivers of blood would flow in massacres, they thought, and the new master would devise new-fangled tortures, the fire, sword, drowning, burial alive, hacking and mutilation seemed child's play. Such had been the behaviour of his predecessors and they expected his measures to be more severe still."[49]

Persecution and Persistence

Although he ruled for only eighteen months and was killed during battle in a foolish campaign against the Persians, Julian's name still terrorized Christians a generation later.[50] However, he was not replaced by another pagan emperor, although his favorite Procopius tried to take the throne, naming himself emperor at Constantinople late in 365. However, Procopius was deserted by the army and executed as a rebel, so it was Jovian who managed to take the throne. Jovian was a Christian who undid some of Julian's anti-Christian actions, but he ruled for only a year before being succeeded by Valentinian in the West and by his brother Valens in the East. Although Valentinian was a devoted Christian, he also was quite tolerant[51] and continued to appoint many pagans to high office. Valens was a rather fanatical Arian Christian who persecuted non-Arian Christians from time to time but who also appointed many pagans.

Nevertheless, in the wake of Julian's campaign for paganism, the Church was able to obtain statutes forbidding certain pagan activities. In three edicts issued during 391–92, Theodosius I banned public and private sacrifices to the gods. These were not only blood sacrifices, but also "such pagan devotions as sprinkling incense on altars, hanging sacred fillets on trees and raising turf altars."[52] However, these prohibitions were so widely ignored that each of the next two emperors, Arcadius and Justinian, reasserted the ban. Pagans obeyed to the extent of no longer conducting massive public animal slaughters, but commitment to paganism remained open and widespread.[53]

It is important to recognize that paganism was not merely a set of superficial practices and only half-believed myths—or, as Lactantius put it, "no more than worship by the fingertips."[54] In past work I have been as guilty as most early Church historians of underestimating the depth of paganism. Indeed, late fourth- and fifth-century pagans often are portrayed as little more than "nostalgic antiquarians." But, in fact theirs was an active faith "premised upon the conviction that the world was filled with the divine, and that proper sacrifice brought the human into intimate communion with the divine."[55] Although the rapid and extensive Christianization of the empire showed that pagans were very susceptible to conversion by their friends and relatives, the failure of legal prohibitions to dent paganism demonstrated that coercion was of no greater deterrent to commitment to the Gods than it had been when used against commitment to the One True God. Moreover, imperial efforts to actually suppress paganism by force were far less sustained and far less vigorous than has long been claimed. Consider that well into the fifth century, men who were openly pagans were still being appointed as consuls and prefects, as were many more who kept their religious preference obscure—something Christians had no reason to do (Table 3.1). As late as the sixth century, temples remained open in many parts of the empire,[56] and some survived into the eighth century.[57]

In the post-Julian era, the public persistence of paganism did not reflect imperial tolerance so much as imperial pragmatism. Emperors often complained that their edicts against paganism were ignored, and it seems revealing that there is "no record of anyone in the fourth century having been prosecuted" for sacrificing to the gods.[58] One imperial letter complained that "Provincial governors set aside imperial commands for the sake of private favors, and they openly allow the [Christian] religion which we [emperors] properly venerate to be openly disturbed, perhaps because they themselves are negligent."[59] Emperor Honorius complained that laws against paganism were not enforced because of the "sloth of the governors . . . [and] the connivance of their office staffs."[60] However, the emperors carefully did not crack down on those provincial governors who justified their inaction on grounds that enforcement of edicts against paganism would create levels of public discontent that "would seriously disrupt the collection of taxes in the province."[61] Hence, in 400 CE, Emperor Arcadius rejected a proposal to destroy the temples in Gaza, remarking, "I know that the city is full of idols, but it shows [devotion] in paying its taxes. . . . If we suddenly terrorize these people, they will run away and we will lose considerable revenues."[62] Roger Brown proposed that persistent paganism served the emperor especially well, as cities would "have been all the more punctual in paying their taxes, it they needed to preserve . . . their ancestral religious practices" from imperial intervention.[63]

It even is questionable whether most emperors expected their various edicts involving Christianity and paganism to be fully observed. For example, when urged to do so by the bishops, Constantine outlawed gladiatorial combats. But when some Umbrian towns petitioned him for permission to celebrate the imperial cult with a festival that would include gladiatorial combats, Constantine granted their request. In similar fashion, Constantius issued an edict to close all pagan temples immediately. Then, in virtually the same breath, he advised the prefect of Rome to care for and sustain the temples around the city. During a subsequent visit to Rome, Constantius toured these temples and expressed his admiration for them.[64] For the fact was that even well into the fifth century "a considerable section of the population of the Roman empire, at all social levels, remained unaffected" by Christianity. "They [remained] impenitently polytheistic, in that the religious common sense of their age, as of all previous centuries, led them to assume a spiritual landscape rustling with invisible presences—with countless divine beings and their ethereal ministers."[65]

In the end, of course, the pagan temples did close and Christianity became, for many centuries, the only licit faith. But to the contrary of early Christian and later antireligious historians, it didn't happen suddenly nor did it involve substantial bloodshed—the latter was mainly limited to conflicts *among* Christians, which sometimes resulted in military action against various heretical movements.[66]

The Decline of Paganism

Gibbon dates the "final destruction of Paganism" to the reign of Theodosius (379–95), noting that this "is perhaps the only example of the total extirpation of any ancient and popular superstition; and may therefore deserve to be considered, as a singular event in the history of the human mind." And, of course, this extirpation occurred because "Rome submitted to the yoke of the Gospel."[67] But as with so much reported by Gibbon, it simply wasn't so. Consider one fact alone: Theodosius, the emperor who, according to Gibbon, extirpated paganism, appointed nearly as many men who were openly pagans as he did Christians to the positions of consuls and prefects, as can be seen in Table 3.1.

This table has often been referred to in the chapter, but here is the appropriate place to consider it in detail. The initial coding was done by Raban von Haehling in 1978. Subsequently, T. D. Barnes corrected von Haehling's statistics through the reign of Constantius (351–61) to eliminate some duplications when the same man was appointed several times. Although Barnes's figures are undoubtedly more accurate, they resulted in no fundamental reinterpretations, and there is no reason to refrain from using von Haehling's original findings for the reign of Julian and later.

Reading across the table, there seem to be three major patterns. First, except narrowly during the reign of Constantine and by a greater margin among those appointed by Constantius, men known to be Christians were not in the majority, and this held for the first half of the fifth century as well. Second, Julian did discriminate against Christians, although not entirely. Third, if it can be assumed that men whose religious affiliation is unknown were unlikely to have been Christians (since it was beneficial to be known as a Christian), then the decline of pagan influence and power was very slow indeed.

Many have argued that paganism held its own far longer among the upper classes and the educated than among persons of lesser rank.[68] But that is mostly inferred from the known paganism of many persons of rank and the "assumption" that Christianity's primary appeal was to the lower classes. However, since it is now recognized that Christianity had as much or more appeal to the upper classes as to the lower, that inference is unjustified.[69] Rather, what Table 3.1 more likely demonstrates is that paganism died slowly in all classes and, as it did, the upper classes became increasingly discreet about their religious identity, seeking to maintain their positions and their access to imperial favor.

And that brings into view a major factor in the Christianization of the empire: opportunism. From the time of Constantine, with the very brief exception of Julian's reign, the imperial throne was in Christian hands and very likely to remain there. Although some identifiable pagans continued to be appointed to high political offices, their prospects were on the downward trend. In addition, the many powerful and increasingly lucrative positions in the Church were closed to them. Understandably, many ambitious individuals and families chose to convert. As Roger Brown put it, "A groundswell of confidence that Christians enjoyed access to the powerful spelled the end of polytheism far more effectively than did any imperial law or the closing of any temple."[70] Even many pagan philosophers broke ranks, some of them becoming leading bishops of the Church.[71]

Assimilation

The word "pagan" derives from the Latin word *paganus*, which originally meant "rural person," or more colloquially "country hick." It came to have religious meaning because after Christianity had triumphed in the cities, most of the rural people remained unconverted. However, even in the cities, as already noted, an elaborate mixture of Christianity and paganism flourished for centuries. As for rural people, most of them seem never to have been fully Christianized, in that they transplanted their familiar Gods, sacred places, rites, and holidays into Christianity. As MacMullen put it: "The triumph of the church was not one of obliteration but of widening embrace and assimilation."[72]

The assimilation of paganism reflected several things. First of all, once established as the official faith of the empire, Christian leaders soon adopted a "trickle down" theory of conversion.[73] It was sufficient that the upper classes in an area acknowledged the authority of the Church and then waited for their example to eventually trickle down the ranks until the peasants were Christians, too. But the peasants tended to respond to Christianity as they always had to the appearance of various new Gods within paganism—to add the new to the old, rather than to replace it. Hence, Jesus and various saints were simply added to the local pantheon. As was written in the Icelandic *Landnánabók*, Helgi the Lean "believed in Christ, but invoked Thor in matters of seafaring and dire necessity."[74]

A second basis for the assimilation of paganism was overt Church policy. In a letter dated 601 and preserved by the Venerable Bede,[75] Pope Gregory the Great advised Abbot Mellitus, who was setting out to missionize Britain: "[I] have come to the conclusion that temples of the idols among that people should on no account be destroyed. . . . For it is certainly impossible to eradicate all errors from obstinate minds at one stroke." Instead, the pope recommended that altars and sacred relics should be placed in the pagan temples, which would transform them into Christian edifices. The same policy was applied to the other pagan sites. "The hundreds of magical springs which dotted the country became 'holy wells,' associated with a saint, but they were still used for magical healing and for divining the future."[76] The famous healing shrine just outside Alexandria, dedicated to the Goddess Isis, underwent an elaborate transformation into a Christian healing site when the remains of two martyrs were placed inside. The same process of assimilation was applied to the plentiful sacred groves, rock formations, and other pagan sites. People continued to visit these traditional sites for the original reasons, even if these sites now took on Christian coloration, although many of the visitors continued to direct their supplications to the old gods.[77]

Traditional pagan ways for celebrating holidays also were quickly assimilated by Church, and in this way, a great deal of festive dancing, bell-ringing, candle-lighting, and, especially, singing became "Christian." As MacMullen noted, "Among Christians, singing was at first limited to psalms, as had always been the custom among Jews. After the mid-fourth century, however, more is heard of a different sort of music not only at private parties . . . but in the very churches as well. . . . The intrusion of music into a sacred setting must obviously be credited to the old cults."[78]

The early church fathers also were careful to assimilate the primary pagan festivals by Christianizing them. This was noted by Augustine (354–430) when "crowds of pagans wishing to become Christians were prevented from doing this because of their habits of celebrating feast days to their idols with banquets and carousing. . . . Our ancestors thought it would be good to make a concession . . . and permit them to celebrate other feasts."[79] The Bible does not say when Jesus was born, and when the Church settled on a date for Christmas, the pagan celebration of Saturnalia was selected. May Day became the feast day for Saints Philip and James; Midsummer Eve became the Nativity of Saint John.[80] Easter occurs at the time of the spring equinox, and the name itself may have come from the Saxon Goddess Eostre. All Saints Eve seems to have been introduced to overlie the traditional harvest festival. It also has been generally accepted that some minor local saints are overlays of equally minor, local pagan deities. Thus, several respected historians insist that "pre-Christian ceremonial" and a "persistent pagan mentality"[81] have lived on among rural and small-town Europeans, among whom "pagan antiquity . . . never disappeared."[82]

Conclusion

In one of his thousands of letters, this one written around 420, the Christian monk Isidore of Pelusium remarked: "The pagan faith, made dominant for so many years, by such pains, such expenditure of wealth, such feats of arms, has vanished from the earth."[83] More than 1,500 years later, the prominent Oxford historian E. R. Dodds (1893–1973) agreed: "In the fourth-century paganism appears as a kind of living corpse, which begins to collapse from the moment when the supporting hand of the State is withdrawn."[84]

But it wasn't true. In the fourth and early fifth centuries, paganism was still quite robust. But to recognize that fact it is necessary, as Peter Brown put it, to attend to "tantalizing fragments" of historical evidence that can be "glimpsed through the chinks in a body of evidence which claims to tell a very different story." That story being that "this one short period of time (under a century) witnessed the 'death of paganism' . . . as a succession of Christian emperors . . . played out their God-given role in abolishing . . . the old gods."[85]

Granted that the early church fathers were certain that theirs was the Only True Faith, and therefore they could not, and did not, commit themselves to ideals of religious freedom. Nevertheless, the Church did not exploit its official standing to quickly stamp out paganism, nor did the emperors accomplish this on behalf of the new faith. Instead, paganism survived relatively unmolested for centuries after the conversion of Constantine, only slowly sinking into obscurity, meanwhile managing to create niches for some of its traditions within Christianity.

The myth of the "Dark Ages:" It is well-known that during the Dark Ages, the Church dominated all intellectual life to such an extent that ignorance prevailed all across Europe. This myth holds that even literacy was severely limited to those in religious orders.

Imposing the Dark Ages   4

~~~~~~

F OR MANY WESTERN intellectuals, the Fall does not refer to the fate of Adam and Eve, but to the fate of civilization after the collapse of Rome. "Christianity conquered the Roman Empire and most of Europe. Then we observe a Europe-wide phenomenon of scholarly amnesia, which afflicted the continent from AD 300 to at least 1300." This occurred because "the leaders of orthodox Christendom built a grand barrier against the progress of knowledge."[1]

These sentences were published in a chapter titled "The Prison of Christian Dogma" in a best-selling book called *The Discoverers* (1983). The author was not just another writer, but Daniel J. Boorstin (1914–2004), onetime professor at the University of Chicago, then the librarian of Congress and senior historian at the Smithsonian Institution. During his illustrious career, Boorstin won both the Bancroft and Pulitzer Prizes. These honors were not inconsistent with Boorstin's view about the harmful effects of the Roman Catholic Church on classical learning. It has long been the received wisdom that following the collapse of Rome, Europe slumbered through a millennium of ignorance that came to be known as the Dark Ages (and sometimes as the Age of Faith). The celebrated Cambridge historian J. B. Bury (1861–1927) noted that when Emperor Constantine adopted Christianity, this "inaugurated a millennium in which reason was enchained, thought was enslaved, and knowledge made no progress."[2] And the distinguished William Manchester (1922–2004) described this as an era "of incessant warfare, corruption, lawlessness, obsession with strange myths, and an almost impenetrable mindlessness . . . The Dark Ages were stark in every dimension."[3]

The Italian humanist Petrarch (1304–74) may have been the first to call "the period stretching from the fall of the Roman Empire down to his own age as a time of 'darkness,'"[4] an anti-Catholic judgment that has echoed down the centuries. Thus, Voltaire (1694–1778) described this long era as one when "barbarism, superstition, [and] ignorance covered the face of the world."[5] According to Rousseau (1712–78), "Europe had relapsed into the barbarism of the earliest ages. The people of this part of the world . . . lived some centuries ago in a condition worse than ignorance."[6] Edward Gibbon (1737–94) also proclaimed that the fall of Rome was the "triumph of barbarism and religion."[7] More recently, Bertrand Russell (1872–1970) lent his awesome authority to the matter, writing in the illustrated edition of his famous college textbook: "As the central authority of Rome decayed, the lands of the Western Empire began to sink into an era of barbarism during which Europe suffered a general cultural decline. The Dark Ages, as they are called . . . it is not inappropriate to call these centuries dark, especially if they are set against what came before and what came after."[8]

As Russell suggested, the prevailing ignorance during the Dark Ages seems magnified by contrast with the Renaissance. Being the French word for "rebirth," the Renaissance identifies the era beginning at the end of the fourteenth century when Europeans rediscovered long-forgotten classical learning, thereby causing new light to break through the prevailing intellectual darkness. According to the standard historical account, the Renaissance occurred because a decline in Church control over major northern Italian cities, such as Florence,[9] allowed a revival of classical Greco-Roman culture. Furthermore, this new appreciation for knowledge, especially for scientific knowledge not hobbled by theology, led directly from the Renaissance to the Enlightenment. Also known as the Age of Reason, the Enlightenment is said to have begun in the sixteenth century when (aided by the Reformation) secular thinkers freed themselves from clerical control and revolutionized both science and philosophy, thereby ushering in the modern world. To quote Bertrand Russell once more: "Enlightenment was essentially a revaluation of independent intellectual activity, aimed quite literally at spreading light where hitherto darkness had prevailed."[10]

To summarize, Western history consists of four major eras: (1) classical antiquity, (2) then the Dark Ages when the Church dominated, followed by (3) the Renaissance-Enlightenment that led the way to (4) modern times.

For several centuries that has been the fundamental organizing scheme for every textbook devoted to Western history,[11] despite the fact that serious historians have known for decades that this scheme is a complete fraud—"an indestructible fossil of self-congratulatory Renaissance humanism."[12] It is appropriate to use the term "Renaissance" to identify a particular period in the arts when there was renewed interest in classical styles and to distinguish this period from the Gothic or the Baroque. But it is inappropriate to apply this term to identify the rebirth of intellectual progress following the Dark Ages because there never were any Dark Ages. Even the respectable encyclopedias now define the Dark Ages as a myth. *The Columbia Encyclopedia* rejects the term, noting that "medieval civilization is no longer thought to have been so dim." *Britannica* disdains the term Dark Ages as "pejorative." And Wikipedia defines the Dark Ages as "a supposed period of intellectual darkness after the fall of Rome." As for the recovery of classical learning, to the extent it ever was lost, Church scholars accomplished the recovery long before the Renaissance. And if one wishes to identify an Age of Reason, it must be redated to have begun very early in the Christian era, for the Western faith in reason originated in Christian theology.

The Myth of the Dark Ages

To assume that the sacking of the city of Rome in 410 by Alaric and his Gothic forces caused "the whole world to perish," as Saint Jerome (347–420) lamented, is to assume that the only civilized people of that time lived in the city itself. But of course, true Romans lived all over the empire, and they didn't suddenly become ignorant when the city fell. Indeed, at the time, Rome was not even still the capital of the empire; the emperor had moved to Ravenna. The fall of the city was, no doubt, of immense symbolic importance, but symbols should not be mistaken for reality.

Of even greater importance, the Goths who conquered Rome were not barbarians, regardless of what the Romans called them. Alaric had served as a commander in the Roman army, and the majority of his troops were Roman army veterans. By the same token, the "barbarian north" had long since been fully "Romanized" and sustained sophisticated manu-facturing centers with active trade routes even to the Far East. For exam-ple, as early at 250 CE, the island city of Helgö near Stockholm, Sweden, was a flourishing industrial center turning out "large quantities of iron tools and weapons, bronze jewelry, gold ornaments, and other products . . . [including] locks and keys . . . [and] glass beads." Coins found at the site of Helgö show it was involved in a vast trade network, and so does the finding of a "bronze Buddha figure made in India."[13] Nor was Helgö an anomaly: there were numerous industrial centers like it all over northern Europe, home of the supposed barbarians.

Incredibly, not only was there no "fall" into "Dark Ages," this was "one of the great innovative eras of mankind," as technology was devel-oped and put into use "on a scale no civilization had previously known" as the French historian Jean Gimpel put it.[14] In fact, it was during the Dark Ages that Europe took the great technological leap forward that put it ahead of the rest of the world.[15] How could historians have so misrepresented things?

In part, the notion that Europe fell into the "Dark Ages" was a hoax perpetrated by very antireligious intellectuals such as Voltaire and Gib-bon, who were determined to claim that theirs was the era of "Enlight-enment." Another factor was that intellectuals too often have no interest in anything but literary matters. It is quite true that after the fall of Rome, educated Europeans did not write nearly as elegant Latin as had the best

Roman writers. For many, that was sufficient cause to regard this as a backward time. In addition, during this era, only limited attention was paid to classical thinkers such as Plato and Aristotle, and that too was taken as proof of widespread ignorance.

Another component contributing to the myth of the Dark Ages was that in this era there were no longer large cities having hundreds of thousands of residents, as had ancient Rome and Alexandria.[16] It seemed obvious that high culture could not have been sustained in the small communities of medieval Europe—in the year 1000 there were only 20,000 inhabitants in Paris, not many more in London, and Rome had shrunk to fewer than 30,000.[17] But perhaps the most important factor in the myth of the Dark Ages was the inability of intellectuals to value or even to notice the nuts and bolts of real life. Hence, revolutions in agriculture, weaponry and warfare, nonhuman power, transportation, manufacturing, and commerce went unappreciated. So too did remarkable moral progress. For example, at the fall of Rome there was slavery everywhere in Europe; by the time of the Renaissance it was long gone. But what is truly difficult to explain is how the creators of the Dark Ages myth could have overlooked what would seem to have been their chief interest: high culture. Nevertheless, they missed or dismissed the enormous progress that took place in music, art, literature, education, and science.

I have written at length in *How the West Won* (2014) on what truly took place during the mythical era of the Dark Ages. Here a summary will suffice.

Progress in Technology

The Romans made little use of water or wind power—preferring manual labor performed by slaves. An inventory conducted in the ninth century found that one-third of the estates along the Seine River in the area around Paris had water mills, the majority of them on Church-owned properties.[18] Several centuries later there was one mill every seventy feet along this stretch of the river![19] Meanwhile, across the channel, the

Domesday Book, compiled in 1086 as a forerunner of the modern census, reported that there were at least 5,624 water-powered mills already operating in England, or one for every fifty families, and this is known to be an undercount.[20] Among many other things, mills such as these mechanized the manufacture of woolen cloth and soon enabled England to dominate the European market.[21] Many dams also were constructed during the Dark Ages; one at Toulouse, built around 1120, was more than thirteen hundred feet across and was constructed by driving thousands of giant oak logs into the riverbed to form a front and rear palisade and then was filled with dirt and stone.[22]

Box 4.1. Some leading historians whose work informed this chapter. Specific studies by each can be found in the bibliography.

MARC BLOCH (1886–1944) was the most influential French historian of the twentieth century. He was born in Lyon to a Jewish family and his father was a professor of ancient history. Bloch studied in Paris, Berlin, and Leipzig before serving as an officer in the French infantry in World War I. After the war he continued his studies at the University of Strasbourg and in 1924 published his first book—it was an immense success. In 1936 he became professor of economic history at the Sorbonne, and in 1939 he published his two-volume masterwork, *Feudal Society*. That same year World War II was declared and Bloch, at age fifty-two, left his university post to serve as a captain in the French army. After France fell to the Germans in 1940, Bloch became active in the French resistance. He was betrayed to the Gestapo and on June 16, 1944—10 days after the Allies had landed in Normandy—Bloch was shot by a German firing squad.

FRANCES (1915–2013) and **JOSEPH** (1916–2006) **GIES** were an American wife-and-husband team of independent scholars who wrote a number of fine and entertaining books about medieval life that helped to dispel the

During this era, Europeans also harnessed the wind. They not only used windmills to power the same equipment as did water mills, they also used them to reclaim huge portions of what are now Belgium and the Netherlands by pumping out the sea—tens of thousands of windmills devoted to this task worked day and night throughout most of the Dark Ages. Indeed, by late in the twelfth century, Western Europe had become so crowded with windmills that owners began to file lawsuits against one another for blocking their wind[23] (Europeans in this era sustained well-organized courts and a host of lawyers, although that may not have amounted to progress).

myth of the Dark Ages, especially their fine *Cathedral, Forge, and Waterwheel: Technology and Invention in the Middle Ages* (1994). Their work is well respected by professional historians.

JEAN GIMPEL (1918–96) was a French historian and medievalist who was independently wealthy and did not need to hold an academic position. Like Bloch, he was active in the French resistance movement during World War II, for which he was awarded both the Croix de Guerre and the Legion of Honor—France's highest medal. In 1987, Gimpel was a founding vice president of the Society of Medieval Technology and Science. He wrote four books, the most influential being *The Medieval Machine: The Industrial Revolution of the Middle Ages*.

LYNN TOWNSEND WHITE JR. (1907–87) was a professor of medieval history at Princeton, then at Stanford, and subsequently became president of Mills College, then a women's school in Oakland, California. In 1958, he left Mills and became a professor at the University of California, Los Angeles and served there until his death. White specialized in the history of technology and was among the first to dismiss the notion of the Dark Ages on the basis of the remarkable progress in technology that had taken place during these supposedly backward centuries. He dedicated his most famous work, *Medieval Technology and Social Change*, to Marc Bloch.

Meanwhile, agriculture was revolutionized.[24] First came the shift to a three-field system wherein one-third of the productive land was left unplanted each year while continuing to be cultivated (to remove weeds) and fertilized. The result of this renewal of the land was far greater production. In addition, the invention of the heavy plow permitted far better cultivation of the wetter, denser soils north of Italy, and the introduction of the horse collar permitted the replacement of teams of slow oxen with teams of horses, thus at least doubling the speed of cultivation. Selective plant breeding also began in the monasteries, resulting in more productive and hardy crops. Altogether these Dark Ages achievements fed a larger population much better and provided sustenance for larger urban populations.

Also of immense importance was the invention of chimneys, which allowed buildings and homes to be heated without needing holes in the roof to let out smoke while letting in rain, snow, and cold air. Another revolutionary innovation was eyeglasses, which were invented in about 1280 and almost immediately went into mass production, thus allowing huge numbers of people to lead productive lives who otherwise could not have done so.[25] In 1492, when Columbus set out on his first voyage west, eyeglasses still were known only in Europe.

Prior to the Dark Ages, there was no heavy cavalry. Mounted troops did not charge headlong at a gallop, putting the full weight of horse and rider behind a long lance. The reason was the lack of stirrups and a proper saddle. Without stirrups to brace against, a rider attempting to drive home a lance would be thrown off his horse. The ability of a rider to withstand sudden shocks was also greatly increased by a saddle with a very high pommel and cantle—the latter being curved to partly enclose the rider's hips. It was not Rome or any other warlike empire that produced heavy cavalry: their mounted troops rode on light, almost flat, pad saddles, or even bareback, and they had no stirrups. Consequently, these mounted warriors could only fire bows, throw spears, or swing swords. They could not bowl over their opponents. It was the "barbarous" Franks who, in 732, fielded the first armored knights astride massive horses and who slaughtered invading Muslim forces on the battlefield of Tours when they charged them behind long lances, secure in their high-backed Norman saddles and braced in their revolutionary stirrups.[26] Nearly four centuries later, when the knights of Europe confronted Muslim armies in the Holy Land, nothing had changed. The Crusaders still were the only ones with stirrups and adequate saddles.

Roman sea power was based on galleys powered by oars and having only an auxiliary sail. Roman ships fought by ramming one another and then by engaging in hand-to-hand combat with swords and spears. But well before the end of the Dark Ages, Europeans had invented true sailing ships and armed them with cannons.[27] That gunpowder was not invented in the West is immaterial. What matters is that within a decade of the arrival of gunpowder from China, church bell manufacturers all over Europe were casting effective cannons that were adopted by every army and navy, transforming the nature of war.[28] In contrast, the Chinese built only a few, ineffective cannons, mostly being content to use gunpowder in fireworks.[29]

These are only a few of the important technological innovations achieved during the Dark Ages. What is clear is that so much important technological progress occurred during these so-called Dark Ages that classical Greece and Rome had been left far behind. In fact, even though they did not yet possess cannons, the Crusader knights who marched off to the Holy Land in 1097 would have made short work of the Roman legions.

Moral Progress

All classical societies were slave societies. In fact, all known societies above the very primitive level have been slave societies—even many of the northwest Indian tribes had slaves long before Columbus's voyage.[30] Amid this universal slavery, only one civilization ever rejected human bondage: Christendom. And it did it twice!

The story of how slavery reappeared and then was prohibited in the Western Hemisphere will be told in chapter 8. But the very first time slavery was eliminated anywhere in the world was not during the Renaissance or the Enlightenment. It was during the Dark Ages. And it was accomplished by clever Church leaders who first extended the sacraments to all slaves, reserving only ordination into the priesthood. Initially, the implications of the Christianization of slaves went unnoticed, but soon the clergy began to argue that no true Christian (or Jew) should be enslaved.[31] Since slaves were Christians, priests began to urge owners to free their slaves as an "infinitely commendable act" that helped ensure their own salvation.[32] Many manumissions were recorded in surviving wills. Soon there was another factor: intermarriage. Despite being against the law in most of Europe, there is considerable evidence of mixed unions by the seventh century, usually involving free men and female slaves. The most celebrated of these unions took place in 649 when Clovis II, king of the Franks, married his British slave Bathilda. When Clovis died in 657, Bathilda ruled as regent until her eldest son came of age. Bathilda used her position to mount a campaign to halt the slave trade and to redeem those in slavery. Upon her death, the Church acknowledged Bathilda as a saint.

At the end of the eighth century, Charlemagne opposed slavery, while the pope and many other many powerful and effective clerical voices echoed Saint Bathilda. As the ninth century dawned, Bishop Agobard of Lyons thundered: "All men are brothers, all invoke one same Father, God: the slave and the master, the poor man and the rich man, the ignorant and the learned, the weak and the strong. . . . None has been raised above the other. . . . There is no . . . slave or free, but in all things and always there is only Christ."[33] Soon, no one "doubted that slavery in itself was against divine law."[34] Indeed, during the eleventh century, both Saint Wulfstan and Saint Anselm successfully campaigned to remove the last vestiges of slavery in Christendom.[35]

The abolition of slavery was merely the most dramatic instance of moral progress during the Dark Ages. Chapter 9 examines the roots of democracy in Christian doctrines of moral equality and in negative theological assessments of the state, which resulted in surprisingly representative elected "parliaments," first in various Italian city-states and then farther north.

Progress in High Culture

Even if Voltaire, Gibbon, and other proponents of the supposed Enlightenment could be excused for being oblivious to engineering achievements and to innovations in agriculture or warfare, surely they must be judged severely for ignoring or dismissing the remarkable achievements in "high culture" accomplished by medieval Europeans in music, art, literature, education, and science.

MUSIC

The Romans and Greeks sang and played monophonic music: a single musical line sounded by all voices or instruments. It was medieval musicians who invented polyphony, the simultaneous sounding of two or more musical lines, hence harmonies. Just when this occurred is unknown, but "it was an established practice when it was described in *Musica enchiriadis*," published around 900.[36] And, in about the tenth century, an adequate system of musical notation was invented and popularized so that music could be accurately performed by musicians who had never heard it.

ART

Unfortunately, the remarkable artistic era that emerged in eleventh-century Europe is known as "Romanesque," despite the fact that it was quite different from anything done by the Romans. This name was imposed by nineteenth-century professors who "knew" that Europe only recovered from the Dark Ages by *going back* to Roman culture. Hence, this could only have been an era of poor imitations of things Roman. In fact, Romanesque architecture, sculpture, and painting were original and powerful in ways that "even the late Roman artists would never have understood."[37] Then, in the twelfth century, the Romanesque period was followed by the even more powerful Gothic era. It seems astonishing, but Gothic architecture and painting were scorned by critics during the Enlightenment for not conforming to "the standards of classical Greece and Rome: 'May he who invented it be cursed.'"[38] These same critics mistakenly thought the style originated with the "barbarous" Goths (hence the name) and, as anyone who has seen one of Europe's great Gothic cathedrals knows, the artistic judgment of these critics was no better than their history, to say nothing of their disregard for the architectural inventions, including the flying buttress, that made it possible for the first time to build very tall buildings with thin walls and large windows, thus prompting major achievements in stained glass. It also was thirteenth-century artists in northern Europe who were the first to use oil paint and to put their work on stretched canvass rather than on wood or plaster. This "allowed the painter to take his time, to use brushes of amazing delicacy, to achieve effects . . . which seemed close to miracles."[39] Anyone who thinks that great painting began with the Italian Renaissance should examine the work of the Van Eycks. So much, then, for notions that the millennium following the collapse of Rome was an artistic blank or worse.

LITERATURE

Gibbon wrote *The Decline and Fall of the Roman Empire* in English, not Latin. Voltaire wrote exclusively in French, Cervantes in Spanish, and Machiavelli and Da Vinci in Italian. This was possible only because these languages had been given literary form by medieval giants such as Dante, Chaucer, the nameless authors of the *chansons de geste*, and the monks who, beginning in the ninth century, devoted themselves to writing the lives of saints—"the first known pages of French literature . . . belong to this genre."[40] Thus, vernacular prose was formulated and popularized. So much for Dark Age illiteracy and ignorance.

EDUCATION

The university was something new under the sun—an institution devoted exclusively to "higher learning." This Christian invention was quite unlike Chinese academies for training Mandarins or a Zen master's school. The new universities were not primarily concerned with imparting the received wisdom. Rather, just as is the case today, faculty gained fame and invitations to join faculties elsewhere by innovation. Consequently, during the Dark Ages, university professors—now known as the Scholastics—gave their primary attention to the pursuit of knowledge.[41] And they achieved many remarkable results, as will be outlined in chapter 7.

The first two universities appeared in Paris (where both Albertus Magnus and Thomas Aquinas taught) and Bologna in the middle of the twelfth century. Oxford and Cambridge were founded around 1200, and then came a flood of new institutions during the remainder of the thirteenth century. There is a widespread misconception that these were not really universities, but consisted of only three or four teachers and a few dozen students. To the contrary, early in the thirteenth century, Paris, Bologna, Oxford, and Toulouse probably enrolled one thousand to fifteen hundred students each—approximately five hundred new students enrolled at the University of Paris every year. Regardless of their enrollments, many "enlightened" recent historians mock these universities as intellectually "hopeless," being "corrupted by scholastic and ecclesiastical overlays."[42] But it was in these "hopeless" early universities that science was born.

SCIENCE

For generations, historians claimed that a "Scientific Revolution" began in the sixteenth century when Nicolaus Copernicus proposed a heliocentric model of the solar system. But recently, specialists in the history of science have concluded that what occurred was an evolution, not a revolution.[43] Just as Copernicus simply took the next implicit step in the cosmology of his day, so too the flowering of science in that era was the culmination of the gradual progress that had been made over previous centuries. This evolution will be properly traced in chapter 7.

This, then, was the era that the intellectual proponents of the Enlightenment described as a tragic decline into ignorance and superstition. Little wonder that many contemporary historians became incensed by use of the term "Dark Ages." As the distinguished medievalist Warren Hollister (1930–97) put it in his presidential address to the Pacific Historical Association, "To my mind, anyone who believes that the era that witnessed the building of Chartres Cathedral and the invention of parliament and the university was 'dark' must be mentally retarded— or at best, deeply, deeply, ignorant."[44] Or they could simply be diehard anti-Catholics.

The Myth of the Renaissance

Obviously, if the Dark Ages are a ridiculous myth, so too must be the Renaissance, since it proposes that Europe was saved from ignorance when intellectuals in various northern Italian city-states broke sufficiently free from Church control to allow the "rebirth" of classical knowledge. Had that really been true, it would have created an era of cultural decline since Christian Europe had long since surpassed classical antiquity in nearly every way. Unfortunately, the creators of the Renaissance myth had no knowledge of the immense progress of the Dark Ages and seem to have based their entire assessment on the extent to which scholars were familiar with Aristotle, Plato, Euclid, Sophocles, Aristophanes, and other stalwarts of classical learning and literature. But even this legacy of classical culture was fully restored long before the Renaissance. The key development was the translation of these writers into Latin, since Greek was no longer the intellectual language of Christendom. And these translations were not made during the Renaissance but rather centuries earlier by pious monastic scholars. Indeed, "between 1125 and 1200, a veritable flood of translations into Latin, made Greek . . . [writing] available, with more to come in the thirteenth century."[45] This is fully supported by surviving monastery library catalogues from as far back as the twelfth century, which reveal extensive holdings of classical authors.[46]

As for the famous "Italian Renaissance," it was not a rebirth of classical learning at all! It was a period of cultural emulation during which people of fashion copied the classical styles in manners, art, literature, and philosophy. Out of this passion for their own ancient days of glory, northern Italians recast history to stress "the achievements of modern Italy and their dislike and contempt for the barbarians of the north."[47] Thus, they imposed the Dark Ages between themselves and their past. But it wasn't so. The Scholastics knew of, and often knew more than, the ancient Greek and Roman authors.

The Myth of Secular Enlightenment

The single most remarkable and ironic thing about the Enlightenment is that those who proclaimed it made little or no contribution to the accomplishments they hailed as a revolution in human knowledge, while those responsible for these advances stressed the continuity with the past. That is, Voltaire, Rousseau, Diderot, Hume, Gibbon, and the rest were literary men, while the primary revolution they hailed as the "Enlightenment" was scientific. Equally misleading is the fact that although the literary men who proclaimed the Enlightenment were irreligious, the central figures in the scientific achievements of the era were deeply religious, and as many of them were Catholics as were Protestants.[48] So much then for the idea that suddenly in the sixteenth century, enlightened secular forces burst the chains of Catholic thought and set the foundation for modern times. What the proponents of Enlightenment actually initiated was the tradition of angry secular attacks on religion in the name of science—attacks like those of their modern counterparts such as Carl Sagan, Daniel Dennett, and Richard Dawkins. Presented as the latest word in sophistication, rationalism, and reason, these assaults are remarkably naïve and simplistic—both then and now.[49] In truth, the rise of science was inseparable from Christian theology, for the latter gave direction and confidence to the former (chapter 7).

Theology, Reason, and Progress

Claims concerning the revolutionary character of the Renaissance and the Enlightenment were plausible because remarkable progress was made in these eras. But rather than being a revolutionary break with the past, these achievements were simply an extension of the accelerating curve of progress that began soon after the fall of Rome. Thus, the historian's task is not to explain why so much progress has been made since the fifteenth century—that focus is much too late. The fundamental questions about the rise of the West are: What enabled Europeans to begin and maintain the extraordinary and enduring period of rapid progress that enabled them, by the end of the Dark Ages, to have far surpassed the rest of the world? Why was it that, although many civilizations have pursued alchemy, it led to chemistry only in Europe? Or, while many societies have made excellent observations of the heavens and have created sophisticated systems of astrology, why was this transformed into scientific astronomy only in Europe?

Several recent authors have discovered the secret to Western success in geography. But, that same geography long sustained European cultures that were well behind those of Asia. Others have traced the rise of the West to steel, or to guns and sailing ships, and still others have credited a more productive agriculture. The trouble is that these answers are part of what needs to be explained: *Why* did Europeans excel at metallurgy, shipbuilding, or farming? I have devoted a book to my answer: that the truly fundamental basis for the rise of the West was an extraordinary faith in *reason* and *progress,* and this faith originated in Christianity.[50]

It has been conventional to date the Age of Reason as having begun in the seventeenth century. In truth, it really began late in the second century, launched by early Christian theologians. Sometimes described as "the science of faith,"[51] *theology* consists of *formal reasoning about God*. The emphasis is on *discovering* God's nature, intentions, and demands and on understanding how these define the relationship between human beings and God. And Christian thinkers have done this, not through meditation, new revelations, or inspiration, but through reason.

Indeed, it was not unusual for Christian theologians to reason their way to a new doctrine; from the earliest days Christian thinkers celebrated reason as the means to gain greater insight into divine intentions. As Quintus Tertullian (155–239) instructed in the second century: "Reason is a thing of God, inasmuch as there is nothing which God the Maker of all has not provided, disposed, ordained by reason—nothing which He has not willed should be handled and understood by reason."[52] In the same spirit, Clement of Alexandria (150–215) warned: "Do not think that we say that these things are only to be received by faith, but also that they are to be asserted by reason. For indeed it is not safe to commit these things to bare faith without reason, since assuredly truth cannot be without reason."[53]

Hence, Augustine (354–430) merely expressed the prevailing wisdom when he held that reason was indispensable to faith: "Heaven forbid that God should hate in us that by which he made us superior to the animals! Heaven forbid that we should believe in such a way as not to accept or seek reasons, since we could not even believe if we did not possess rational souls." Augustine acknowledged that "faith must precede reason and purify the heart and make it fit to receive and endure the great light of reason." Then he added that although it is necessary "for faith to precede reason in certain matters of great moment that cannot yet be grasped, surely the very small portion of reason that persuades us of this must precede faith."[54] Christian theologians always have placed far greater faith in reason than most secular philosophers are willing to do today.[55]

In addition, from very early days, Catholic theologians have assumed that the application of reason can yield an *increasingly more accurate* understanding of God's will. Augustine noted that although there were "certain matters pertaining to the doctrine of salvation that we cannot yet grasp . . . one day we shall be able to do so."[56] This universal faith in progress among Catholic theologians had immense impact on secular society as well. Thus, Augustine celebrated not only theological progress but earthly, material progress as well. Writing early in the fifth century, he exclaimed: "Has not the genius of man invented and applied countless astonishing arts, partly the result of necessity, partly the result of exuberant invention, so that this vigour of mind . . . betokens an inexhaustible wealth in the nature which can invent, learn, or employ such arts. What wonderful—one might say stupefying—advances has human industry made in the arts of weaving and building, of agriculture and navigation!" He went on to admire the "skill [that] has been attained in measures and numbers! With what sagacity have the movements and connections of the stars been discovered!" All of this was due to the "unspeakable boon" that God conferred upon his creation, a "rational nature."[57]

Augustine's optimism was typical among medieval intellectuals; progress beckoned. As Gilbert de Tournai wrote in the thirteenth century, "Never will we find truth if we content ourselves with what is already known. . . . Those things that have been written before us are not laws but guides. The truth is open to all, for it is not yet totally possessed."[58] Especially typical were the words preached by Fra Giordano in Florence in 1306: "Not all the arts have been found; we shall never see an end to finding them. Every day one could discover a new art."[59] Compare this with the prevailing view in China at this same time, well expressed by Li Yen-chang, "If scholars are made to concentrate their attention solely on the classics and are prevented from slipping into study of the vulgar practices of later generations, then the empire will be fortunate indeed!"[60]

It is widely believed, even by very secular scholars, that the "idea of progress" was crucial to the rise of Western civilization.[61] Because Europeans believed progress was possible, desirable, and to some extent inevitable, they eagerly pursued new methods, ideas, and technologies. As it turned out, these efforts were self-confirming: faith in progress prompted efforts that repeatedly produced progress. The basis for the unique European belief in progress was not a triumph of secularity, but of religion. As John Macmurray put it: "That we think of progress at all shows the extent of the influence of Christianity upon us."[62]

So much, then, for nonsense about the "triumph of barbarism and religion." So too for silly claims that the Age of Reason dawned in about 1600. Perhaps the most utterly revealing aspect of this nonsense is the claim that it was René Descartes who led the way into and epitomized the Age of Reason. In fact, Descartes very explicitly modeled himself on his Scholastic predecessors as he attempted to reason his way from the most basic of axioms ("I think, therefore I am") to the essentials of Christian faith. Various philosophers have subsequently attacked the validity of steps in his deductive chains, but what is important is that Descartes was not revolting against an Age of Faith, but instead was entirely comfortable extending the long tradition of Christian commitment to reason.

In contrast, the "age of reason" is a phrase that originated as the title of a book by Thomas Paine, written in 1793–94 while he was in prison during the French Revolution. Despite its title, this was not primarily a work of reason but one of invective in the name of reason, much of it devoted to militant attacks on the Bible and all religions as "fabulous inventions."

Conclusion

When one examines the conventional outline of Western history, one encounters some truly fabulous inventions. These were not invented by the Church but by secular intellectuals, who coined the Dark Ages, the Renaissance, the Enlightenment, and the Age of Reason. These were great historical eras that never really happened.

The myth of the Crusades: Even American presidents and the editors of the *New York Times* have erroneously charged that much of the conflict today between Christians and Muslims can be traced to the Crusades, when European armies—like the one led by Richard the Lionheart—attempted to invade and colonize the Muslim Middle East.

Crusading for Land, Loot, and Converts 5

I N THE IMMEDIATE aftermath of the destruction of the World Trade Center by Muslim terrorists, frequent mention was made of the Crusades as a basis for Islamic fury. It was argued that Muslim bitterness over their mistreatment by the Christian West could be dated back to 1096 when the First Crusade set out for the Holy Land. Far from being motivated by piety or by concern for the safety of pilgrims and the holy places in Jerusalem, the Crusades were but the first extremely bloody chapter in a long history of brutal European colonialism.[1] More specifically: the Crusaders marched east not out of idealism, pursuing lands and loot; the Crusades were promoted "by power-mad popes" seeking to greatly expand Christianity through conversion of the Muslim masses,[2] constituting "a black stain on the history of the Catholic Church"; the knights of Europe were barbarians who brutalized everyone in their path, leaving "the enlightened Muslim culture . . . in ruins."[3] As Akbar Ahmed, chair of Islamic studies at American University in Washington, DC, suggested: "the Crusades created a historical memory which is with us today—the memory of a long European onslaught."[4]

Two months after the attack on New York City, former president Bill Clinton informed an audience at Georgetown University that "those of us who come from various European lineages are not blameless" vis-à-vis the Crusades as a crime against Islam, and then he summarized a medieval account about all the blood that was shed when Godfrey of

Bouillon and his forces conquered Jerusalem in 1099. That the Crusades were a crime in great need of atonement was a popular theme even before the Islamic terrorists crashed their hijacked airliners. In 1999, the *New York Times* had solemnly proposed that the Crusades were comparable to Hitler or to the ethnic cleansing in Kosovo.[5] Also in 1999, to mark the nine-hundred-year anniversary of the Crusader conquest of Jerusalem, hundreds of devout Protestants took part in a "Reconciliation Walk" that began in Germany and ended in the Holy Land. Along the way, the walkers wore T-shirts bearing the message "I apologize" in Arabic. Their official statement explained the need for a Christian apology:

> Nine hundred years ago, our forefathers carried the name of Jesus Christ in battle across the Middle East. Fueled by fear, greed, and hatred . . . the Crusaders lifted the banner of the Cross above your people. . . . On the anniversary of the First Crusade . . . we wish to retrace the footsteps of the Crusaders in apology for their deeds. . . . We deeply regret the atrocities committed in the name of Christ by our predecessors. We renounce greed, hatred and fear, and condemn all violence done in the name of Jesus Christ.[6]

And, of course, in February 2015, in response to criticisms of his unwillingness to identify the terrorists who were transmitting videos of their many beheadings of "infidel" enemies as being Muslims, President Barack Obama said to those attending the National Prayer Breakfast: "And lest we get on our high horse and think this is unique to some other place, remember that during the Crusades and the Inquisition, people committed terrible deeds in the name of Christ."

These are not new charges. Western condemnations of the Crusades originated in the Enlightenment, that utterly misnamed era during which French and British intellectuals invented the Dark Ages in order to glorify themselves and vilify the Church (chapter 4). Hence, Voltaire

(1694–1778) called the Crusades an "epidemic of fury which lasted for two hundred years and which was always marked by every cruelty, every perfidy, every debauchery, and every folly of which human nature is capable."[7] According to David Hume (1711–76), the Crusades were "the most signal and most durable monument to human folly that has yet appeared in any age or nation."[8] Denis Diderot (1713–84) characterized the Crusades as "a time of the deepest darkness and of the greatest folly . . . to drag a significant part of the world into an unhappy little country in order to cut the inhabitants' throats and seize a rocky peak which was not worth one drop of blood."[9] These attacks reinforced the widespread "Protestant conviction that crusading was yet another expression of Catholic bigotry and cruelty."[10] But the notion that the Crusaders were early Western imperialists who used a religious excuse to seek land and loot probably was originated by Edward Gibbon (1737–94), who claimed that the Crusaders really went in pursuit of "mines of treasures, of gold and diamonds, of palaces of marble and jasper, and of odoriferous groves of cinnamon and frankincense."[11]

During the twentieth century, Gibbon's thesis was developed into a quite elaborate "materialist" account of why the Crusades took place.[12] As summed up by Hans Mayer, the Crusades alleviated a severe financial squeeze on Europe's "knightly class." According to Mayer and others who share his views, at this time there was a substantial and rapidly growing number of "surplus" sons, members of noble families who would not inherit and who were unable to receive even modest incomes from their families. Hence, as Mayer put it, "the Crusade acted as a kind of safety valve for the knightly class . . . a class which looked upon the Crusade as a way of solving its material problems."[13] Indeed, a group of American economists recently proposed that the Crusaders hoped to get rich from the flow of pilgrims (comparing the shrines in Jerusalem to modern amusement parks) and that the pope sent the Crusaders east in pursuit of "new markets" for the church, presumably to be gained by converting people away from Islam.[14] The prolific Geoffrey Barraclough wrote: "Our verdict on the Crusades [is that the knightly settlements established in the East were] centers of colonial exploitation."[15] It is thus no surprise that a leading college textbook on Western civilization informs students that "from the perspective of the pope and European monarchs, the crusades offered a way to rid Europe of contentious young nobles . . . [who] saw an opportunity to gain territory, riches, status, possibly a title, and even salvation."[16] Or, as the popular writer Karen Armstrong confided, these "were our first colonies."[17]

To sum up: during the Crusades, an expansionist, imperialistic Christendom, directed by the pope, brutalized, looted, and colonized a tolerant and peaceful Islam.

In recent years, these claims have been utterly refuted by a group of distinguished historians.[18] They propose that the Crusades were precipitated by Islamic provocations— by centuries of bloody attempts to colonize the West and by sudden new attacks on Christian pilgrims and holy places. Although the Crusades were initiated by a plea from the pope, this had nothing to do with hopes of converting Islam. Nor were the Crusades organized and led by surplus sons, but by the heads of great families who were fully aware that the costs of crusading would far exceed the very modest material rewards that could be expected; most went at immense personal cost, some of them knowingly bankrupting themselves to go. Moreover, the Crusader kingdoms that they established in the Holy Land, and which stood for two centuries, were not sustained by local exactions, but instead required immense subsidies from Europe. In addition, it is utterly unreasonable to impose modern notions about proper military conduct on medieval warfare—both Christians and Muslims observed quite different rules of war. Finally, claims that Muslims have been harboring bitter resentments about the Crusades for a millennium are nonsense; Muslim antagonism about the Crusades did not appear until about 1900 in reaction against the decline of the Ottoman Empire and the onset of European colonialism in the Middle East.

Now for the details.

Provocations

Muslims began raiding Christian areas in the lifetime of Muhammad. Then, a year after his death, Muslim invasions began in earnest when their forces entered Syria, then a Christian province of the Eastern Roman Empire. Muslim forces soon won a series of battles, taking Damascus and some other cities in 635, and by 636 the Byzantine army was forced to abandon Syria. Next, the Arabs marched into the Holy Land—Jerusalem was taken in 638, Caesarea Maritima in 640. From there, Muslim armies invaded Christian Egypt, taking Cairo; Alexandria fell to them in 642. A major Muslim Empire now ruled most of the Middle East and was spreading along the North African coast—then a major Christian region. Thirty years later, the empire stretched past Tangier and reached the Atlantic. By 714, much of Spain was occupied. Soon, major thrusts were made deep into France before the Franks managed to repel the Muslim forces at Tours (or Poitiers) in 732. In 831, Muslim forces invaded Sicily and held it until 1072, and in 846 they sacked Rome and then withdrew to rule over southern Italy for the next two centuries.

It seems very odd that those who are so vociferous about the misery and injustice imposed by Europeans on their former colonial empires fail to admit any such consequences of Muslim imperialism. But the fact remains that the Crusades were fundamentally defensive, and it is against this general background of chronic and longstanding Western grievances that the very specific provocations for the Crusades must be considered. These involved the destruction of, and threat to, holy places in Jerusalem and the murder, torture, enslavement, robbery, and general harassment of Christian pilgrims.

In 1009, at the direction of Fatimid Caliph al-Hakim, Muslims destroyed the Church of the Holy Sepulcher in Jerusalem—the splendid basilica that Constantine had erected over what was believed to be the site of the tomb where Christ lay before the Resurrection. As word of the desecration of the holiest of all Christian shrines reached Europe, it prompted considerable anger and concern. But the crisis soon passed because al-Hakim was killed by political opponents and religious tolerance was restored in Jerusalem, thus permitting resumption of the substantial flow of Christian pilgrims. Indeed, the value of the pilgrim traffic probably was the primary factor in the very liberal policies that had prevailed in Muslim-controlled Jerusalem through the centuries. Despite the great distances involved and the limited means of transportation, pilgrimages to Jerusalem were surprisingly common. In the first of his famous three volumes on the Crusades, Sir Steven Runciman (1903–2000) reported "an unending stream of travellers poured eastward, sometimes travelling in parties numbering thousands, men and women of every age and every class, ready . . . to spend a year or more on the [journey]."[19] A major reason for going to the Holy Land was the belief that a pilgrimage would absolve even the most terrible sins. Thus, many pilgrims came all the way from Scandinavia—some even from Iceland. As Runciman explained, the Norse "were violent men, frequently guilty of murder and frequently in need of an act of penance."[20]

But then, later in the eleventh century, everything changed. The Seljuk Turks, recent converts to Islam, became the new rulers of Asia Minor, pushing to within one hundred miles of Constantinople. Perhaps because they were new to Islam, or perhaps because they were still seminomadic tribesmen untainted by city dwelling, the Turks were unflinching particularists. There was only One True God and his name was Allah, not Yahweh or Jehovah. Tolerance was at an end. Not that the Turks officially prohibited Christian pilgrimages, but they made it clear that Christians were fair game. Hence, every Anatolian village along the route to Jerusalem began to exact a toll on Christian travelers. Far worse, many pilgrims were seized and sold into slavery while others were tortured, often seemingly for entertainment. Those who survived these perils "returned to the West weary and impoverished, with a dreadful tale to tell."[21]

Thus, anger and anxiety about the Holy Land grew. It is important to understand just how vivid was the image of the Holy Land to sincere medieval Christians. It was where Christ and the disciples had lived and, to an almost palpable degree, still did. In the words of Robert Payne, in Palestine Christians "expected to find holiness in a concrete form, something that could be seen, touched, kissed, worshipped, and even carried away. Holiness was in the pathways trodden by Christ, in the mountains and valleys seen by Christ, in the streets of Jerusalem where Christ had wandered."[22] In Jerusalem, a Christian could even climb the hill on which the cross had borne the Son of God. But no longer. Living "enemies of Christ, the spawn of Satan," now barred Christians from walking in Christ's footsteps.

It was in this climate of opinion that Alexius Comnenus, emperor of Byzantium, wrote from his embattled capital to the count of Flanders requesting that he and his fellow Christians in the West come to the rescue. In his letter, the emperor detailed gruesome tortures of pilgrims and vile desecrations of churches, altars, and baptismal fonts. Should Constantinople fall to the Turks, not only would thousands more Christians be murdered, tortured, and raped, but "the most holy relics of the Saviour" gathered over the centuries, would be lost. "Therefore in the name of God . . . we implore you to bring this city all the faithful soldiers of Christ . . . in your coming you will find your reward in heaven, and if you do not come, God will condemn you."[23]

When Pope Urban II read this letter, he was determined that it be answered in deeds. He arranged for a great gathering of clergy and laity in the French city of Clermont on November 27, 1095. Standing on a podium in the middle of a field, and surrounded by an immense crowd that included poor peasants as well as nobility and clergy, the pope gave one of the most effective speeches of all time. Blessed with an expressive and unusually powerful voice, he could be heard and understood at a great distance. Subsequently, copies of the speech (written and spoken in French) were circulated all across Europe.[24]

The pope began by graphically detailing the torture, rape, and murder of Christian pilgrims and the defilement of churches and holy places:

Many of God's churches have been violated. . . . They have ruined the altars with filth and defilement. They have circumcised Christians and smeared the blood on the altars or poured it into baptismal fonts. It amused them to kill Christians by opening up their bellies and drawing out the end of their intestines, which they then tied to a stake. Then they flogged their victims and made them walk around and around the stake until their intestines had spilled out and they fell dead on the ground. . . . What shall I say about the abominable rape of women? On this subject it may be worse to speak than to remain silent.

At this point, Pope Urban raised a second issue to which he already had devoted years of effort—the chronic warfare of medieval times. The pope had been attempting to achieve a "Truce of God" among the feudal nobility, many of whom seemed inclined to make war, even on their friends, just for the sake of a good fight. After all, it was what they trained to do every day since early childhood. Here was their chance! Pope Urban spoke: "Christian warriors, who continually and vainly seek pretexts for war, rejoice, for you have today found a true pretext. . . . If you are conquered, you will have the glory of dying in the very same place as Jesus Christ, and God will never forget that he found you in the holy battalions. . . . Soldiers of Hell, become soldiers of the living God!"

Now, shouts of "Dieu li volt!" (God wills it!) began to spread through the crowd, and men began to cut up cloaks and other pieces of cloth to make crosses and to sew them on their shoulders and chests. Everyone agreed that next spring they would march to Jerusalem. And they did.

It has often been suggested that we should not trust the pope or the emperor on what was taking place in the Holy Land. Perhaps they were misinformed. Perhaps they were lying to arouse a military venture for reasons of their own. James Carroll has even suggested that the pope cynically used the Muslims as threatening outsiders in order to unite the European princes "against a common enemy."[25] But as Runciman pointed out, Europeans, especially the nobility, had trustworthy independent information on the brutalization of the Christian pilgrims— from their own relatives and friends who had managed to survive. Even had the pope and emperor been cynical propagandists, that would not alter the motivation of the Crusaders, for that depended entirely on what the knights believed.

Economic Aspects of the Crusades

Had there been a financial squeeze on the knightly class, about the last thing they would have done was march off on a crusade to the Holy Land. As Peter Edbury explained, "Crusading was expensive, and the costs were borne by the crusaders themselves, their families, their lords and, increasingly from the end of the twelfth century, by taxes levied on the Church in the West."[26] Even the many Crusader castles and the garrisons by which Christians held portions of the Holy Land for two centuries were not built or sustained by local exactions, but by funds sent from Europe. Indeed, the great wealth of the knightly crusading orders was not loot—it came from donations and legacies in Europe.[27] All told, "large quantities of Western silver flowed into the crusader states."[28] The Crusades were possible only because this was not a period of economic decline, but one of *growth* "which put more resources and money into the hands of the ruling elites on Western Europe."[29]

Moreover, it was not "surplus" sons who went. Because the "cost of crusading was truly enormous"[30] only the heads of upper-class households could raise the money to go: it was kings, princes, counts, dukes, barons, and earls who enrolled, led, and paid the expenses for companies of knights and infantry.[31] Even so, they raised the needed funds at a very great sacrifice. Many sold all or substantial amounts of their holdings, borrowed all they could from relatives, and impoverished themselves and their families in order to participate.[32] As for making up their losses by looting and colonizing in the Holy Land, most of them had no such illusions; indeed, most of them had no plans to remain in the East once the fighting was done, and all but a small garrison did return home.

Why They Went

The knights of Europe sewed crosses on their breasts and marched East for two primary reasons: one generic and the other specific to crusading. The generic reason was their perceived need for penance. The specific reason was to liberate the Holy Land.

BOX 5.1. Some leading historians whose work informed this chapter. Specific studies by each can be found in the bibliography.

THOMAS F. MADDEN is professor of history and director of the Center for Medieval and Renaissance Studies at Saint Louis University. He earned his bachelor's degree at the University of New Mexico and his PhD at the University of Illinois. In addition to his ten very well-written books, Madden has been outspoken in his efforts to change the public image of the Crusades—to inform the public that this was "a defensive war."

JONATHAN RILEY-SMITH is the most prominent living historian of the Crusades. Formerly the Dixie Professor of Ecclesiastical History at Cambridge, he is now a fellow of Emmanuel College, Cambridge. He was the founder of the Society for the Study of the Crusades and the Latin East (to which I belong) and is a Knight of Malta. It was Riley-Smith who realized that a huge trove of solid evidence about who actually went on the Crusades and why could be recovered from surviving records of loans and property sales. Thus far his research on the Crusades has produced sixteen books.

Just as it has today, the medieval Church had many profound reservations about violence, and especially about killing. This created serious concerns among the knights and their confessors because war was chronic among the medieval nobility, and any knight who survived for very long was apt to have killed someone. Even when victims were evil men without any redeeming worth, their deaths were held to constitute sins,[33] and in most instances the killer enjoyed no obvious moral superiority over the victim—sometimes quite the reverse. Consequently, knights were chronically in need of penance, and their confessors imposed all manner of acts of atonement. Confessors sometimes

SIR STEVEN RUNCIMAN (1903–2000) wrote a three-volume study of the Crusades (1951, 1952, and 1954) that long dominated the field. They were brilliant books in many respects, but they did a great deal of harm by depicting the Crusaders as brutal barbarians who invaded a far superior culture, not Islam, but Byzantium. Born into the English nobility, he was extremely wealthy and able to travel and study where he wished, becoming proficient in Latin and Greek as well as French, Russian, and German and also in Arabic, Turkish, Persian, Hebrew, Syriac, and Armenian. Long associated with Cambridge University, he spent World War II as professor of Byzantine Art and History at Istanbul University in Turkey.

CHRISTOPHER TYERMAN received a most remarkable honor in July 2015, when Oxford University created an endowed chair for him as professor of the history of the Crusades. This was in recognition of his immense (1,040 pages) study, *God's War: A New History of the Crusades* (2007). No single work does a better job of showing that the Crusaders went for religious reasons and knowingly paid an immense price in money and lives for their ventures.

required a pilgrimage to a famous shrine and, for particularly hideous sins, a journey all the way to the Holy Land.

As already noted, pilgrimages to Jerusalem were remarkably common for several centuries before the First Crusade. Thousands went every year, often in large groups; for example, in 1026 a group of seven hundred persons from Normandy made a pilgrimage to the Holy Land and along the way they were joined by many other groups of Western pilgrims.[34] A major reason pilgrimages were so common was that the knights of Europe were both very violent and very religious. Thus, when Count Thierry of Trier murdered his archbishop in 1059, his confessor demanded that he undertake a pilgrimage, and he went.[35] Perhaps the most notorious pilgrim was Fulk III, count of Anjou (972–1040), who was required to make four pilgrimages to the Holy Land, the first as penance for having his wife burned to death in her wedding dress, allegedly for having had sex with a goatherd. All things considered, four pilgrimages may have been far too few, given that Fulk was a "plunderer, murderer, robber, and swearer of false oaths, a truly terrifying character of fiendish cruelty. . . . Whenever he had the slightest difference with a neighbor he rushed upon his lands, ravaging, pillaging, raping and killing; nothing could stop him."[36] Nevertheless, when confronted by his confessor, Fulk "responded with extravagant expressions of devotion."[37]

Thus, the call to crusade was not a call to do something novel—no doubt many knights had long been considering a pilgrimage. Indeed, the pope himself had assured them that crusading would wash away all their sins and, at the same time, they could rescue the Holy Land, including Christ's tomb, from further damage and sacrilege at the hands of the enemies of God. It was an altogether noble and holy mission, and the knights treated it as such. The Burgundian Stephen I of Neublans put it this way: "Considering how many are my sins and the love, clemency and mercy of Our Lord Jesus Christ, because when he was rich he became poor for our sake, I have determined to repay him in some measure for everything he has given me freely, although I am unworthy.

And so I have decided to go to Jerusalem, where God was seen as man and spoke with men and to adore the place where his feet trod."[38]

Had the Crusaders not been motivated by religion but by land and loot instead, the knights of Europe would have responded earlier, in 1063, when Pope Alexander II proposed a crusade to drive the infidel Muslims out of Spain. Unlike the Holy Land, Moorish Spain was extremely wealthy, possessed an abundance of fertile lands, and was close at hand. But hardly anyone responded to the pope's summons. Yet, only twenty years later, thousands of Crusaders set out for the dry, impoverished wastes of faraway Palestine. What was different? Spain was not the Holy Land. Christ had not walked the streets of Toledo nor was he crucified in Seville.

So finally, on June 7, 1099, and against all odds, the Crusaders arrived at Jerusalem. Of the original force of about forty-five hundred knights and thirty thousand infantry, disease, privation, misadventure, desertion, and fighting had so reduced their ranks that the Crusaders now numbered only about thirteen hundred knights and perhaps ten thousand infantry,[39] although Muslim historians placed their numbers at three hundred thousand.[40] Following a brief siege, on July 15, 1099, the Crusaders burst into the city. Thus, after about 460 years of Muslim rule, Jerusalem was again in Christian hands, although it was nearly destroyed and depopulated in the process.

The Crusader Kingdoms

Having defeated several Muslim armies that had attempted to turn them back and with Jerusalem in their possession, the Crusaders had to decide what to do to preserve their victory. Their solution was to create four kingdoms—independent states along the Mediterranean Coast. These were the County of Edessa, named for its major city; the Princedom of Antioch, which surrounded the city of Antioch in what is now southern Turkey; the County of Tripoli, which was just south of the Princedom and named for the Lebanese coastal city of that name; and the Kingdom of Jerusalem, an enclave on the coast of Palestine roughly equivalent to modern Israel.[41]

Unlike the other three kingdoms, Edessa was landlocked. When the main body of Crusaders marched south in 1098 to attack Antioch, Baldwin of Boulogne led a smaller force east to Edessa and managed to convince Thoros, the ruler of the city (who was a Greek Orthodox Christian), to adopt him as his son and heir! When Thoros was assassinated by angry subjects, Baldwin took over. Edessa was the first Crusader state (founded in 1098) and the first to be retaken by Islam (1149).

Crusaders captured the city of Antioch in 1098 after a long siege during which the knights ran so short of supplies that they ate many of their horses. Almost immediately after the Crusades had taken the city, a new Muslim army appeared and laid siege to the knights. Against staggering odds, Bohemond of Taranto led his troops out from the city and somehow defeated the Muslims—subsequent accounts claim that an army of saints had miraculously appeared to help the knights. Following this victory, Bohemond named himself prince. The area remained an independent state until 1119 when it was joined to the Kingdom of Jerusalem. In 1268, Antioch fell to an army led by Baybars, sultan of Egypt, whose troops killed every Christian they could find (see below).

The County of Tripoli was the last of the four Crusader states to be established—in 1102. It came into being when Count Raymond IV of Toulouse, one of the leaders of the First Crusade, laid siege to the port city of Tripoli. When Raymond died suddenly in 1105, he left his infant son as heir, so when the knights finally took the city, the county became a vassal state of the Kingdom of Jerusalem. It was captured by Mameluke forces in 1289.

By far the most important and powerful of the Crusader states was the Kingdom of Jerusalem, which was also known at Outremer, the French word for overseas (*outremer*). Initially, that term applied to all the Crusader states, but it came to refer primarily to the Kingdom of Jerusalem. Like the other states, Outremer was never a European colony, it being fully independent. Godfrey of Bouillon, who led the capture of

Jerusalem, was installed as the first ruler, with the title defender of the Holy Sepulcher. Godfrey was chosen not only for his integrity, but also for his military talent, which was just as well since no sooner was he in command than he was confronted by a very large Egyptian army intent on recapturing Jerusalem. Rather than shelter his outnumbered forces behind the walls of the city, Godfrey marched them out for a night attack that found the Egyptians sleeping and defeated them with a great loss of life.

This terrible defeat long deterred Muslim leaders from mounting new attacks. The Muslim historian Ibn Zafir recorded reproachfully: "He [the Egyptian vizier] had given up hope of the Syrian coastline remaining in Muslim hands and he did not personally wage war against them after that."[42] This was fortunate for the Crusaders, since following their victory over the Egyptians, nearly all of the forces of the First Crusade boarded ships and sailed home, leaving the Outremer to be protected by a small company of about three hundred knights and perhaps two thousand infantry.[43] Eventually their ranks were substantially reinforced by two knightly religious orders in which "monastic discipline and martial skill were combined for the first time in the Christian world."[44] The Knights Hospitaller were founded initially to care for sick Christian pilgrims traveling to the Holy Land. Eventually, the order kept its "medical" name, but in about 1120 expanded its vows from chastity, poverty, and obedience to include the armed protection of Christians in Palestine. The Knights Templar originated as a military religious order in about 1119. Hospitallers wore black robes with a white cross on the left sleeve; the Templars wore a white robe with a red cross on the mantel. The two orders hated one another quite intensely, but together they provided the Kingdom of Jerusalem with a reliable force of well-trained soldiers who built and garrisoned a chain of extremely well-situated castles along the frontiers of the kingdom.

Nevertheless, the existence of the kingdoms remained perilous, surrounded as they were by a vast and populous Muslim world. For many years, whenever the Muslim threat loomed especially large, new

Crusades were mounted in Europe bringing fresh troops east in support of the Crusader kingdoms. But eventually, Europeans lost their fervor to defend the "Holy Land," and Islamic forces began to eat away at the Crusader areas. Still, that the Kingdom of Jerusalem lasted until 1291, when its last fortress at Acre fell to a huge Mameluk army, seems a remarkable achievement.

As already noted, not only the defenders, but most of the funds for all of this came from Europe.[45] Both of the knightly orders established many religious houses in Europe from which they not only sent young recruits, but also a constant, substantial flow of cash, some of it raised by productive activities of the houses—each owned great estates, including some towns and villages—but most of it was donated by wealthy Europeans. About seventy years after the conquest of Jerusalem, the trade routes from Asia shifted to pass through Jerusalem's ports. This seems to have enriched Genoa and Pisa (and perhaps Venice), since these cities controlled maritime trade on the Mediterranean, but it had little impact on the general economy of the kingdom and surely played no role in motivating Crusaders.[46] Thus, the Crusader states "remained dependent on Christendom for men and money, endured as long as Christendom retained enough interest to keep supplying them, and withered and collapsed when that interest was lost."[47] Since a colony is normally defined as a place that is politically directed and economically exploited by a homeland, the Crusader states were not colonies[48]—unless one places a high material value on spiritual profits.

Nevertheless, the Crusaders made no attempt to impose Christianity on the Muslims. In fact, "Muslims who lived in Crusader-won territories were generally allowed to retain their property and livelihood, and always their religion."[49] Consequently, the Crusader kingdoms always contained far more Muslim residents than Christians. In the thirteenth century, some Franciscans initiated conversion efforts among Muslims, but these were based on peaceful persuasion, were quite unsuccessful, and were soon abandoned.[50] In fact, the Church generally opposed any linkage between crusading and conversion until the issue arose during the "Crusades" against Christian heretics in Europe.[51]

Crusader "War Crimes"

In the last paragraph of his immensely influential three-volume work on the Crusades, Runciman regretted this "tragic and destructive episode." The "high ideals" of the Crusaders "were besmirched by cruelty and greed . . . by a blind and narrow self-righteousness."[52] In the wake of Runciman's huge work, many more historians adopted the tradition that the Crusades pitted a barbarian West against a more sophisticated and more civilized East. Thus, the emphasis has been given to evidence that the Crusaders were brutal, blood-thirsty, religious zealots.

The attacks on Jews in the Rhineland are often cited in support of these claims. However, as was reported in chapter 1, these did not involve the major Crusader forces, but only peripheral groups such as Emich of Leisinger and his motley band of reinforcements, or disorganized mobs.

It is the massacre subsequent to the fall of Jerusalem that is taken as certain proof that the Crusaders were brutal even for their era and especially so in comparison with their Muslim opponents. Following a siege, the Christian knights took the city by storm and this was said to have been followed by an incredibly bloody massacre of the entire population. Unfortunately, these claims were written by Christian chroniclers "eager to portray a ritual purification of the city."[53] Did it really happen? The chroniclers' accounts seem farfetched—streets don't run knee-deep in blood—but it seems likely that a major massacre did occur. However, it is important to realize that, according to the norms of warfare at that time, a massacre of the population of Jerusalem would have been seen as justified because the city had refused to surrender and had to be taken by storm, thus inflicting many casualties on the attacking forces. In such cases, commanders (Muslims as well as Christians) believed they had an obligation to release their troops to murder, loot, and burn as an example to other cities that might be tempted to hold out excessively long in the future. Thus, Muslim victories in similar circumstances resulted in wholesale slaughters too. The point is that, however much we may condemn these practices today, they were not exclusive to the crusaders but were considered proper and practiced by both sides.

The remarkable bias of so many Western histories of the Crusades could not be more obvious than in the fact that massacres by Muslims receive so little attention. As Robert Irwin pointed out, "In Britain, there ha[s] been a long tradition of disparaging the Crusaders as barbaric and bigoted warmongers and of praising the Saracens as paladins of chivalry. Indeed, it is widely believed that chivalry originated in the Muslim East. The most perfect example of Muslim chivalry was, of course, the twelfth-century Ayyubid Sultan Saladin."[54] In fact, this is not a recent British invention. Since the Enlightenment, Saladin has "bizarrely" been portrayed "as a rational and civilized figure in juxtaposition to credulous barbaric crusaders."[55] For example, in 1898, Germany's Kaiser Wilhelm visited Damascus and placed a bronze laurel wreath on Saladin's tomb. The wreath was inscribed: "From one great emperor to another."[56]

Much has been made of the fact that Saladin did not murder the Christians when he retook Jerusalem in 1187. Writing in 1869, the English historian Barbara Hutton claimed that although Saladin "hated Christians . . . when they were suppliants and at his mercy, he was never cruel or revengeful."[57] But neither Hutton nor most other modern, Western fans of Islam have had anything to say about the fact, acknowledged by Muslim writers, that Jerusalem was an exception to Saladin's usual butchery of his enemies. Indeed, Saladin had planned to massacre the knights holding Jerusalem but instead offered a safe conduct in exchange for their surrender of Jerusalem without resistance (and unlike many other Muslim leaders, he kept his word). In most other instances, Saladin was quite unchivalrous. Following the Battle of Hattin, for example, he personally participated in butchering some of the captured knights and then sat back and enjoyed watching the execution of the rest of them.

As told by Saladin's secretary, Imad ed-Din: "He [Saladin] ordered that they should be beheaded, choosing to have them dead rather than in prison. With him was a whole band of scholars and sufis and a certain number of devout men and ascetics; each begged to be allowed to kill one of them, and drew his sword and rolled back his sleeve. Saladin, his face joyful, was sitting on his dais; the unbelievers showed black despair."[58] It thus seems fitting that during one of his amazing World War I adventures leading irregular Arab forces against the Turks, T. E. Lawrence "liberated" the kaiser's wreath from Saladin's tomb, and it now resides in the Imperial War Museum in London.

Not only have many Western historians ignored the real Saladin, they have given little or no coverage to Baybars (also Baibars), sultan of Egypt, although he is much more celebrated than Saladin in Muslim histories of this period. When Baybars took the Knights of the Templar fortress of Safad in 1266, he had all the inhabitants massacred even though he had promised to spare their lives during negotiations.[59] Later that same year, his forces took the great city of Antioch. Even though the city surrendered after four days, Baybars ordered all inhabitants, including all women and children, to be killed or enslaved. What followed was "the single greatest massacre of the entire crusading era."[60]

Since Count Behemund VI, ruler of Antioch, was away when this disaster befell his city, Baybars sent him a letter telling him what he had missed:

> You would have seen your knights prostrate beneath the horses' hooves, your houses stormed by pillagers. . . . You would have seen your Muslim enemy trampling on the place where you celebrate Mass, cutting the throats of monks, priests and deacons upon the altars, bringing sudden death to the Patriarchs and slavery to the royal princes. You would have seen fire running through your palaces, your dead burned in this world before going down to the fires of the next.[61]

The massacre of Antioch is seldom reported in the many apologetic Western histories of the Crusades. Karen Armstrong did report this massacre, but attributed it to "a new Islam" that had developed in response to the dire Crusader threat and with a "desperate determination to survive." Armstrong also noted that because Baybars was a patron of the arts, he "was not simply a destroyer . . . [but also] a great builder."[62] Even so, Armstrong's evaluation of Baybars is faint praise compared with that of the Muslims. An inscription from about 1266 calls him: "The pillar of the world and religion, the sultan of Islam and the Muslim, the killer of infidels and polytheists, the tamer of rebels and heretics . . . the Alexander of the age."[63] Many other inscriptions also compare him with Alexander the Great.

Of course, even though most of the Crusaders went to war for God and at considerable personal cost, few of them adopted a religious lifestyle. They ate and drank as well as they were able, and most of them routinely violated many commandments, especially those concerned with murder, adultery, and coveting wives. Moreover, they did not disdain the spoils of battle and looted as much as they were able—which wasn't much when balanced against the costs of crusading. And, of course, they were often cruel and bloodthirsty; after all, they had been trained from childhood to make war, face to face, sword to sword, and Pope Urban II called them "Soldiers of Hell." No doubt it was very "unenlightened" of the Crusaders to be typical feudal warriors, but it strikes me as even more unenlightened to anachronistically impose the Geneva Convention on the Crusaders while pretending that their Islamic opponents were either UN Peacekeepers or hapless victims.

Rediscovering the Crusades

Karen Armstrong would have us believe that the Crusades were "one of the direct causes of the conflict in the Middle East today."[64] That may be so, but not because the Muslim world has been harboring bitterness over the Crusades for the past many centuries. As Jonathan Riley-Smith explained: "One often reads that Muslims have inherited from their medieval ancestors bitter memories of the violence of the crusaders. Nothing could be further from the truth. Before the end of the nineteenth-century Muslims had not shown much interest in the crusades . . . [looking] back on [them] with indifference and complacency."[65] Even at the time they took place, Muslim chroniclers paid very little attention to the Crusades, regarding them as invasions by "a primitive, unlearned, impoverished, and un-Muslim people, about whom Muslim rulers and scholars knew and cared little."[66] Moreover, most Arabs dismissed the Crusades as having been attacks upon the hated Turks, and therefore of little interest.[67] Indeed, in the account written by Ibn Zafir at the end of the twelfth century, it was said that it was better that the Franks occupied the Kingdom of Jerusalem, as this prevented "the spread of the influence of the Turks to the lands of Egypt."[68]

Muslim interest in the Crusades seems to have begun in the nineteenth century, when the term itself[69] was introduced by Christian Arabs who translated French histories into Arabic—for it was in the West that the Crusades first came back into vogue during the nineteenth century. In Europe and the United States "the romance of the crusades and crusading" became a very popular literary theme, as in the many popular novels of Sir Walter Scott.[70] Not surprisingly, this development required that, at least in Britain and America, the Crusades be "de-Catholicized."[71] In part, this was done by emphasizing the conflict between the Knights Templar and the pope, transforming the former into an order of valiant anti-Catholic heroes. In addition, there developed a strong linkage between the European imperial impulse and the romantic imagery of the Crusades "to such an extent that, by World War One, war campaigns and war heroes were regularly lauded as crusaders in the popular press, from the pulpit, and in the official propaganda of the British war machine."[72]

Meanwhile in the East, the Ottoman Empire was fully revealed as "the sick man of Europe," a decrepit relic unable to produce any of the arms needed for its defense, which highlighted the general backwardness of Islamic culture and prompted "seething anger"[73] against the West among Muslim intellectuals, eventually leading them to focus on the Crusades.

Thus, current Muslim memories and anger about the Crusades are a twentieth-century creation,[74] prompted in part by "post–World War I British and French imperialism and the post–World War II creation of the state of Israel."[75] It was the last sultan of the Ottoman Empire to rule with absolute authority, Abdulhamid II (reigned from 1876–1909), who began to refer to European Crusades. This prompted the first Muslim history of the Crusades, published in 1899. In the introduction, its author, Sayyid Ali al-Hariri, noted that: "The sovereigns of Europe nowadays attack our Sublime Empire in a manner bearing great resemblance to the deeds of those people in bygone times [the Crusaders]. Our most glorious sultan, Abdulhamid II, has rightly remarked that Europe is now carrying out a Crusade against us."[76]

This theme was eagerly picked up by Muslim nationalists: "Only Muslim unity could oppose these new crusades, some argued, and the crusading threat became an important theme in the writings of the pan-Islamic movement."[77] Even within the context of Muslim weakness in the face of the modern West, Islamic triumphalism flourished; many proposed that through the Crusades the "savage West . . . benefited by absorbing [Islam's] civilized values." As for Crusader effects on Islam, "How could Islam benefit from contacts established with an inferior, backward civilization?"[78]

Eventually, the brutal, colonizing Crusader imagery proved to have such polemical power that it drowned out nearly everything else in the ideological lexicon of Muslim antagonism toward the West, except, of course, for Israel and paranoid tales about the worldwide Jewish conspiracy.

Conclusion

The Crusades were not unprovoked. They were not the first round of European colonialism. They were not conducted for land, loot, or converts. The Crusaders were not barbarians who victimized the cultivated Muslims. The Crusades are not a blot on the history of the Catholic Church. No apologies are required.

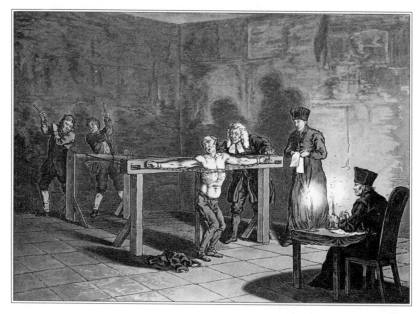

The myth of unjust and excessive torture during the Spanish Inquisition: While images like this are meant to represent the rampant use of torture and resulting deaths of the Spanish Inquisition, the reality is that the Spanish Inquisition was a relative source of justice in its time.

Monsters of the Inquisition 6

THE TERM "Spanish Inquisition" brings to mind one of the most frightening and bloody chapters in Western history. Created in 1478 by the Spanish monarchs Ferdinand and Isabella, the Inquisition was charged with ridding Spain of heretics, especially Jews and Muslims who were pretending to be Christians. But the Inquisition also set its sights on all Protestants, witches, homosexuals, and other doctrinal and moral offenders.

For the first several years, the Inquisition was rather inactive, but after the fanatical Tomás de Torquemada was appointed Grand Inquisitor in 1483, this hideous Catholic institution tortured and murdered huge numbers of innocent people. Every Saturday in every major Spanish city there was an auto-de-fe, and the air was filled with ashes as screaming victims were burned at the stake, usually after having been mercilessly tortured. On many Saturdays, piles of offensive books, especially scientific treatises, also were burned during the autos-de-fe.

The Inquisition did not even pretend to observe any semblance of legal procedure, seizing people right and left on the flimsiest accusations, as the Inquisitors grew rich from confiscating the wealth of the accused. Writing in 1554, the English Protestant John Foxe reported, "The extreme dealing and cruel ravening of these Catholic Inquisitors of Spain, who, under the pretended visor of religion, do nothing but seek their private gain and spoiling of other men's goods."[1] Thirteen years later came the truly devastating exposé, written in Latin by Reginaldus Montanus, *A Discovery and Plaine Declaration of Sundry Subtill Practices of the Holy Inquisition of Spain.* Translated into English, French, Dutch, and German it was widely circulated. Montanus's account "emphasize[d] the deviousness and trickery of the interrogation techniques, the variety of horrors in its torture chambers, and the appalling behavior of its familiars, prison keepers, and torturers."[2] The main part of the book follows an innocent victim through the entire ordeal, ending at the stake, and the book concludes with twelve case histories of Lutherans martyred for their faith.

Montanus's volume became the standard account. According to *The Columbia Encyclopedia*, "Torture of the accused . . . soon became customary and notorious . . . [m]ost trials resulted in a verdict of guilty."[3] On these grounds, the very popular historian Will Durant (1885–1981) informed several generations of readers that "we must rank the Inquisition . . . as among the darkest blots on the record of mankind, revealing a ferocity unknown in any beast."[4]

Not only historians, but novelists, painters, and screenwriters have repeatedly re-created scenes of brutal Inquisitorial sadism—Edgar Allen Poe's story of "The Pit and the Pendulum" (1842) being a classic among them. Another is Dostoyevsky's passage in *The Brothers Karamazov* (1880) wherein the Grand Inquisitor encounters Christ as he raises a child from the dead, whereupon he has Jesus seized and informs him: "Tomorrow I shall condemn thee and burn thee at the stake as the worst of heretics."

How many victims were there? Microsoft's *Encarta* says that Torquemada "executed thousands." The *Encyclopedia of Religious Freedom* puts Torquemada's total at 10,000, as did Edmond Paris,[5] who also claimed that another 125,000 died of torture and privation in Torquemada's prisons. Some historians have estimated that during the effective lifetime of the Inquisition, more than 31,000 people were burned at the stake,[6] but Simon Whitechapel claims that well over 100,000 died during Torquemada's tenure alone.[7] Another historian has proposed that the Inquisition burned "nearly two hundred thousand . . . in thirty-six years."[8] Yet,

David Hunt claims that overall the Inquisition condemned more than 3 million, "with about 300,000 burned at the stake."[9]

Despite these immense variations in estimated fatalities, everyone agrees that the Inquisition was a bloodbath. And perhaps nothing has so poisoned attitudes toward the Catholic Church. As recently as 2003, Simon Whitechapel began his book on the Inquisition's "atrocities" thus: "I should make one thing clear from the start: I despise the Catholic Church."[10]

Enough!

The standard account of the Spanish Inquisition is mostly a pack of lies, invented and spread by English and Dutch propagandists in the sixteenth century during their wars with Spain and repeated ever after by the malicious or misled historians eager to sustain "an image of Spain as a nation of fanatical bigots."[11] Consider that "Montanus" was the pen name used by a renegade Spanish monk who became a Lutheran and fled to the Netherlands where he wrote his book. As the distinguished Edward Peters noted, "Part of Montanus' appeal lay in the base of accuracy upon which he erected an otherwise extremely misleading description of the Inquisition to an audience prepared to believe the worst . . . Montanus portrays every victim of the Inquisition as innocent, every Inquisition official as venal and deceitful, every step in the procedure as a violation of natural and rational law."[12]

That such lies flourished during Europe's era of religious wars is not so surprising. But there is no such excuse for the irresponsible contemporary "scholars" who continue to support such claims while ignoring the remarkable research on the Inquisition that has been accomplished in the past generation. Astonishing as it may seem, the new historians of the Inquisition have revealed that, in contrast with the secular courts all across Europe, the Spanish Inquisition was a consistent force for justice, restraint, due process, and enlightenment.[13]

Box 6.1. Some leading historians whose work informed this chapter. Specific studies by each can be found in the bibliography.

CARLO GINZBURG is the son of a Jewish father who was murdered by the Gestapo in 1943 for publishing an underground newspaper in Turin, Italy. Ginzburg received his PhD in history from the University of Pisa in 1961 and then joined the faculty of the University of Bologna. In 1988, he moved the University of California, Los Angeles and then returned to the University of Pisa in 2006.

HENRY KAMEN is a British historian who was born in Rangoon and received his PhD from Oxford. He accepted a distinguished professorship at the University of Wisconsin in 1984 and was elected a fellow of the Royal Historical Society in 1992. Kamen moved to the University of Barcelona in 1993, in order to study the files of the Inquisition. In 1997, he helped put the record straight with *The Spanish Inquisition: A Historical Revision*.

E. WILLIAM MONTER received his PhD from Princeton University and went on to be professor of history at Northwestern University. Before playing a leading role analyzing the Inquisition files, Monter gained an international reputation for his major studies of the European witchcraft craze. As a result, he was elected to membership at the Institute for Advanced Studies at Princeton, an honor mainly reserved for distinguished physical scientists.

JOHN TEDESCHI is an American historian who served for many years as curator of rare books and special collections at the University of Wisconsin. In addition to writing major works on the Inquisition based on the files, he wrote studies of the Reformation and, with his wife, Anne, he has translated important books from Italian.

The revisionist historians (see Box 6.1) base their dissenting views on having gained full access to the complete archives of the Inquisitions of both Aragon and Castile, which together constituted the Spanish Inquisition. Subsequently, they have read the careful records made of each of the 44,674 cases heard by these two Inquisitions between 1540 and 1700. At the time they were written, these records were secret so there was no reason for the clerks to have misrepresented the actual proceedings. Not only are these cases a goldmine of historical detail, historians have entered each in a database in order to facilitate statistical analysis.[14] In addition, these historians have done an immense amount of more traditional research, pouring over diaries, letters, decrees, and other old documents. The results are solidly undeniable. The remainder of the chapter offers a summary of the major discoveries.

Deaths

The term "auto-de-fe" does not mean execution, let alone burning at the stake, but is best translated as "act of faith." The Inquisitors were far more concerned with repentance than with punishment, and therefore an auto-de-fe consisted of a public appearance by persons convicted of various sins who offered public confessions of their guilt and were thereby reconciled to the Church. Only very rarely did an auto-de-fe end with the offender being surrendered to the civil authorities for execution (the Inquisition did not ever conduct an actual execution). Even so, autos-de-fe were not frequent. In the city of Toledo, between 1575 and 1610, only twelve autos-de-fe were held, "at which 386 culprits appeared."[15] Obviously then, the tales of weekly mass burnings all across Spain are malicious fantasies. So, how many did die?

The first fifty years of the Inquisition's operations are poorly documented, but historians now agree that these were its bloodiest days and that perhaps as many as fifteen hundred people may have been executed, or about thirty a year.[16] Turning to the fully recorded period, of the 44,674 cases, only 826 people were executed, which amounts to 1.8

percent of those brought to trial.[17] All told, then, during the entire period 1480 through 1700, only about ten deaths *per year* were meted out by the Inquisition all across Spain, a small fraction of the many thousands of Lutherans, Lollards, and Catholics (in addition to two of his wives) that Henry VIII is credited with having boiled, burned, beheaded, or hanged.[18] Then, during the subsequent century (1530 to 1630), the English averaged 750 hangings a year, many of them for minor thefts.[19] In contrast, the few who were sentenced to death by the Spanish Inquisition usually were repeat offenders who would not repent.

Torture

In popular culture, the term "Inquisition" is nearly a synonym for torture. As John Dowling (1808–78) explained, "Of all the inventions of popish cruelty the Holy Inquisition is the masterpiece. . . . It was impossible for even Satan himself to conceive a more horrible contrivance of torture and blood."[20] Thus, as noted above, it has been taken for granted that many more poor souls died in the Inquisition's prisons and torture chambers than survived long enough to go to the stake.

This may be the biggest lie of all!

All the courts of Europe used torture, but the Inquisition did so *far less* than other courts. For one thing, Church law limited torture to one session lasting no more than fifteen minutes, and there could be no danger to life or limb. Nor could blood be shed![21] There are, of course, very painful techniques that can be applied within these rules. But even so, torture was rarely used, perhaps because the "[i]nquisitors themselves were sceptical of the efficacy and validity of torture as a method of conviction."[22] If torture was used, its progress was carefully recorded by a clerk, and this material was included with the record of the case.[23] Based on these data, Thomas Madden has estimated that the Inquisitors resorted to torture in only about 2 percent of all the cases that came before them.[24] Moreover, it is widely agreed that prisons operated by the Inquisition were by far the most comfortable and humane in Europe—

instances have been reported of "criminals in Spain purposely blaspheming so as to be transferred to the Inquisition's prisons."[25]

So there it is. Contrary to the Black Legend, the Inquisition made little use of the stake, seldom tortured anyone, and maintained unusually decent prisons. But what about its procedures? The remainder of the chapter examines the workings of the Inquisition, organized on the basis of the alleged offenses.

Witchcraft

Perhaps no historical statistics have been so outrageously inflated as the numbers executed as witches during the craze that took place in Europe from about 1450 to 1700. Many writers have placed the final death toll at nine million, drawing comparisons with the Holocaust.[26] And while it is acknowledged that Protestants burned a lot of witches too, historians have stressed the leading role played by the Inquisition.[27] Several have blamed the whole thing on the dire effects of celibacy, which inflamed priests to "a raging campaign of revenge and annihilation" against women.[28] Finally, it is widely claimed that the witch hunts ended only when the so-called Dark Ages of religious extremism were overthrown by the supposed Enlightenment.[29]

Vicious nonsense, all of it.

Consider that the witch hunts reached their height *during* the so-called Enlightenment! Indeed, writing in his celebrated book *Leviathan* (1651), Thomas Hobbes (1599–1679), the famous English philosopher and proponent in the Enlightenment, wrote that "as for witches . . . they are justly punished."[30] Another leading figure of the Enlightenment, Jean Bodin (ca. 1530–96), served as a judge at several witchcraft trials and advocated burning witches in the slowest possible fires.[31] In fact, many of the distinguished scientists of the seventeenth century, including Robert Boyle, encouraged witch hunts.[32]

As for the death toll, in recent years, competent scholars have carefully assembled the evidence nation by nation and found the "accepted" totals to be utterly fantastic. For example, it had long been assumed that in England from 1600 to 1680, "about forty-two thousand witches were burnt,"[33] but the most trustworthy figure turns out to be fewer than a thousand over a period of three centuries.[34] In similar fashion, the best estimate of the final death toll is not nine million, but about sixty thousand![35] Even that is a tragic total, but it needs to be recognized that a mere handful of these victims were sentenced to death by the Spanish Inquisition—so few that the very distinguished historian William Monter entitled a chapter in his statistical study of the Inquisition as "Witchcraft: The Forgotten Offense."[36] This was in response to data showing that during the century 1540–1640, when the witch hunts were at their peak in most of Europe, the Inquisition of Aragon (one of the two Inquisitions functioning in Spain) executed only twelve people for "superstition and witchcraft."[37] This should have been acknowledged all along. Even the virulently anti-Catholic historian Henry C. Lea (1825–1909) agreed that witch-hunting was "rendered comparatively harmless" in Spain and that this "was due to the wisdom and firmness of the Inquisition."[38] Let us examine this wisdom and firmness in some detail.

To begin, it is important to recognize what sustained the charge of witchcraft, since it is not the case that the accusations were nothing but unfounded hysteria; many people actually were "doing something" that led them to be charged. What they were doing was practicing magic. As would be expected in an era that was extremely deficient in medical knowledge, medical magic abounded in Europe and so did magical attempts to influence weather, crops, love, wealth, and other human concerns. The critical distinction was between Church and non-Church magic.

Church magic was plentiful: sacred wells, springs, groves, and shrines abounded where supplicants could seek all sorts of miracles and blessings. In addition, priests had an extensive array of incantations, prayers, and rites available for dealing with many human concerns, especially for treating illness—there were many priests who specialized in exorcism. Parallel to this elaborate system of Church magic was an extensive culture of folk or traditional magic, a substantial portion of which also was devoted to treating medical problems. Some of this magic dated from pre-Christian times, and much of it was a somewhat jumbled adaptation of Church magic. This non-Church magic was sustained by local practitioners, sometimes referred to as "Wise Ones." Often these practitioners performed nonmagical functions too, as in the case of midwives who combined their practical skills with magical spells to deliver babies. It should be mentioned that sometimes priests engaged in "corruptions" of Church magic, as in the case of a village priest who baptized coins in holy oil in hopes that they would be replaced as soon as they were spent,[39] and the many priests who baptized various objects, such as magnets, in hopes of creating love potions, despite love potions being vigorously condemned by the Church.[40] Even though performed by priests, such activities were regarded as non-Church magic by the religious authorities.

All magic appears to work, some of the time. Thus, some sufferers who turned to their local priest got well. But so did some who turned to their local "Wise One." This posed a serious theological issue, and the attempt to find a logical explanation resulted in tragedy. The question was posed: If Church magic works because God invests it with the power to do so, why does non-Church magic work too? Surely, these powers do not come from God. The conclusion seemed obvious: Non-Church magic works because Satan empowers it! Hence, to practice non-Church magic constituted invoking Satan and his demons. That is the definition of witchcraft.[41]

Efforts to expose and suppress evil in the form of non-Church magic soon led to public panics in many parts of Europe. All sorts of lurid tales and fears spread rapidly and, especially in places where governance was weak, mobs and local authorities were swept up in the witchcraft craze. The very same towns and cities along the Rhine where violent attacks on Jews had been concentrated in earlier centuries (chapter 1) became the hotbeds of the witchcraft craze.[42] These same fears and impulses arose among people in Spain too, but there they were effectively squelched by the Inquisition.

One reason that the Inquisition prevented a witch craze in Spain is that, during its very first cases involving the use of non-Church magic, the Inquisitors paid close attention to what the accused had to say. What they learned was that magical practitioners had no intention whatever of invoking Satanic forces. In fact, many thought they were using Church magic! This was because the practices and procedures involved were very similar to those authorized for use by the clergy—reciting of fragments of liturgy, appealing to saints, sprinkling holy water taken from a local church on an afflicted area, and repeatedly making the sign of the cross. As a result, the accused seemed sincerely surprised to learn they had been doing anything wrong.

In fact, the main reason these efforts did not qualify as Church magic was because the accused were not ordained, and therefore they were not authorized to conduct such activities. Hence, if the magic worked, it was not God's doing. That is, the Spanish Inquisitors agreed with their colleagues elsewhere that non-Church magic worked only because of Satanic intervention. However, because they had listened to the accused with a sympathetic ear, the Spanish Inquisitors initiated a crucial distinction "between the implicit and explicit invocation of demons."[43] Thus, they assumed that most accused of using non-Church magic (including priests) were sincere Catholics who meant no harm and had been unaware of invoking demons. While it was wrong even to have implicitly invoked demons, it should be forgiven in the ordinary way, through confession and absolution. Consequently, the Spanish Inquisition sent nearly no witches to the stake, and those who were had been convicted for the third or fourth time.

Even more important, the Inquisition used its power and influence to suppress witch-hunting by local mobs or secular authorities. An example occurred in Barcelona in 1549, just as the most ferocious witch hunts broke out in other parts of Europe. Local officials accused seven women as witches, and the official of the local branch of the Inquisition approved that they be burned. The members of the Suprema (the ruling body of the Inquisition) were appalled that such a thing could happen and sent the Inquisitor Francisco Vaca to investigate. Upon arrival, he sacked the local representative of the Inquisition and ordered the immediate release of two women still being held under sentence of death. After further investigation, he dismissed all pending charges and required the return of all confiscated property to the families of the victims. In his report, Vaca dismissed the charges of witchcraft as "laughable" and wrote, "One of the most damning indictments of witch persecution ever recorded."[44] His colleagues on the Suprema agreed and thereafter turned their vengeance upon those who *conducted* unauthorized witch hunts, having several of them executed and sending others to serve long sentences in the galleys.[45]

Even so, in 1610 six persons were burned as witches by local officials in Logroño. When they heard of this, the Suprema dispatched Alonso de Salazar y Frias, who spent more than a year interviewing the local inhabitants and inviting them to repudiate their errors (mostly having to do with superstition and magic). At the end of his mission, Salazar reported that he had reconciled 1,802 persons to the Church. He also reported the negative results of his investigation of witchcraft: "I have not found the slightest evidence that a single act of witchcraft has really occurred."[46] Salazar went on to suggest that efforts should be made to prevent public discussion and agitation concerning the topic; the preaching of sermons about witchcraft should especially be avoided, because he had discovered "that there were neither witches nor bewitched until they were talked and written about."[47]

Salazar's report soon circulated widely among Churchmen all across Europe. Other Catholic clergy, including the Jesuit Friedrich von Spee, soon joined in denouncing witch hunts, and it was their influence, and especially their discrediting of evidence gained by torture, that brought witch-burning to an end in Catholic areas—an effect that soon seeped into the Protestant areas as well. Some historians like to claim that witch-hunting finally ended because it was attacked by participants in the Enlightenment, such as Balthasar Bekker. But none of these "enlightened" attacks on witch hunts appeared until nearly a century after efforts by Catholic clergy had discredited the witch craze and made it entirely safe to say such things.[48]

Heresy

The Spanish Inquisition was founded to deal with a social crisis concerning the *conversos*, or converts—former Jews and Muslims who had become Catholics. The standard story misrepresents everyone involved. It portrays the conversos, especially those of Jewish background, as overwhelmingly having only pretended to become Christians, while continuing to live as "crypto-Jews." And it portrays the Inquisition as brutally determined to unmask all these pretenders and burn them for heresy. The truth is that nearly all of the Jewish and most of the Muslim converts were sincere, and the Inquisition was founded to suppress and replace the chronic outbreaks of mob violence against them with due process, as well as to expose those whose conversions were insincere. Soon after the Inquisition began to operate, Luther's Reformation rocked the religious consciousness of Europe, soon joined by other Protestant movements. Although the Spanish Crown was steadfastly Catholic, a small underground Lutheran movement arose in Spain (often involving priests and monks), and the Inquisition was directed to repress it.

MARRANOS

For more than a thousand years, more Jews lived in Spain than in "all the countries of medieval Europe combined."[49] It was in Spain that the renaissance of the Hebrew language was made possible by the creation of a Hebrew grammar—the Jews of the diaspora had so completely lost the ability to read and write Hebrew that their scriptures had to be translated into Greek several centuries before the birth of Jesus. But in Spain, beginning in the tenth century, there was a sudden flowering of Hebrew poetry and other writing.[50] Moreover, the center of this Hebrew renaissance was in the Christian areas of Spain, and as Christian forces slowly drove the Muslims south, Jews continued to migrate north. When

Jewish minorities have enjoyed amicable relations with their social environment, a substantial amount of conversion often has occurred,[51] and that is what happened in Spain. A wave of Jewish conversions to Christianity began in the fourteenth century, as tens of thousands accepted baptism and came to be known as conversos.[52] This caused immense bitterness in the Spanish Jewish community—Maimonides proposed that conversos be stoned as idolaters. Worse yet, since Jewish leaders in Spain presumed that no Jew would willingly abandon the faith, they concluded that these conversions somehow must have been forced and insincere—a falsehood that has lived on to corrupt historical accounts ever after.[53] In fact, these conversions were so sincere that soon many of the leading Christians in Spain, including bishops and cardinals, were of converso family origins. Indeed, in 1391 the chief rabbi of Burgos had himself and his whole family baptized and eventually he became the bishop of Burgos.[54] The sheer number of Jewish converts as well as their prominence (King Ferdinand had a converso grandmother)[55] impeded assimilation and led to antagonisms between "old" and "new" Christians that eventually resulted in armed conflicts between the two. Not surprisingly, "old" Christians were inclined to accuse "new" ones of being insincere "crypto-Jews," and too often some Spanish Jews were eager to support such charges. That turned out to be misguided because antagonism toward the conversos soon was expanded to include attacks on the Jews by "old" Christians.

It was this mess that the Inquisition was commissioned to sort out. The Inquisitors were able to stifle much of the mob action and disorder, but they could not forge a lasting peace, with the tragic result being the edict of 1492 ordering that Spain's remaining Jews either convert or leave. However, the Inquisition eventually dissipated the conflicts over "crypto-Jews." It did so largely by failing to discover many offenders. Although many cases were tried, the actual total was far below what would have been expected given the huge and angry literature on the topic that often seems to suggest that most conversos were dragged before the Inquisitors. The data for the Inquisition in Aragon (1540–

1640)—one of the two divisions of the Spanish Inquisition, and the one for which executions were broken down by offense—show that only 942 or 3.6 percent of all the cases tried involved charges of being a *Marrano*, far below the numbers tried for being *Moriscos* (Muslims) or *Luteranos* (Protestants). Some of these alleged Marranos were exonerated. Not only that, but only 16 of the 942 defendants (1.7%) were executed.[56] So much then for claims such as that by Cecil Roth (1899–1970), who wrote that Marranos "furnished a disproportionately large number . . . of those condemned to death."[57]

Moriscos

Morisco refers to a Muslim who falsely converted rather than leave Spain subsequent to the Christian Reconquest. Moriscos posed a far more serious threat than did Jews or converts from Judaism. They were far more numerous, they had a distinctive geography wherein they often constituted the majority of residents, they spoke their own language, and their conversions often had been compelled. Indeed, the Moriscos mounted several bloody insurrections.[58] Even so, many Jewish historians have claimed that Moriscos were treated far more leniently than Marranos by the Inquisition: "Far fewer Moriscos than conversos [crypto-Jews] were sentenced."[59] Wrong! The Inquisition in Aragon tried 7,472 cases based on accusations of being a Morisco, or 29 percent of all the cases it heard. Of these, 181 were executed, or 2.4 percent, which was slightly more than the rate for Marranos.

Luteranos

The various Protestant Reformations made little headway in Spain. In large part this was because earlier attempts at Church reform had been extremely successful in Spain. As Yale's celebrated Roland Bainton (1894–1984) put it: "Spain originated the Catholic reformation before ever the Protestant had begun."[60] The result was a remarkable increase in popular support for the Church and the lack of the substantial discontent that elsewhere favored Lutheranism and Calvinism. In fact, most who embraced or even dabbled in Protestantism (referred to in Spain as Luteranos) seem to have been clergy. In any event, 2,284 people were brought before the Inquisition in Aragon charged with being Luteranos, or 8.8 percent of all the cases heard. These cases resulted in 122 executions, or 5.3 percent of those charged—more than twice the rate as for those charged as Moriscos.

During the life of the Spanish Inquisition, all European nations persecuted religious minorities and dissenters.[61] In addition to hunting for Lollards and Lutherans, the English searched high and low for undercover Catholic priests and executed those they found. The French martyred thousands of Huguenots, and the Dutch Calvinists also hanged priests. Anabaptists were harassed in both the Lutheran and the Catholic parts of Germany, while in Geneva, Calvin persecuted both Anabaptists and Catholics. But somehow, these activities have been treated as "different" from the Spanish Inquisition's persecution of Luteranos.

Sexuality

The Inquisitors also concerned themselves with sexual misbehavior, dividing the offenses into four main categories.

Solicitation involved a priest using the confessional and his powers of granting or withholding absolution to have sexual activities with a woman. Of the 44,674 cases in the main database, there are 1,131 cases of solicitation, or 2.5 percent of all cases. A priest convicted of this offense could at the very least expect a severe flogging, followed by lifelong shame. Those discovered to have had an extensive career of solicitations were sentenced to long terms of penal servitude, and several notorious cases resulted in executions.

Bigamy probably was quite widespread in this era when divorce was nearly unavailable, but only rarely did it become such a public scandal as to attract the attention of the Inquisition (on grounds that it was sacrilegious). Even so, the major database includes 2,645 cases of big-amy (or 5.9 percent of the total). In addition to cancellation of the second marriage, the usual penalty involved only public disgrace and a period of banishment from the community of residence—women made up 20 percent of those convicted of bigamy.[62]

Sodomy primarily consisted of male homosexuality, but some cases of female homosexuality also were tried, as were some cases involving heterosexual anal intercourse (usually based on accusations by a wife). Sodomy is not broken out in the statistics based on the 44,674 cases because in 1509 the Suprema ordered that "no action be taken against homosexuals except when heresy was involved"[63] (i.e., only when claims were made that sodomy was not a sin). Consequently, the Inquisition of Castile, having by far the larger jurisdiction of the two Spanish Inqui-sitions, "never again exercised jurisdiction over sodomy,"[64] although the Inquisition of Aragon continued to do so. However, the published data on sexuality are based only on the cities of Barcelona, Valencia, and Saragossa (1560–1700). Of the 1,829 cases of sexual offenses in these three cities, sodomy prosecutions made up 38 percent.[65] In the execu-tion data, also based only on the Aragon Inquisition (1540–1640), 167 were executed for "Sodomy," as compared with 12 for "Superstition and Witchcraft" and 122 for being "Protestants."[66]

Even so, the Inquisition was more lenient toward sodomy (and most sexual offenses) than were the secular courts. Most of those convicted of sodomy by the Inquisition were whipped or given short terms in the galleys, and even many of the death sentences were commuted. By contrast, in this era the secular courts in most of Europe treated homo-sexuality as a capital offense.[67] For example, from the twelfth century on, civil courts in France and Italy sent "sodomites" to the stake. Henry VIII requested that parliament pass an "anti-buggery" law, and in 1533 a statute was passed making sodomy punishable by hanging. In 1730, Holland also made sodomy a capital crime. In practice, however, the general public was reluctant to accuse people of sodomy, and the courts, both secular and religious, were not eager to bring them to trial.

Bestiality accounted for 27 percent of the cases of sexual offenses in the three cities, although sometimes bestiality was included in the sodomy category rather than being separated. This offense usually involved young, single men, often those employed as herders, although several women also were convicted of sex with pet dogs. Bestiality was "almost invariably punished ruthlessly"[68] by the Inquisition. But even here, as in all other cases involving sexual offenses, "penalties to women remained far milder than those punishing male sexuality."[69]

Book Burning

It is true that the Inquisition did burn some books. Many of these contained theological heresies, such as Lutheran doctrines, but very few, if any, scientific books were burned—the Spanish never even put Galileo on their list of forbidden books.[70] It strikes me as of particular interest that of the books that the Inquisition did burn, most were condemned as pornographic![71] It seems that although the first printed books were Bibles and prayer books, quite soon printers discovered an eager, if underground, market for smut.[72]

Conclusion

Great historical myths die hard, even when there is no vested resistance to new evidence. But in this case, many recent writers continue to spread the traditional myths about this "holy terror" even though they are fully aware of the new findings.[73] They do so because they are determined to show that religion, and especially Christianity, is a dreadful curse upon humanity. As Helen Ellerbe explained, the Church "has left a legacy . . . that fosters sexism, racism, the intolerance of differences, and the desecration of the natural environment."[74] So these writers casually dismiss the new studies as written by "apologists"[75] and go on as before about the "men in black . . . [who] killed countless thousands of innocent men, women, and children," as Jonathan Kirsch put it in 2008.

The myth of the Church's suppression of science: This image is one of the many drawings and paintings that depict the brave scientific genius Galileo Galilei in prison, having been sentenced by the pope for writing that the Earth circles the sun. Galileo never spent a day in prison.

Scientific Heresies 7

I N 1829, Pope Leo XII prohibited vaccination for smallpox on
grounds that "small pox is a judgement from God."[1] He did
so because he "was a ferocious fanatic, whose object was to
destroy all the improvements of modern times, and force society back to
the government, customs, and ideas of mediaeval days. In his insensate
rage against progress he stopped vaccination for smallpox."[2] Of course,
Leo's attack on smallpox vaccination was entirely consistent with the
many centuries during which the Church opposed science and persecuted scientists—rejecting Copernicus's discovery that the earth travels
around the sun and condemning Galileo to "groan . . . away his days
in the prisons of the Inquisition," as Voltaire put it.[3] Indeed, it is well
known that those who created the great "scientific revolution" were
men of the Enlightenment, who had freed themselves of the blinders of
Catholicism. Indeed, it was mainly because the Protestant Reformation
had freed England and many parts of the Continent from the "dead
hand of the Catholic Church"[4] that real scientific thinking had become
possible.

However, Pope Leo never said anything of the sort! He had no objections to vaccination, and the Church had actively promoted vaccina-
tions from the very start. The story of his opposition was as fraudulent
as so many other seemingly reputable attacks on the Church. Moreover,
the great scientific achievements of the seventeenth and eighteenth centuries were not made despite the Church; they were the culmination of

135

normal scientific progress that took place through the centuries in the universities founded, controlled, and staffed by the Church. Indeed, the leading figures in the "scientific revolution" were unusually devout and about half of them were Catholics, many of them clergy. As for Galileo, he never spent a day in prison, and he didn't really get in trouble for his science (the Spanish Inquisition never banned his books), but for arrogant duplicity.

The Pursuit of Knowledge

The most fundamental key to the rise of Western civilization has been the dedication of so many of its most brilliant minds to the pursuit of knowledge. Not illumination. Not enlightenment. Not wisdom. Knowledge! And the basis for this commitment to knowledge was the Christian commitment to *theology*.

Theology has long been in disrepute among most Western intellectuals. The word is taken to mean a passé form of religious thinking that embraces irrationality and dogmatism. Consequently, as Ludwig Feuerbach (1804–74) put it, "The task of the modern era was the transformation of theology into anthropology."[5] So too, *Scholasticism*. According to most dictionaries, this word means "pedantic and dogmatic," denoting the sterility of medieval Church scholarship. John Locke, the eighteenth-century British philosopher, dismissed the Scholastics as "the great mintmasters" of useless terms meant "to cover their ignorance."[6] More recently, Sir William Dampier (1867–1952) spoke for most conventional academics when he complained that scientific thought was "quite foreign to the prevailing mental outlook" of the Scholastics, who were enmeshed in a "tangle of astrology, alchemy, magic and theosophy" and were absolutely hostile to experimentalism.[7] Not so! The Scholastics were fine scholars who founded Europe's great universities and who were the first to formulate and teach the experimental method; it was they who launched the rise of Western science.

As for theology, it has little in common with most religious thinking, as it is a sophisticated, highly *rational* discipline that has its roots in Judaism and in Greek philosophy and has been fully developed only in Christianity. The pursuit of knowledge was inherent in theology as efforts to more fully understand God were extended to include God's creation—thus inaugurating an academic enterprise known as *natural philosophy*, defined as the study of nature and of natural phenomena. During medieval times, a long line of brilliant Scholastic natural philosophers advanced Western knowledge in ways leading directly to the Copernican "Revolution" and the subsequent extraordinary scientific achievements.

Theology and Natural Philosophy

As noted in chapter 4, theology consists of *formal reasoning about God*. The emphasis is on *discovering* God's nature, intentions, and demands and on understanding how these define the relationship between human beings and God. Christian theologians have devoted centuries to reasoning, not only about God's nature but also about what God may really have meant by various passages in scripture. And over time, the interpretations often have "evolved" in quite dramatic and extensive ways. For example, not only does the Bible not condemn astrology, the story of the Wise Men following the star even seems to suggest that it is valid. However, in the fifth century, Saint Augustine *reasoned* that astrology was sinful because to believe that one's fate is predestined in the stars stands in opposition to God's gift of free will.[8] This was not a mere amplification of scripture; it is an example of careful deductive reasoning leading to a *new doctrine*: the Church did then prohibit astrology. In similar fashion, as outlined in chapter 4, medieval Christian theologians deduced that previous doctrines that accommodated slavery were wrong—that slavery was in fact against divine law. As these examples demonstrate, great minds could, and often did, greatly alter or even reverse Church doctrines, not on the basis of new revelations but on the basis of nothing more than persuasive reasoning.

As this suggests, leading Christian theologians such as Saint Augustine of Hippo (354–430) and Saint Thomas Aquinas (1225–74) were not what might be called "strict constructionists" today. Rather, they celebrated reason as the means to gain greater insight into divine intentions. For, as Quintus Tertullian instructed in the second century: "Reason is a thing of God, inasmuch as there is nothing which God the Maker of all has not provided, disposed, ordained by reason—nothing which He has not willed should be handled and understood by reason."[9] But, perhaps the most compelling and influential linkage of faith and reason was proclaimed by Clement during the third century:

> Do not think that we say that these things [Christian doctrines] are only to be received by faith, but also that they are to be asserted by reason. For indeed it is not safe to commit these things to bare faith without reason, since assuredly truth cannot be without reason. And therefore he who has received these things fortified by reason, can never lose them; whereas he who receives them without proofs, by an assent to a simple statement of them, can neither keep them safely, nor is certain if they are true; because he who easily believes, also easily yields. But he who has sought reason for those things which he has believed and received, as though bound by the chains of reason itself, can never be torn away or separated from those things he hath believed. And therefore, according as any one is more anxious in demanding a reason, by so much will he be the firmer in preserving his faith.[10]

Such views prompted R. W. Southern (1912–2001) to reflect that, if anything, Scholastic theologians tended "to make man appear more rational, human nature more noble, the divine ordering of the universe more open to human inspection, and the whole complex of man, nature and God more fully intelligible, than we now can believe to be plausible. . . . But—regarded simply as an effort to comprehend the structure of the universe and . . . to demonstrate the dignity of the human mind by showing that it can know all things—this body of thought is one of the most ambitious displays of scientific humanism ever attempted."[11]

This commitment to the pursuit of knowledge reflects that the link between Christian theology and natural philosophy was extremely close during medieval times. As the distinguished Edward Grant noted, "Within Western Christianity in the late Middle Ages . . . almost all professional theologians were also natural philosophers. The structure of medieval university education also made it likely that most theologians had early in their careers actually taught natural philosophy."[12] In contrast, natural philosophy was a highly controversial subject within Islam, something to be "taught privately and quietly" at some risk, and it was never taught by prominent Muslim religious thinkers. However, in "the West natural philosophy could attract talented individuals who believed that they were free to present their opinions publicly on a host of problems that formed the basis of the discipline."[13] It would be difficult to exaggerate the intellectual importance of the bond between theology and natural philosophy, for it made the pursuit of knowledge about the natural world central to "the graduate curriculum of the medieval universities"[14] and led, ultimately, to the rise of Western science—as will be seen.

Inventing Universities

Perhaps in deference to the political correctness of our times, or perhaps due entirely to ignorance, there have been many recent efforts to place the first universities in China, India, or Persia. Of course, from ancient times and in many of the ancient empires, there were schools devoted to teaching religious culture, as well as institutions that sheltered those devoted to contemplation and meditation, as there were in the West. But, just as there are no theologians in the East, none of these ancient institutions was devoted to the pursuit of knowledge. Rather, as the prolific Harvard scholar Charles Homer Haskins (1870–1937) put it, "Universities, like cathedrals and parliaments, are a product of the Middle Ages."[15] More specifically, they were the product of the medieval Church.

The word *university* is a shortened version of the Latin *universitas magistrorum et scholarium*, which can be translated as "community of teachers and scholars." Most of what became medieval universities had long been schools imparting religious culture, maintained by cathedrals and monasteries, many dating from the sixth century. The first universities were created specifically to go beyond such instruction. Their mission was stated as the exclusive devotion to "higher learning"—to the active pursuit of knowledge. To do so, of course, faculty did not limit themselves to reciting the received wisdom. Instead, the Scholastics who founded universities esteemed innovation. Marcia L. Colish's description is enlightening:

Box 7.1. Some leading historians whose work informed this chapter. Specific studies by each can be found in the bibliography.

EDWARD GRANT is distinguished professor of history at the University of Indiana and has received many awards for his authoritative and literate books on the central role of religion in the rise of science, including *God and Reason in the Middle Ages* (2001) and *The Foundations of Modern Science in the Middle Ages: Their Religious, Institutional and Intellectual Contexts* (1996).

DAVID C. LINDBERG (1935–2015) was Hilldale Professor of History of Science at the University of Wisconsin. He earned a degree in physics from Northwestern University and then a PhD in history from the University of Indiana. Author of more than a dozen books, mainly on medieval and early modern science, he also was general editor of the eight-volume *The Cambridge History of Science*.

They [the Scholastic faculty] reviewed past authorities and current opinions, giving [their] analysis of them and [their] reasons for rejecting some and accepting others. Altogether, the methodology already in place by the early twelfth century shows the scholastics' willingness, and readiness, to criticize the foundation documents in their respective fields. More than simply receiving and expanding on the classical and Christian traditions, they set aside ideas of those traditions deemed to have outlived their usefulness. They also freely realigned the authorities they retained to defend positions that those authorities might well have thought strange and novel. [Commentaries] were now rarely mere summaries and explications of their author's views. Scholastic commentators were much more likely to take issue with their chosen author or to bring to bear

STANLEY JAKI (1924–2009) was a Hungarian Benedictine priest who earned his doctorate in theology from the Pontifical Institute in Rome and then pursued the study of physics at Fordham University, followed by studies at Stanford University, the University of California, Berkeley, and finally at the Institute for Advanced Studies at Princeton. In 1975, he became distinguished professor of physics at Seton Hall University. Beginning in 1966 he published a book nearly every year (sometimes two); the last book came out the year before his death. Of these, I learned much from his *The Savior of Science* (1988).

SIR R. W. SOUTHERN (1912–2001) spent his academic career at Oxford, as a student, as a fellow of Balliol, then as Chichele Professor of Modern History, and finally as president of St. John's College. He was president of the Royal Historical Society from 1969 to 1973 and was knighted in 1974. His *Making of the Middle Ages* (1953) was one of the most influential historical works published in the twentieth century.

on his work ideas from emerging schools of thought or the scholastics' own opinions.[16]

Of crucial importance, from the start, the great medieval universities were dominated by empiricism. If it was possible to put an intellectual claim to observational tests, then that was what should be done. Nowhere was the Scholastic commitment to empiricism more fully displayed than in the study of human physiology. It was the Scholastics, not the Greeks, Romans, Muslims, or Chinese, who based their studies on *human dissection.*[17] In fact, during classical times, the "dignity of the human body forbade dissection,"[18] which is why Greco-Roman works on anatomy are so faulty. Aristotle's studies were limited entirely to animal dissections, as were those of Celsius and Galen. Human dissection was also prohibited in Islam. But, with the founding of Christian universities came a new outlook on dissection. The starting assumption was that what was unique to humans was a soul, not a body. Therefore, dissections of the human body had no theological implications. To this, two justifications were added. The first was forensic. Too many murderers escaped detection because the bodies of their victims were not subjected to a careful postmortem. The second was that adequate medical knowledge required direct observation of human anatomy.

Consequently, in the thirteenth century, local officials (especially in Italian university towns) began to authorize postmortems in instances when the cause of death was uncertain. Then, late in the century, Mondino de'Luzzi (1270–1326) wrote a textbook on dissection, based on his study of two female cadavers.[19] Subsequently, in about 1315, he performed a human dissection in front of an audience of students and faculty at the University of Bologna. From there, human dissection spread quite rapidly throughout the Italian universities—given added impetus by the calamity of the Black Death. Public dissections began in Spain in 1391, and the first one in Vienna was conducted in 1404.[20] Nor were these rare occurrences—dissection became a customary part of anatomy classes. The "introduction [of human dissection] in the Latin west, made without serious objection from the Church, was a momentous occurrence."[21]

Moreover, the popularity of human dissections reflected the autonomy of medieval universities. As Nathan Schachner (1895–1955) explained:

> The university was the darling, the spoiled child of the Papacy and Empire, of king and municipality alike. Privileges were showered on the proud Universities in a continuous golden stream; privileges that had no counterpart, then, before, or since. Not even the sacred hierarchies of the Church had quite the exemptions of the poorest begging scholar who could claim protection of a University. Municipalities competed violently for the honour of housing one within their walls; kings wrote siren letters to entice discontented groups of scholars from the domains of their rivals; Popes intervened with menacing language to compel royalty to respect the inviolability of this favoured institution.[22]

Not only were universities autonomous, to a considerable extent so too were faculty. It was amazing how often scholars moved from one university to another, facilitated by the fact that all instruction, everywhere, was in Latin so there were no language barriers to their mobility. Indeed, it was a time when, despite slow transportation, all the leading scholars—spread from Poland to England—knew of one another. Many had actually met, and all had many mutual acquaintances. Then, as today, one gained fame and invitations to join other faculties by *innovation*. It was not who knew Aristotle word for word, but who had found errors in Aristotle. As William of Auvergne (1180–1249), a professor of theology at the University of Paris, put it: "Let it not enter your mind that I want to use the words of Aristotle as authoritative for the proof of things I am about to say, for I know that a proof from an authority is only dialectical and can only produce belief, though it is my aim, both in this treatise and whenever I can, to produce demonstrative certitude."[23] Better yet was to have discovered something unknown to the classical world. So much, then, for the ignorant claims that Scholastics merely recited dogma or debated fatuous theological minutia.

The first university was founded in Bologna, in northern Italy, in about 1088—just after the Norman invasion of England and just before the First Crusade. Next was the University of Paris in about 1150, Oxford in 1167, Palencia in 1208, and Cambridge in 1209, followed by twenty-four others before the end of the fourteenth century: Montpellier, Siena, Toulouse, Orleans, Naples, Salamanca, Seville, Lisbon, Grenoble, Padua, Rome, Perugia, Pisa, Modena, Florence, Prague, Cracow, Vienna, Heidelberg, Cologne, Ofen, Erfurt, Leipzig, and Rostock. At least twenty-eight more were added during the next century, including one as far north as Uppsala in Sweden (in 1477).

The Road to the Scientific "Revolution"

Just as there were no Dark Ages, there was no Scientific Revolution. Rather, the notion of a Scientific Revolution was invented to discredit the medieval Church by claiming that science burst forth in full bloom (thus owing no debts to prior Scholastic scholars) only when a weakened Christianity no longer could suppress it. But, as will be seen, the great scientific achievements of the sixteenth and seventeenth centuries were produced by a group of scholars notable for their piety, who were based in Christian universities, and whose brilliant achievements were carefully built upon an invaluable legacy of centuries of brilliant Scholastic scholarship.[24]

Since the start of the so-called Scientific Revolution is usually attributed to Nicolaus Copernicus (1473–1543), it is appropriate to examine him and his intellectual predecessors to demonstrate that his was a work of "normal" science.

According to the fashionable account, Copernicus was an obscure Catholic canon in far-off Poland, an isolated genius who somehow discovered that, contrary to what everyone believed, the earth revolved around the sun. Moreover, the story goes, the Church made unrelenting efforts to suppress this view.

There is far more fiction than fact in this account. Rather than being some obscure Pole, Copernicus received a superb education at the best Italian universities of the time: Bologna, Padua, and Ferrara. The idea that the earth circled the sun did not come to him out of the blue; he was taught the essential fundamentals leading to the heliocentric model of the solar system by his Scholastic professors. What Copernicus added was not a leap but was the implicit next step in a long line of discovery and innovation stretching back for centuries. I have traced this line of distinguished Scholastic scholars in some detail in *How the West Won* (2014). Here it is sufficient to mention only a few.

ROBERT GROSSETESTE (1168–1253)[25]

A Norman raised in England, Grosseteste attended Oxford, studied and taught at the University of Paris from 1208 to 1213, returned to become chancellor of Oxford, and then became bishop of Lincoln, the largest diocese in England, within which was Oxford. Grosseteste was a remarkable polymath who made important contributions to optics, physics, and tides, and he refuted Aristotle's theory of the rainbow—Grosseteste was the first to realize that rainbows involved refracted light.[26] He also pursued astronomy, being very careful to distinguish it from astrology, as many of his contemporaries did not. But, perhaps his most important contributions were in what has come to be called the scientific method. One of these contributions was what he called the principle of "resolution and composition"—which involved reasoning from the particular case to the general and then back again. For example, by looking at a particular case, one could formulate a universal law about nature and then apply this law to make predictions about all the other relevant cases (e.g., to formulate a "law" about eclipses of the moon and then test that law by applying it to eclipses of the sun). Note the emphasis on observation as the basis of all science. In fact, Grosseteste's commitment to empiricism was such that it led him to introduce the notion of the controlled scientific experiment to Western thought, with the fundamental principle that "when one controls his observations by eliminating any other possible cause of the effect, he may arrive at an experimental universal of provisional truth."[27]

ALBERTUS MAGNUS (C. 1200–1280)[28]

The son of the count of Bollstädt in Bavaria, Albertus was educated in Italy at the University of Padua and then taught at a number of German universities before taking the position of master of theology at the University of Paris (where Thomas Aquinas was his dedicated student). In 1248, Albertus returned to Germany, and in 1260, he was appointed bishop of Regensburg. He resigned after three years to return to his scholarship. Author of thirty-eight books, he was so celebrated during his lifetime that his colleagues, including Roger Bacon, began to add the title "Magnus" (the great) to his name. Although he is regarded as one of the theological giants of medieval times, he also often put claims made about nature by Aristotle and other classical Greek philosophers to empirical tests and in doing so became "perhaps the best field botanist of the entire Middle Ages."[29] His biological studies were not only observational, but also experimental. Albertus made significant contributions to many other fields, including geography, astronomy, and chemistry— hence his colleagues bestowed upon him the title "Doctor Universalis." Perhaps his most important contribution was to inspire his colleagues and students to not merely accept classical scholarship but to challenge the received wisdom and seek reliable observations.

ROGER BACON (1214–94)[30]

This brilliant Englishman is often identified as "the first scientist" in that he fully embraced Grosseteste's commitment to the experimental method and expanded on it at length. Born in Somerset, he entered Oxford at thirteen and eventually became a master there, lecturing on Aristotle. Moving on to the University of Paris in about 1240, he spent a few years on the faculty and then joined the Franciscan Order and ceased teaching—devoting his time to writing.

Initially, Bacon was prevented from publishing by his Franciscan superiors, but Pope Clement IV "ordered" Bacon to write for him, and Bacon responded by sending him his *Opus Majus*. It is an amazing work. Written in only a year of frantic effort, the available modern edition runs to 1,996 pages." A veritable library covering all aspects of natural science,"[31] Bacon displayed knowledge of many different fields: mathematics; the size and position of heavenly bodies; the physiology of eyesight; optics, including refraction, mirrors, and lenses, the magnifying glass, and spectacles; an accurate recipe for gunpowder; calendar reform; and on and on.

Bacon also stressed empiricism as opposed to authority, for "authority has no savor, unless reason for it is given, and it does not give understanding, but belief. For we believe on the strength of authority, but we do not understand through it. Nor can we distinguish between sophism and demonstration, unless we know to test the conclusion by works, as I will show later in the experimental sciences."[32] As illustration, Bacon noted that it had been argued (wrongly) that Aristotle claimed that hot water freezes faster than does cold water. This was not a matter to be accepted on Aristotle's authority or by consulting other learned persons, but only by taking a container of hot water and one of cold and putting them outside in cold weather and *seeing* which froze first.

Bacon's general discussion of the experiment rested greatly on the work of his predecessor Robert Grosseteste—that theories must be put to further tests of their implications or predictions before they could be regarded as valid. That is, making appropriate observations is what Grosseteste, Bacon, and probably most Scholastic scientists meant by the experimental method, although they all recognized the difference between controlled and uncontrolled procedures. This was an extraordinary departure from the Greeks as well as from early Christian thinkers, who all believed in the superiority of ideas and abstract forms to empirical reality, and who therefore concluded that reason, not observation, was always the true test of any "philosophical" claim. It followed that to make an experimental or observational test of an idea was to accept the superiority of the imperfect to the perfect. That was the powerful tradition that proponents of experimentalism had to overcome. Only because Bacon, Grosseteste, and other Scholastics fought and won the battle for empiricism was it possible for the rise of science to occur.

Finally, *Opus Majus* was filled with remarkable predictions about future inventions including microscopes, telescopes, and flying machines. The Oxford historian John Henry Bridges (1832–1906) noted that Bacon's "scientific imagination" made these forecasts possible. Further, he noted, "What may [best] be said is that he set the world on the right track towards their discovery; experiment and observation combined with mathematics, when mathematics were available, and when they were not available, then experiment and observation pursued alone."[33]

WILLIAM OF OCKHAM (1295–1349)[34]

Another Englishman who studied at Oxford, Ockham joined the Franciscans and then spent his academic career on the Continent. He was constantly in trouble with the pope while enjoying the protection of the Holy Roman Emperor, Louis IV of Bavaria. Ockham died during the outbreak of the Black Death, but it is unknown whether that was the cause of his death.

Today, Ockham is remembered primarily for his principle known as Ockham's razor, which stresses parsimony in the formulation of explanations. As he expressed it, explanations should "not be multiplied beyond necessity." Too often this is misrepresented as saying one should prefer the simplest explanation, but the simplest might well be an inferior explanation. What Ockham meant was that theories should include no more terms and principles than needed to explain the matters in question. Hence, if two theories are equally efficient, prefer the one that is simpler. However, Ockham's razor was not Ockham's important contribution to understanding the cosmos.

Because the Greeks thought vacuums could not exist, they assumed that the universe was a sphere filled with transparent matter. If so, the movement of all heavenly bodies would need to constantly overcome friction. If so, how did they keep moving? To solve this problem, many Greek philosophers transformed the sun, moon, stars, and other bodies into living creatures having the capacity to move on their own, while others imagined various sorts of pushers in the form of gods and spirits. Early Christian scholars assumed that angels pushed the heavenly bodies along their courses. It was Ockham who did away with the need for pushers by recognizing that space was a frictionless vacuum. He then anticipated Newton's first law of motion by proposing that once God had set the heavenly bodies in motion, they would remain in motion ever after since there was no friction to counter their motion.

NICOLE D'ORESME (1325–82)[35]

The next vital step toward the heliocentric model was taken by the most brilliant (and sadly neglected) of the Scholastic scientists. Nicole d'Oresme was born in Normandy, attended the University of Paris, and then joined the faculty. In 1364, he was appointed dean of the Cathedral of Rouen, and in 1377, he was appointed bishop of Lisieux.

Among his many major achievements, d'Oresme firmly established that the earth turned on its axis, thus giving the illusion that the other heavenly bodies circled the earth. He began by noting that if the earth turned, the movements observed of the heavenly bodies would appear exactly the same as they would if these bodies were circling the earth. There were no observational data to settle the matter. However, d'Oresme reasoned, for the earth to turn was a far more economical explanation than for the immense number of heavenly bodies all to be circling the earth.

The idea that the earth rotated had occurred to many people through the centuries, but two objections had always made it seem implausible. First, if the earth turned, why wasn't there a constant and powerful wind from the east, caused by the rotation of the earth in that direction? Second, why did an arrow shot up into the air not fall well behind (or in front of) the shooter? Since there was not a powerful eastern wind and since the arrow came straight back down, the earth could not turn. D'Oresme proposed that there was no wind from the east because the motion of the earth was imparted to all objects on the earth or close by, including the atmosphere. This also explained why arrows fell straight back down; they not only had vertical impetus imposed on them by the bow, they also had horizontal impetus conferred on them by the turning earth.

NICHOLAS OF CUSA (1401–64)[36]

A German who became bishop of Brixen and then was elevated to cardinal in 1448, Nicholas of Cusa was educated at the great Italian University of Padua, where he learned that the earth turned in response to "an impetus conferred upon it at the beginning of time." Having noted that "as we see from its shadow in eclipses . . . the earth is smaller than the sun" but larger than the moon, Nicholas went on to observe that "whether a man is on the earth, or the sun, or some other star, it will always seem to him that the position he occupies is the motionless center, and that all other things are in motion."[37] It followed that humans need not trust their perceptions that the earth was stationary in space. Indeed, according to Nicholas, the earth moved though space.

NICOLAUS COPERNICUS (1473–1543)[38]

All of this prior theorizing was well known to Copernicus, since it was taught at all three of the Italian universities he attended. So what did Copernicus contribute? He put the sun in the middle of the solar system and had the earth circling it as one of the planets. What gave such special luster to his work was that he expressed it all in mathematics[39]

and worked out the geometry of his system so as to permit the calcula-
tion of future positions of the bodies involved, which was essential for
setting the dates of Easter, the solstices, and the like. However, these
calculations were no more accurate or any easier to calculate than those
based on the prior Ptolemaic system dating from the second century
CE, because Copernicus failed to realize that the orbits in the solar system were elliptical, not circular. Therefore, to make his system work,
Copernicus had to postulate that there were loops in the orbits of the
heavenly bodies that delayed them sufficiently so they did not complete
their orbits too soon—it would not do for the earth to circle the sun
in only three hundred days. However, these loops lacked any observational support; had they existed, a heavenly body should have been
observed looping. Consequently, everything in Copernicus's famous
book, *On the Revolutions of the Heavenly Spheres,* is wrong, other than
the placement of the sun in the center. It was nearly a century later that
Johannes Kepler (1571–1639), a German Protestant, got things right by
substituting ellipses for Copernicus's circles. Now each heavenly body
was always where it was supposed to be, was on time, and required no
loops.

Of course, even with Kepler's additions, there still was no *explanation*
of why the solar system functioned as it did, or of why, for example,
bodies remained in their orbits rather than flying off into space. The
achievement of such an explanation awaited Isaac Newton (1642–1727).
But over several prior centuries, many essential pieces of such a theory
had been assembled: that the universe was a vacuum; that no pushers
were needed because once in motion, the heavenly bodies would continue in motion; that the earth turned; that the sun was the center of the
solar system; that the orbits were elliptical.

This record of systematic progress is why the distinguished historian of science, I. Bernard Cohen (1914–2003) noted that "the idea that a
Copernican revolution in science occurred goes counter to the evidence
. . . and is the invention of later historians."[40] Most of Cohen's sophisticated colleagues agree.[41] Copernicus added a small step forward in a

long process of normal science, albeit one having immense polemical and philosophical implications. It should be noted, too, that the scholars involved in this long process were not rebel secularists. Not only were they devout Christians, they all were priests or monks, and four of them were bishops and one a cardinal.

Science Comes of Age

Isaac Newton famously remarked, "If I have seen further it is by standing on the shoulders of giants." Unfortunately, too few who quote this line realize that not only was Newton quite serious, he was quite correct. Science did not suddenly erupt in a great intellectual revolution during Newton's time; this era of superb achievements was the culmination of centuries of sustained, normal scientific progress. Nevertheless, the notion that a Scientific Revolution erupted in the sixteenth century is so ingrained in our intellectual culture that Steven Shapin began his recent study with the charming line: "There was no such thing as the Scientific Revolution, and this is a book about it."[42] However, it seems more accurate to positively identify what occurred in this era as the "coming of age" of Western science. Two questions shape our interest in this era. Were these great scientists "Enlightened" rebels against the Church? Were they mainly Protestants?

Historians often are misled (and mislead) by relying on atypical examples. This problem can be solved by proper use of quantitative methods. Rather than cite examples of famous early scientists who were Protestants, or irreligious, or ordained clergy, far more trustworthy results can be based on analysis of *all* of the famous scientists of this era. Hence, in my analysis I identified all of the significant scientific stars of the era, beginning with the publication of Copernicus's *De revolutionibus* in 1543 and including all born prior to 1680. I based my selections by studying the rosters provided in a number of specialized encyclopedias and biographical dictionaries, among which Isaac Asimov's *Encyclopedia of Science and Technology* (1982) was especially useful and reliable. I limited my selections to *active scientists*, thereby excluding some well-known intellectual figures of the day, such as Francis Bacon and Joseph Scaliger. In selecting great scientists, I paid no attention to their religion, whether Protestant, Catholic, or irreligious. Then, having assembled a list, I consulted various sources, including individual biographies, to determine the facts I wished to code for each case. In the end, I had a data set consisting of fifty-two scientists.[43]

"Enlightened" Scientists

Just as a group of eighteenth-century philosophers invented the notion of the Dark Ages to discredit Christianity, they labeled their own era the Enlightenment on grounds that religious darkness had finally been dispelled by secular humanism. As Bertrand Russell (1872–1970) explained, the "Enlightenment was essentially a revaluation of independent intellectual activity, aimed quite literally at spreading light where hitherto darkness had prevailed."[44] Thus did Voltaire, Rousseau, Locke, Hume, and others wrap themselves in the achievements of the "Scientific Revolution" as they celebrated the victory of secularism, eventuating in the Marquis Laplace's claim that God was now an unnecessary hypothesis. Of course, not one of these "enlightened" figures had played *any* part in the scientific enterprise. What about those who had? Were they a bunch of skeptics too? Hardly.

First of all, thirteen of the scientific stars (25%) were members of the clergy, nine of them Roman Catholics. In addition, I coded each of the fifty-two stars as to their personal piety. To code someone as *devout*, I required clear evidence of especially deep religious involvement. For example, Robert Boyle spent a great deal of money on translations of the Bible into non-Western languages. Isaac Newton wrote far more on theology than he did on physics—he even calculated that the Second Coming would take place in 1948. By the same token, Johannes Kepler was deeply interested in mysticism and in biblical questions—he devoted great effort to working out the date of the Creation, settling for 3992 BC.

I used the code *conventionally religious* to identify those whose biography offers no evidence of skepticism, but whose piety does not stand out as other than satisfactory to their associates. An example is Marcello Malpighi, whose observations of a chick's heart are regarded as one of the most remarkable achievements of seventeenth-century biology. Malpighi's biography offers no direct evidence of concerns about God similar to Boyle's or Newton's. On the other hand, he did retire to Rome to serve as the personal physician of Pope Innocent XII, a very pious Counter-Reformation pontiff, who surely expected a similar level of piety from those around him. If anything, then, I have underrated Malpighi's level of personal piety, and I may well have done so in other cases, but I certainly have not overstated anyone's level of piety.

Finally, I reserved the label *skeptic* for anyone about whom I could infer disbelief, or at least profound doubt, in the existence of a conscious God. Only one of the fifty-two qualified: Edmund Halley—he was rejected for a professorship at Oxford on grounds of his "atheism."

Table 7.1 displays the religious profile of these fifty-two scientific stars.

TABLE 7.1. Personal Piety

PIETY	NUMBER	PERCENT
Devout	31	60%
Conventional	20	38%
Skeptic	1	2%
Total	52	100%

Clearly, the superb scientific achievements of the sixteenth and seventeenth centuries were not the work of skeptics, but of very Christian men—at least 60 percent were devout. The era of the Enlightenment is as imaginary as the era of the Dark Ages, both perpetrated by the same people for the same reasons.

Protestantism

In 1938, Robert K. Merton (1910–2003), soon to become one of America's most influential sociologists, published a lengthy study, "Science, Technology and Society in Seventeenth-Century England," in the history of science journal *Osiris*. Rejecting the Marxist and secularist orthodoxies of the day that science was the triumph of irreligion, Merton proposed that it was Protestant Puritanism that had given birth to the Scientific Revolution. According to Merton, this occurred because the Puritans had reasoned (and, presumably, they were the first Christians to do so) that since the world was God's handiwork, it was their duty to study and understand this handiwork as a means of glorifying God. Thus, Merton argued, among Puritan intellectuals in England during the seventeenth century, science was defined as a religious calling.

Merton's whole argument was, of course, merely an extension of Max Weber's claims about the role of the Protestant ethic in the rise of capitalism (chapter 10). And, like Weber's, Merton's position is untenable. However, contrary to Merton's early critics who claimed that the evidence of personal piety that he cited must have been merely faked by the early scientists in order to avoid trouble, Merton was most certainly correct in that regard. Where he went wrong was to misidentify English Protestant scientists as Puritans, when most of them were conventional Anglicans,[45] and, by keeping a narrow focus on England, he ignored the very substantial Catholic participation in science at this time. Indeed, Merton's definition of "Puritan" was so broad that essentially no Christian was excluded, not even Catholics.[46] In Barbara J. Shapiro's pithy summation, "What [Merton] is essentially saying is that Englishmen contributed to English science."[47]

The claim that the supposed Scientific Revolution was the work of Protestants of any kind is clearly undermined by the data in Table 7.2. Only half of the fifty-two stars were Protestants, and with the English removed, Catholics outnumbered Protestants by twenty-six to eleven, which approximates the distribution of Protestants and Catholics on the Continent in this era. Indeed, "there was nothing in the dogmas of Catholicism, Anglicanism, or Puritanism which made any one of them more or less favorable to science in general than any of the others. . . . [In each, the majority held] that science should be welcomed as a faithful handmaid of theology."[48]

Why England?

Many have claimed that England was the primary setting for this scientific era. Merton focused exclusively on England in pushing his Puritan explanation, and the prominence of nonacademics among the London scientific set encouraged many to disdain the role of the universities. Although both of these interpretations are false, there is some basis for the view that England was exceptionally productive of scientists, as can be seen in Table 7-3.

In fact, England does stand out, especially when we consider that in this era Italy had about twice the population of England.[49] It is legitimate to ask, "Why England?" My explanation is that England led the way in science for the same reasons that it led the way in the Industrial Revolution—its substantially greater political and economic liberty had produced a relatively open class system that enabled the emergence of an ambitious and creative upper middle class, sometimes called the *bourgeoisie*. While the rise of the bourgeoisie occurred all across western Europe, it did so earlier and to a far greater degree in England (and Holland).

From earliest days, the pursuit of knowledge has been the work of

TABLE 7.2. Religious Affiliation

	ALL	CONTINENT ONLY
Protestants	26	11
Catholic	26	26
Total	52	37

TABLE 7.3. Nationality

NATIONALITY	NUMBER	PERCENT
English	14	27%
Italian	11	21%
French	9	17%
German	8	15%
Dutch	4	8%
Danish	3	6%
Flemish	1	2%
Polish	1	2%
Scottish	1	2%
Total	52	100%

persons whose status was less than aristocratic. Aristotle tutored future kings, but he was the son of a physician. As noted in chapter 8, the students at medieval universities "were of a social position intermediate between the highest and the very lowest—sons of knights and yeomen, merchants, tradesmen or thrifty artisans."[50] There were, of course, many universities educating these sons all across western Europe, but it was the case that in the seventeenth century more students enrolled in "the English universities than at any time until the nineteenth century."[51] In fact, beginning in the 1540s, there was a remarkable explosion of education at all levels in England, resulting in a huge increase in literacy and a corresponding leap in the sale of books.[52] This was, of course, fully consistent with the Elizabethan court—"commoners" such as John Hawkins and Francis Drake having played prominent roles in the Queen's service.

Something else equally remarkable was taking place in England at this time as well: the lesser aristocracy were, in effect, joining the bourgeoisie from above. As Lawrence Stone (1919–99) reported, "They were pouring into the universities and the Inns of Court."[53] As a consequence of these developments, the segment of the population from which scientists were most apt to be drawn was much larger in England than on the Continent. Perhaps for that reason, English scientific stars in the era were far more likely to have been of bourgeois origins than were Continental scientists, as can be seen in Table 7-4.

These codes apply to each scientist's family. *Nobility* means one's father had a title. *Gentry* includes people of high social status but with no title, such as government officials and large landowners, or, as Deirdre McCloskey put it, "any dignified people just below the aristocracy."[54] *Bourgeois* fathers were in business or were members of the professions, clergy, professors, and the like. *Lower* refers to those who rose from peasant or laboring backgrounds, there being only three among these stars—Marin Mersenne's parents were peasants, Johann Glauber's father was a barber, and John Ray was the son of a blacksmith.

But, even though England was somewhat more productive in scien-

TABLE 7.4. Class Origins		
	ENGLAND	CONTINENT
Nobility	7%	14%
Gentry	7%	38%
Bourgeois	79%	43%
Lower	7%	5%
Total	100%	100%

tists, the principal fact about this wonderful era of science is that it was spread across all of western Europe. And for good reason: it was the normal result of the organized pursuit of knowledge that was fundamental to Christianity.

The Religious Origins of Science

Science arose only in Christian Europe because only medieval Europeans believed that science was *possible* and *desirable*. And the basis of their belief was their image of God and his Creation. This was dramatically asserted to a distinguished audience of scholars attending the 1925 Lowell Lectures at Harvard by the great English philosopher and mathematician Alfred North Whitehead (1861–1947), who explained that science developed in Europe because of the widespread "faith in the possibility of science . . . derivative from medieval theology."[55] This claim shocked not only his audience, but Western intellectuals in general when his lectures were published. How could this world-famous thinker, coauthor with Bertrand Russell of the landmark *Principia Mathematica* (1910–13), not know that religion is the unrelenting enemy of science? In fact, Whitehead knew better!

Whitehead had recognized that Christian theology was essential for the rise of science, just as non-Christian theologies had stifled the scientific enterprise everywhere else. He explained:

> The greatest contribution of medievalism to the formation of the scientific movement [was] the inexpungeable belief . . . that there was a secret, a secret which can be unveiled. How has this conviction been so vividly implanted in the European mind? . . . It must come from the medieval insistence on the rationality of God, conceived as with the personal energy of Jehovah and with the rationality of a Greek philosopher. Every detail was supervised and ordered: the search into nature could only result in the vindication of faith in rationality.[56]

Whitehead was, of course, merely summarizing what so many of the great early scientists had said—René Descartes justified his search for the "laws" of nature on ground that such laws must exist because God is perfect and therefore "acts in a manner as constant and immutable as possible."[57] That is, the universe functions according to rational rules or laws. As that great medieval Scholastic Nicole d'Oresme put it, God's creation "is much like that of a man making a clock and letting it run and continue its own motion by itself."[58] Furthermore, because God has given humans the power of reason it ought to be possible for us to discover the rules established by God.

Indeed, many of the early scientists felt morally obliged to pursue these secrets, just as Whitehead had noted. The great British philosopher concluded his remarks by noting that the images of God and creation found in the non-European faiths, especially those in Asia, were too impersonal or too irrational to have sustained science. Any particular natural "occurrence might be due to the fiat of an irrational despot" god, or might be produced by "some impersonal, inscrutable origin of things. There is not the same confidence as in the intelligible rationality of a personal being."[59] It should be noted that given their common roots, the Jewish conception of God is as suitable to sustaining science as is the Christian conception. But Jews were a small, scattered, and often repressed minority in Europe during this era and took no part in the rise of science—although Jews have excelled as scientists since their emancipation in the nineteenth century.

In contrast, most religions outside the Judeo-Christian tradition do not posit a creation at all. The universe is said to be eternal, without beginning or purpose, and never having been created, it has no creator. From this view, the universe is a supreme mystery, inconsistent, unpredictable, and (perhaps) arbitrary. For those holding this view, the only paths to wisdom are meditation or inspiration—there being nothing to reason about. But if the universe was created in accord with rational rules by a perfect, rational creator, then it ought to yield its secrets to reason and observation. Hence, the scientific truism that nature is a *book* meant to be read.

Of course, the Chinese "would have scorned such an idea as being too naïve for the subtlety and complexity of the universe as they intuited it,"[60] as explained by the esteemed Oxford historian of Chinese technology, Joseph Needham (1900–95). As for the Greeks, many of them also regarded the universe as eternal and uncreated—Aristotle condemned the idea "that the universe came into being at some point in time . . . as unthinkable."[61] Indeed, none of the traditional Greek gods would have been capable of such a creation. But, worst of all, the Greeks insisted on turning the cosmos, and inanimate objects more generally, into living things. Consequently, they attributed many natural phenomena to *motives*, not to inanimate forces. Thus, according to Aristotle, heavenly bodies moved in circles because of their affection for doing so, and objects fall to the ground "because of their innate love for the centre of the world."[62] As for Islam, the orthodox conception of Allah is hostile to the scientific quest. There is no suggestion in the Qur'an that Allah set his creation in motion and then let it run. Rather, it is assumed that he often intrudes in the world and changes things as it pleases him. Thus, through the centuries, many of the most influential Muslim scholars have held that all efforts to formulate natural laws are blasphemy in that they would seem to deny Allah's freedom to act. Thus did their images of God and the universe deflect scientific efforts in China, ancient Greece, and Islam.[63]

It was only because Europeans believed in God as the Intelligent Designer of a rational universe that they pursued the secrets of creation. In the words of Johannes Kepler, "The chief aim of all investigations of the external world should be to discover the rational order and harmony imposed on it by God and which he revealed to us in the language of mathematics."[64] In similar fashion, in his last will and testament, the great chemist Robert Boyle (1627–91) wrote to the members of the Royal Society of London, wishing them continuing success in "their laudable attempts to discover the true Nature of the Works of God."[65]

Perhaps the most remarkable aspect to the rise of science is that the early scientists not only searched for natural laws, confident that they existed, but *they found them*! It thus could be said that the proposition that the universe had an Intelligent Designer is the most fundamental of all scientific theories and that it has been successfully put to empirical tests again and again. For, as Albert Einstein (1879–1955) once remarked, the most incomprehensible thing about the universe is that it is comprehensible: "*A priori* one should expect a chaotic world which cannot be grasped by the mind in any way. . . . That is the 'miracle' which is constantly being reinforced as our knowledge expands."[66] And that is the "miracle" that testifies to a creation guided by intention and rationality.

Of course, the rise of science did engender some conflicts with the Catholic Church, as well as with the early Protestants. That in no way diminishes the essential role of the Christian conception of God in justifying and motivating science; it merely reflects that many Christian leaders failed to grasp the important differences between science and theology as to domain and evidence. That is, Christian theologians attempt to deduce God's nature and intentions from scripture; scientists attempt to discover the nature of God's creation by empirical means. In principle, the two efforts do not overlap, but in practice theologians have sometimes felt that a scientific position was an attack on faith (and some modern scientists have, in fact, attacked religion, albeit on spurious grounds). In the early days, a major dispute took place because both Catholic and Protestant theologians were reluctant to accept that the earth was not the center of the universe, let alone not the center of solar system. Both Luther and the pope were opposed to the Copernican claim, and both attempted to defeat it, but their efforts had little impact and were never very vigorous. Unfortunately, this modest conflict has been blown into a monumental event by those determined to show that religion is the bitter enemy of science by turning Galileo Galilei into a heroic martyr to blind faith. As Voltaire reported: "The great Galileo, at the age of fourscore, groaned away his days in the dungeons of the Inquisition, because he had demonstrated by irrefutable proofs the motion of the earth."[67] The Italian gadfly Giuseppe Baretti (1719–89) added that Galileo was "put to the torture, for saying that *the earth moved*."[68]

So, What about Galileo?

It is true that Galileo was called before the Roman Inquisition and charged with the heretical teaching that the earth moves—around the sun or otherwise. And he was forced to recant. But he was neither imprisoned nor tortured; he was sentenced to a comfortable house arrest during which he died at age seventy-eight. More important, what got Galileo in trouble with the Church were not his scientific convictions nearly as much as his arrogant duplicity. It happened this way.

Long before he became Pope Urban VIII (serving from 1623 to 1644), while still a cardinal, Maffeo Barberini knew and liked Galileo. In 1623, when he published *Assayer,* Galileo dedicated the book to Barberini (the Barberini family crest appeared on the title page of the book), and the new pope was said to have been delighted by the many nasty insults it directed against various Jesuit scholars. *Assayer* was mainly an attack on Orazio Grassi, a Jesuit mathematician, who had published a study that (correctly) treated comets as small heavenly bodies; Galileo ridiculed this claim, arguing wrongly that comets were but reflections on vapors arising from the earth.[69] In any event, *Assayer* prompted Pope Urban VIII to write an adulatory poem on the glory of astronomy. So, what went wrong?

It is important to put the Galileo affair in historical context. At this time, the Reformation stood defiant in northern Europe, the Thirty Years' War raged, and the Catholic Counter-Reformation was in full bloom. Partly in response to Protestant charges that the Catholic Church was not faithful to the Bible, the limits of acceptable theology were being narrowed, and this led to increasing Church interference in scholarly and scientific discussions. However, Urban VIII and other leading officials were not ready to clamp down on scientists, but instead proposed ways to avoid any conflicts between science and theology by separating their domains. Thus, Friar Marin Mersenne advised his network of leading scientific correspondents to defend their studies on grounds that God was free to place the earth anywhere he liked, and it was the duty of scientists to find out where he had put it.[70] More cautious early scientists adopted the tactic of identifying scientific conclusions as hypothetical or mathematical, hence being without direct theological implications. And that was what the pope asked Galileo to do—to acknowledge in his publications that "definitive conclusions could not be reached in the natural sciences. God in his omnipotence could produce a natural phenomenon in any number of ways and it therefore was presumptuous for any philosopher to claim that he had determined a unique solution."[71]

That seemed an easy evasion. And, given Galileo's propensity to claim false credit for inventions made by others, such as the telescope, and to have conducted empirical research he probably did not really perform, such as dropping weights from the Leaning Tower of Pisa, it would not seem to have stretched his ethical standards to have gone along with the pope. But to defy the pope in a rather offensive way was quite consistent with Galileo's ego.

In 1632, Galileo published his awaited *Dialogue Concerning the Two Chief World Systems*. Although the ostensible purpose of the book was to present an explanation of tidal phenomena, the two systems involved were Ptolemy's, in which the sun circles the earth, and Copernicus's, wherein the earth circles the sun. The dialogue involves three speakers, two of them philosophers and the third a layman. It is the layman, Simplicio, who presents the traditional views in support of Ptolemy—the resemblance of the name to "simpleton" was obvious to all. This allowed Galileo to exploit the traditional "straw man" technique to ridicule his opponents. Although Galileo did include the disclaimer suggested by the pope, he put it in the mouth of Simplicio, thereby disowning it.

The book caused an immense stir and, understandably, the pope felt betrayed—although Galileo never seemed to have grasped that fact and continued to blame the Jesuits and university professors for his troubles. Despite that, the pope used his power to protect Galileo from any serious punishment. Unfortunately, Galileo's defiant action stimulated a general crackdown by the Counter-Reformation Church on intellectual freedom that otherwise may never have occurred. Ironically, much that Galileo presented in the book as correct science was not; his theory of the tides, for example, was nonsense, as Albert Einstein pointed out in his foreword to a 1953 translation of Galileo's notorious book.[72] Equally ironic is the fact that the judgment against Galileo was partly motivated by efforts on the part of Church leaders to suppress astrologers—some theologians mistakenly equating the claim that the earth moved with doctrines that fate was ruled by the motion of heavenly bodies.

So, what does the case of Galileo reveal? It surely demonstrates that powerful groups and organizations often will abuse their power to impose their beliefs, a shortcoming that certainly is not limited to religious organizations—the Communist regime in the Soviet Union outlawed Mendelian genetics on grounds that all characteristics are caused by the environment. But it also shows that Galileo was not some naïve scholar who fell victim to a bunch of ignorant bigots—these same "bigots" ignored dozens of other prominent scientists, many of them resident in Italy! In any event, this celebrated case does nothing to alter the fact that the rise of science was rooted in Christian theology—indeed, for all his posturing, Galileo remained deeply religious. As William Shea noted, "Had Galileo been less devout, he could have refused to go to Rome [when summoned by the Inquisition]; Venice offered him asylum."[73] But he did not flee to Venice and often expressed his personal faith to his daughter and friends after his trial was over.

Conclusion

Although Christianity was essential for the development of Western science, that dependency no longer exists. Once properly launched, science has been able to stand on its own, and the conviction that the secrets of nature will yield to prolonged inquiry is now as much a secular article of faith as it originally was Christian. The rise of an independent scientific establishment has given birth to new tensions between theology and science. If the church fathers were leery of the implications of science for theology, there now exists a militant group of atheists, only some of them actually scientists, who devote a great deal of effort to attacking religion as superstitious nonsense and to claiming that science refutes the existence of God and the possibility of miracles. They fail to grasp that science is limited to the empirical, natural world and can say nothing about a nonempirical, spiritual realm—except to deny it exists.

Amazingly, several of the most prominent of these angry atheists are confident that "god-like" beings have evolved on distant planets. As Richard Dawkins explained in *The God Delusion* (2006): "Whether we ever get to know about them or not, there are very probably alien civilizations that are superhuman, to the point of being god-like in ways that exceed anything a theologian could possibly imagine."[74]

The myth of sanctifying slavery: It is a common myth that not only did the Catholic Church fail to oppose slavery, it was very comfortable with members of the clergy owning slaves, as seen here.

Blessed Be Slavery 8

I<small>T HAS LONG</small> been the received wisdom that until very recently the Catholic Church accepted slavery. As John Francis Maxwell put it in his well-received *Slavery and the Catholic Church* (1975): "Since the sixth century and right up until the twentieth century it has been the common Catholic teaching that . . . slavery is morally legitimate."[1] Although some historians have claimed that the Church did not repudiate slavery until 1890,[2] Maxwell charged that this did not take place until 1965!

But, as noted in chapter 4, the Church opposed and eliminated slavery in Europe more than a thousand years ago. Then, when European colonists began to reestablish slavery in the New World, the popes vigorously opposed it. Unfortunately, the popes lacked the power to impose their will—the Spanish had recently sacked Rome and ruled much of Italy. However, the Church was able to formulate and enforce codes as to the treatment of slaves that spared them many of the worst features of slavery that prevailed in Protestant areas. Moreover, to prevent enslavement and exploitation of Native Americans, the Jesuits guided the creation of a remarkable, and strangely forgotten, sophisticated Indian civilization that eventually was utterly destroyed by Portuguese and Spanish armies, who brutalized the Jesuits and expelled them from the continent.

Papal Opposition to Slavery

The best place to begin is with Thomas Aquinas (1225–74), for his theological conclusion that slavery is a sin has guided papal policy ever since. Keep in mind that in Aquinas's day, slavery no longer existed in Europe, so his conclusion was a by-product of his overall analysis of morality in human relationships. Aquinas placed slavery in opposition to natural law, deducing that all "rational creatures" are entitled to justice. Hence, he found no natural basis for the enslavement of one person by another, "thus removing any possible justification for slavery based on race or religion."[3] Right reason, not coercion, is the moral basis of authority, for "one man is not by nature ordained to use another as an end."[4] Here Aquinas distinguished two forms of "subjection" or authority, just and unjust. The former exists when leaders work for the advantage and benefit of their subjects. The unjust form of subjection "is that of slavery, in which the ruler manages the subject for his own [the ruler's] advantage."[5] Based on the immense authority vested in Aquinas by the Church, it became the official view that slavery was sinful.

It is true that several popes who served soon after Aquinas's day did not observe the moral obligation to oppose slavery. Indeed, in 1488 Pope Innocent VIII accepted the gift of a hundred Moorish slaves from King Ferdinand of Aragon, giving some of them to his favorite cardinals. Of course, Innocent violated other moral standards as well—he fathered many children, for example. In addition, the fact that the Moors held huge numbers of slaves, and routinely enslaved Christians, was felt by many, including Innocent, to mitigate against the prohibition on slavery so far as Moors were concerned. However, subsequent popes disagreed and strictly interpreted Aquinas's conclusion, as had popes prior to Innocent VIII.

During the 1430s, the Spanish colonized the Canary Islands and began to enslave the native population. When word of these actions reached Pope Eugene IV (1431–47), he issued a bull, *Sicut dudum*. In it, the pope did not mince words. With a threat of excommunication, the pope gave everyone involved fifteen days from receipt of the bull "to restore to their earlier liberty all and each person of either sex who were once residents of said Canary Island. . . . These people are to be totally and perpetually free and are to be let go without the exaction or reception of any money."[6] Pope Pius II (1458–64) and Pope Sixtus IV (1471–84) followed with additional bulls condemning enslavement of Canary Islanders, which, obviously, had continued. What this episode displays is the weakness of papal authority at this time, not the indifference of the Church to the sin of slavery.

With the successful Spanish and Portuguese invasions of the New World, enslavement of the native peoples and the importation of Africans ensued, and some slavers offered the rationale that this was not a violation of Christian morality, as these were not "rational creatures" entitled to liberty but were a species of animals and therefore legitimately subject to human exploitation. This theological subterfuge by slave traders was used, perhaps cynically, by Norman F. Cantor to indict Catholicism: "The church accepted slavery. . . . In sixteenth-century Spain, Christians were still arguing over whether black slaves had souls or were animal creations of the Lord."[7] Cantor gave no hint that Rome utterly rejected the claim that Africans were not fully human and that popes repeatedly denounced New World slavery as grounds for excommunication.

But that is precisely what Pope Paul III (1534–49) had to say about the matter. He not only recognized the moral challenge of Protestantism and organized the Counter-Reformation, he issued a magnificent bull against New World slavery. But, it was somehow "lost" from the historical record until very recently, as were similar bulls by other popes.[8] In the case of Pope Paul's bull, its loss may well not have been due only to the Protestant bias of historians but also to scornful reactions to the fact that the pope attributed slavery to Satan:

> [Satan,] the enemy of the human race, who always opposes all good men so that the race may perish, has thought up a way,

unheard of before now, by which he might impede the saving word of God from being preached to the nations. He has stirred up some of his allies who, desiring to satisfy their own avarice, are presuming to assert far and wide that the Indians of the West and the South who have come to our notice in these times be reduced to our service like brute animals, under the pretext that they are lacking in Catholic faith. And they reduce them to slavery, treating them with afflictions they would scarcely use with brute animals.

Therefore, we . . . noting that the Indians themselves indeed are true men . . . by our Apostolic Authority decree and declare by these present letters that the same Indians and *all other peoples*—even though they be outside the faith—. . . should not be deprived of their liberty or their other possessions . . . and are not to be reduced to slavery, and that whatever happens to the contrary is to be considered null and void.[9]

In a second bull on slavery, Paul imposed the penalty of excommunication on anyone, regardless of their "dignity, state, condition, or grade . . . who may in any way presume to reduce said Indians to slavery or despoil their goods."[10]

But nothing happened. Soon, in addition to the brutal exploitation of the Indians, Spanish and Portuguese slave ships began to sail between Africa and the New World. And just as overseas Catholic missionaries had aroused Rome to condemn enslavement of Indians, similar appeals were filed concerning imported black slaves. On April 22, 1639, Pope Urban VIII (1623–44), at the request of the Jesuits of Paraguay, issued a bull *Commissum nobis* reaffirming the rule by "our predecessor Paul III" that those who reduced others to slavery were subject to excommunication.[11] Eventually, the Congregation of the Holy Office (the Roman Inquisition) took up the matter. On March 20, 1686, it ruled in the form of questions and answers:

It is asked:

Whether it is permitted to capture by force and deceit Blacks and other natives who have harmed no one?	Answer: no.
Whether it is permitted to buy, sell or make contracts in their respect Blacks and other natives who have harmed no one and been made captives by force or deceit?	Answer: no.
Whether the possessors of Blacks and other natives who have harmed no one and been captured by force or deceit, are not held to set them free?	Answer: yes.
Whether the captors, buyers and possessors of Blacks and other natives who have harmed no one and who have been captured by force or deceit are not held to make compensation to them?	Answer: yes.

Nothing ambiguous here. The problem wasn't that the Church failed to condemn slavery; it was that few heard it and most did not listen. In this era, popes had little or no influence over the Spanish or the Portuguese since at that time the Spanish ruled most of Italy; in 1527, under the leadership of Charles V, they had even sacked Rome. If the pope had little influence in Spain or Portugal, he had next to none in their New World colonies, except indirectly through the work of the religious orders. In fact, it was illegal even to publish papal decrees "in the Spanish colonial possessions without royal consent," and the king also appointed all the bishops.[12]

Nevertheless, Urban VIII's bull was read in public by the Jesuits in Rio de Janeiro, with the result that rioters attacked the local Jesuit college and injured a number of priests. In Santos, a mob trampled the Jesuit vicar-general when he tried to publish the bull, and the Jesuits were expelled from Sào Paulo when word spread of their involvement in obtaining the bull.[13]

Clearly, although not formally published in the New World, Urban's bull was not a secret. Then, why was it "unknown" to modern historians? Indeed, why were the many papal attacks on slavery not mentioned in even the most respected histories?

The papal bulls were not unknown to the distinguished Stanley M. Elkins. In his celebrated *Slavery: A Problem in American Institutional and Intellectual Life* (1959), he wrote: "The papacy itself would denounce it [slavery] in various ways in 1462, 1537, 1639, 1741, 1815, and 1839." But, that was it! One sentence. No quotations. Nothing more. Yet, Elkins paid far more attention to the popes than did many other equally celebrated historians of slavery. The only entry for "pope" in the index of David Brion Davis's highly praised book on slavery in Western culture, *The Problem of Slavery in Western Culture* (1966), is the British poet Alexander Pope. Precisely the same can be said for Robin Blackburn's extensive study, *The Making of New World Slavery* (1998). Nor is any mention made of popes in Drescher and Engerman's encyclopedic *A Historical Guide to World Slavery* (1998), although one fails to understand how popes could be omitted from the book's lengthy sections devoted to "Moral Issues" and to "Religion." But, that's the way things have been.

Of course, Catholics were not the only slavers in the New World. And it should be noted that initially the introduction of slaves into the Dutch and English colonies did not prompt any outcries from leading Protestants.

Slave Codes

Even though the papal bulls against slavery were hushed up and ignored by slavers in the New World, the strong antislavery views of the Church did have significantly moderating effects in the Catholic Americas. This occurred via the formulation and successful enforcement of the *Code Noir* and the *Código Negro Español*.

The *Code Noir* was formulated by Louis XIV's minister of finance, Jean-Baptist Colbert (1619–83), with the aid of leading French clergy. What it did was set down an extensive legal code governing slavery in the French colonies. The *Code* has been outrageously misrepresented by nearly all modern historians of slavery. Many have mentioned only Article 3, which prohibited the instruction of slaves in any religion other than Roman Catholicism, to show how biased it was. None of these historians noted that public worship by Roman Catholics was prohibited in all British colonies other than Maryland at this same time, and that it was forbidden to provide slaves with religious instruction or baptism in British colonies. More important is that these historians ignored the many articles of the *Code* that expanded on the stated premise that a slave is "a being of God." It was in this spirit that the *Code* required owners to baptize their slaves, provide them with religious instruction, and allow them the sacrament of holy matrimony, which, in turn, became the basis for prohibiting the selling of family members separately. Slaves also were exempted from work on Sundays and holy days (from midnight to midnight), with masters being subject to fines or even confiscation of their slaves for violating this provision. Other articles specified minimum amounts of food and clothing that masters must provide and ordered that the disabled and elderly must be properly cared for, including their hospitalization.

It surely is no surprise that Article 12 prohibited slaves from carrying guns or clubs or that Article 13 outlawed "slaves belonging to different masters to gather in a crowd." Article 38, which forbade masters to torture their slaves, allowed that they might be whipped. As will be seen, these articles have been seized upon by some historians who misrepresented them as the entire *Code* in an effort to claim that it was devoted solely to "the protection of whites." Peter Gay wrote that the *Code* was "extraordinarily severe—toward the slave, of course."[14] And the *Columbia Encyclopedia* (2nd ed.), in the entry for Louisiana, explained "[T]he Code Noir, adopted in 1724, provided for the rigid control of their [slaves'] lives and the protection of whites. Additional provisions established Catholicism as the official religion." And that's it! For this fraud to be perpetrated, it is necessary that there be no mention of the many articles already noted, as well as Article 39, which ordered officers of justice "to proceed criminally against masters and overseers who will have killed their slaves or mutilated them," a matter of some importance from a slave's perspective.

It also is fashionable to dismiss the *Code* on grounds that it often wasn't fully observed or enforced—David Brion Davis complained that "there is apparently no record of a French master being executed for killing a slave."[15] The weight of that statement would shift substantially if Davis had quoted the entire sentence he cited as his source. It reads: "Masters maltreating or killing slaves were liable to prosecution, and there are records of cases being brought against them, although no master appears to have suffered the death penalty for killing a slave."[16] No doubt masters enjoyed advantages when the *Code* was interpreted vis-à-vis their actions. But given that French slave owners were aware that the *Code* was enforced even some of the time must have modified their behavior as compared with that of British and Dutch owners who faced no legal limits or peril.

From the start, Spanish treatment of slaves was more humane even than that of the French because it was even more greatly modified by Church influence. Toward the end of the eighteenth century, Spain adopted the *Código Negro Español* (Spanish Black Code), based on a thirteenth-century Castilian code formulated to set standards for the treatment of enslaved Moorish prisoners of war. The *Código* not only included most of the provisions of the French *Code*, but it was far more liberal in that it guaranteed slaves the right to own property and to purchase their freedom. Specifically, slaves were enabled to petition the courts "to have themselves appraised and to purchase themselves from even unwilling masters or mistresses at their judicially appraised market value."[17] This was greatly facilitated by terms of the *Código* that gave slaves the right to work for themselves on their days off, including the eighty-seven days a year they were at liberty because of not having to work for their owners on Sundays and holy days. In rural areas, slaves were typically permitted to sell produce raised in their own gardens and keep the proceeds.[18]

Many skeptics have dismissed the rights given by the *Código* as merely "symbolic." But how then to account for the fact that in 1817 there were 114,058 free blacks in Cuba alone, many times more than in *all* of the British West Indies? Or that Spanish slaves were married in church at almost the same rate as whites? As for enforcement of the *Código*, bishops held frequent synods to "deal with local conditions," during which they "always legislated in favor of the fullest freedom and rights [for slaves] that were permissible" under the *Código*. Meanwhile, "the lower clergy, especially at the parish level, effectively carried this law into practice."[19] They did this not only by maintaining close contacts with their black parishioners but also by imposing religious definitions on many aspects of the master-slave relationship. Not only were new-born slaves baptized in formal church services that emphasized their "humanity," church weddings were held for slave couples, and even manumission (freeing of a slave) was made a religious ceremony held in church.[20]

In contrast, the British and the Dutch did not baptize slaves—several colonies imposed heavy fines for anyone who did so. There were no limits at all on slave owners until Barbados adopted a code in 1661 which later was adopted in other British colonies.[21] This code gave masters the right to "apply unlimited force to compel labor," without penalty even if it resulted in death.[22] Slaves were not permitted to marry, and owners were prohibited from freeing any slave. That was later changed to place such a heavy tax on manumission as to prohibit it—the avowed purpose was to prevent any increase in "free Negros" as they were a "great inconvenience."[23] Thus, for many years it was accepted by historians that slaves were far better off in Spanish colonies. As Sir Harry Johnson put it: "Slavery under the flag . . . of Spain was not a condition without hope, a life of hell, as it was for the most part in the British West Indies."[24]

But, during the 1960s, revisionists arose who were determined to impose the view that slaves were not one bit better off under Spanish rule (and maybe worse). Why? Marxists such as Marvin Harris denounced the notion that any aspect of "culture" such as legal codes or ideals could influence anything! Only material factors *could* matter, and these were the same everywhere![25] Unfortunately, non-Marxist historians were as determined to deny that Catholic slave codes could have mattered, if on different, but as specious, grounds. Here the most influential voice was that of David Brion Davis, who won the Pulitzer Prize for his 1996 book. Davis condemned as "idealized models" all claims that conditions of servitude were milder in Catholic areas, equating those who support such a view with "Southern apologists" for slavery. He argued, instead, that "Negro bondage was a single phenomenon, or *Gestalt*, whose variations were less significant than underlying patterns of unity."[26] This pronouncement was followed by many claims that more humane slave codes were of no consequence, owing to dishonest magistrates and sadistic, greedy masters. Finally, Davis concluded that for "lack of detailed statistical information," and because the subject is "too complex" it is "impossible to assume that the treatment of slaves was substantially better in Latin America than in the British colonies, taken as a whole."[27]

I am inclined to attribute Davis's pettifogging to his sensitivity to "political correctness." His colleagues were swift to level the charge of "being soft on slavery" if one admitted that any slave system could have been less brutal than another, charges that subsequently were heaped on the very fine scholars Robert Fogel and Stanley Engerman when they published their superb *Time on the Cross* in 1974. The politically correct, hence safe, position was to assert that slavery was equally inhumane in all its manifestations.

But that isn't true. Nor was Davis correct when he noted the lack of pertinent statistics—they were lying there in plain sight all along but ignored until I published them in *For the Glory of God: How Monotheism Led to Reformations, Science, Witch-Hunts and the End of Slavery* (2003). All that was required was to know something about American history and to be familiar with early American census publications. Census data on free blacks, available in most college and university libraries for nearly two centuries, offer an opportunity for a "natural experiment" to assess the effectiveness of Catholic slave codes. What's involved is to compare "Catholic" Louisiana with the rest of the "Protestant" Deep South.

Louisiana came under the *Code Noir* in 1724 as the French consolidated their administration. When control of Louisiana shifted to Spain in 1769, the circumstances of slaves were greatly improved owing to the more liberal provisions of the *Código Negro Español*, concerning the right of slaves to own property and to purchase their freedom. France regained control of Louisiana in 1802 and sold it to the United States the next year, but by then Catholic norms concerning slavery and the treatment of free blacks were deeply rooted in the local culture. This is evident in the fact that the US Census of 1830 reported that a far higher percentage of blacks in Louisiana were free (13.2 percent) than in any other slave state. The contrast was especially sharp in comparison with neighboring states having similar plantation economies: Alabama (1.3 percent), Mississippi (0.8 percent), and Georgia (1.1 percent).

The contrast between New Orleans and other major cities of the Deep South is even more revealing, as shown in Table 8.1. In New Orleans, 41.7 of the blacks were free in 1830. In Charleston, South Carolina, 6.4 percent were free, and all the other Deep South cities had even fewer free blacks.

Can such immense differences stem from anything other than the effects of the Catholic codes and attitudes toward slavery? I am not a historian of slavery. Why was it left to me to bring these statistics to light? They have been easily available since about 1833. In any event, the recent revisionists are wrong. Culture matters, and slave codes made a

TABLE 8-1. Free Blacks in Deep South Cities, 1830		
	% BLACKS FREE	BLACK POPULATION
New Orleans, LA	41.7	28,545
Charleston, SC	6.4	56,116
Columbia, SC	5.2	9,534
Savannah, GA	4.3	9,901
Augusta, GA	3.6	6,481
Montgomery, AL	1.0	6,515
Selma, AL	0.9	7,723
Natchez, MS	1.2	11,077
Vicksburg, MS	0.5	4,505

Source: US Census, 1830. Note: Atlanta did not yet exist.

substantial difference. Granted that, in the end, Protestants played a very major role in ending slavery. But for many generations, the Catholic Church stood alone in its efforts to mitigate the horrors of slavery. So much for claims that the Church taught that slavery was morally legitimate.

The Jesuit/Indian Civilization

We come now to one of the most extraordinary omissions from the history of the New World. As you read about it you will wonder, as

I do, how this extensive episode possibly could be blanked out of all the standard histories, even though well-documented accounts have been published.[28] What is involved is a huge Indian civilization—complete with its own symphony orchestras—created under the guidance of the Jesuits and then utterly stamped out by Spanish and Portuguese armies.

Welcome to the Jesuit Republic of Paraguay, founded in 1609. It covered an area twice the size of France and was located south of Brazil and west of the territory ceded to Portugal by the Treat of Tordesillas (1494). Here, a tiny group of Spanish Jesuits (probably never numbering more than two hundred) founded, protected, educated, and advised a remarkable civilization encompassing at least thirty "Reductions,"[29] or communities, of Guarani Indians. Not only did the arts and industry flourish in the Jesuit Republic—cities had paved streets and impressive buildings—but a valid attempt was made at representative government. The Jesuits' purpose in founding this republic, as explained by the Jesuit superior Antonio Ruiz de Montoya in 1609, was to Christianize and "civilize" the Indians so they could be free subjects of the Crown, equal to the Spaniards, and thus to "bring about peace between the Spaniards and the Indians, a task so difficult that, since the discovery of the West Indies more than a hundred years ago, it still has not been possible."[30]

The Republic flourished, but rather than becoming the basis for equality and peace, its existence offended many colonial officials and planters and provided a tempting plum for expropriation. Nevertheless, the Jesuits managed to forestall and outmaneuver their opponents for well over a century. But then things began to go sour. The first step in the downfall of the Republic came in 1750 when the Portuguese and the Spanish signed a new treaty, redividing South America along natural boundaries. As a result, seven of the Reductions fell within Portuguese jurisdiction. Ordered to turn these settlements over to the civil authorities, the Jesuits resisted and appealed to the Portuguese and Spanish Crowns to have the Reductions spared. But the opposition was too strong and too unscrupulous, planting rumors and false evidence of Jesuit conspiracies against both Crowns. So in 1754, the Spanish sent troops against the seven Reductions from the west, while the Portuguese advanced from the east. But both forces of European troops were defeated by the Indians, who were quite well trained in Western military tactics and possessed muskets and cannons. Although the Jesuits had not participated in the battles, they were blamed as traitors and in response were banned from Portuguese and Spanish territories in 1758. Soon additional plots against the Jesuits succeeded in Spain, as

---

Box 8.1. Some leading historians whose work informed this chapter. Specific studies by each can be found in the bibliography.

EUGENE GENOVESE (1930–2012) was the twentieth century's most respected and influential historian of American slavery. Born in Brooklyn, he received his PhD from Columbia University and taught at a number of American schools, including Rutgers University and the University of Rochester, before becoming an independent scholar. He was still a committed Marxist when he wrote his great work: *Roll, Jordan, Roll: The World the Slaves Made* (1974), but the scrupulous regard for evidence displayed in this work not only earned it the Bancroft Prize (the top award for a historical study), but it presaged his break with the Left.

SIR HENRY (HARRY) HAMILTON JOHNSON (1858–1927) was a British explorer, botanist, historian, and colonial administrator. After graduating from King's College London, he studied painting at the Royal Academy, but later abandoned art to go exploring in Africa, meeting Henry Morton Stanley in the Congo and then, in 1884, leading an expedition to Mount Kilimanjaro. In 1886, he became vice-consul in Cameroon, and in 1889, he was shifted to Mozambique. Later he helped to establish North Eastern

all members of the order in Spain were arrested in 1767 and deported to the Papal States. In July of that year, colonial authorities were ready to move against the Jesuits in Latin America, and the roundup began in Buenos Aires and Cordoba. But it wasn't until the next year that Spanish troops moved against the final twenty-three Reductions and seized the remaining Jesuits, whereupon even very sick and elderly fathers were tied to mules and transported over the mountains in bad weather, many to their deaths. Thus, the Jesuits were expelled from the Western Hemisphere. Soon their Republic lay in ruins, defeated and looted by

Rhodesia. Through this entire time Johnson published books, many of them focused on slavery, both in Africa and the New World.

HERBERT S. KLEIN is a research fellow and Latin American curator at the Hoover Institution at Stanford University. Before that he served as professor of history at Columbia University. He earned his PhD at the University of Chicago. He has specialized in comparative studies of slavery, writing twenty books and more than 160 articles. I was most influenced by his *African Slavery in Latin America and the Caribbean* (1986).

FRANK TANNENBAUM (1893–1969) climaxed his rather tumultuous life by becoming professor of Latin American history at Columbia University until his retirement in 1965. In 1914, Tannenbaum was one of the leaders of a demonstration of Industrial Workers of the World members in New York City, which led to his arrest for inciting a riot and a year in jail. Upon his release, he continued his radical activities for several more years. But then he enrolled in Columbia University and after graduation continued his studies and earned his PhD at Brookings Institution. After a hitch in the US army, Tannenbaum spent several years in Mexico, and in 1935 joined the faculty at Columbia. In 1947, he published his very influential *Slave and Citizen*.

civil authorities. Disheartened by their mistreatment and the loss of the Black Robed Fathers, the surviving Guarani drifted away.

It is depressing, but no surprise, that among the very few historians who bother to mention the Jesuit Republic, too many attack it as naked Catholic colonialism, condemn the "fanatical" Jesuits for imposing religion and civilization on the "gentle" Indians, and denounce Jesuit efforts to sustain a republic as cruel paternalism and "ruthless exploitation."[31]

But even if one were to accept the most extreme version of these claims, one is still faced with sincere and effective efforts by the Jesuits to protect the Indians against planters and colonial authorities who wished to reduce them to servitude or to eradicate them entirely. To have constructed an advanced Indian civilization in this historical context was an extraordinary feat. Moreover, the antagonistic historians at least have reported this remarkable event, while most other historians have utterly ignored it. In the section on "Paraguay, History of," the *Encyclopaedia Britannica* (15th ed.) offers this sentence: "During most of the colonial era, Paraguay was known chiefly for a huge Jesuit mission group of 30 *reducciones*." We are not even told what "reduccionies" are, and nothing more is said anywhere else in the many volumes. As for the major works on New World slavery, all of which have bitter (and often anti-Catholic) things to say about the enslavement and abuse of the Indians in Latin America, not a word!

Conclusion

In contrast, considerable attention has been paid by historians to the fact that not all of the Catholic clergy, including not all Jesuits, accepted the claim that slavery was sinful. Indeed, sometimes in the midst of slave societies, Catholic clergy themselves kept slaves (as did many Protestant clergy)—during the eighteenth and early nineteenth centuries. For example, Jesuits in Maryland were slave owners. Other clergy were confused about the issue. For example, the Dominican Bartolomé de las Casas (1474–1566) waged a bitter and quite unsuccessful campaign against enslaving Indians, during which he proposed that slaves be brought from Africa instead. Later he came to so deeply regret this proposal that he expressed doubt whether God would pardon him for this terrible sin.[32] Nevertheless, claims that the Church failed to oppose slavery and that slave codes merely served the masters simply aren't true.

The myth of Holy Authoritarianism: During the Spanish Civil War, it was charged that because the Church opposed democracy that it supported the right-wing dictator Francisco Franco, seen here with a group of Catholic prelates. In fact, the Church was given no choice in Spain because the Soviet-backed leftists had begun the civil war by murdering thousands of priests, monks, and nuns.

Holy Authoritarianism 9

IT IS COMMON knowledge that the Catholic Church favors tyrannical governments, the Divine Right of Kings having long been an official doctrine. Indeed, the current *Wikipedia* article on "Relations between the Catholic Church and the state" flatly asserts that "belief in the God-given authority of monarchs was central to the Roman Catholic vision of governance in the Middle Ages."[1] Subsequently, the Church has been the implacable enemy of all forms of liberal politics, which provoked the many dire warnings about the "Catholic threat" to democracy issued by leading American intellectuals during the 1940s and 1950s.

- ▶ Reinhold Niebuhr—then considered the leading Protestant spokesman—denounced the gap "between the presuppositions of a free society and the inflexible authoritarianism of the Catholic religion."[2]

- ▶ John Dewey, the most prominent educator of the day, warned that the Church was a threat to democracy, being a "reactionary world organization."[3]

- ▶ Sidney Hook, one of the nation's leading philosophers, charged that Catholicism is "the oldest and greatest totalitarian movement in history."[4]

- ▶ And Talcott Parsons, Harvard's very influential sociologist, expressed his concern about an "authoritarian element in the basic structure of the Catholic church itself which may weaken individual self-reliance and valuation of freedom."[5]

Today, critics of the Church are a bit more circumspect, but the belief that the Church favors tyrants lingers, fueled by its "history" of opposition to left-wing parties and revolutionary regimes.

All of these charges are either greatly exaggerated or simply false. The *Wikipedia* article on the "Divine right of kings" correctly reports that this doctrine originated with Protestants during the seventeenth century! And there is abundant evidence that from early days the church fathers took a rather dim view of the state and its rulers. This certainly is not to claim that the Church was an early advocate of democracy, although it did support republican forms of government when they arose in many medieval Italian city-states. Mostly the Church dealt with the forms of government with which it was confronted, although it often acted to moderate and limit repression and exploitation by rulers. In general, however, relations between the Church and state have been dominated by conflict—the state often seeking to control the Church, and the Church always asserting its independence.

But, the primary basis for accusing the Church of favoring authoritarian government is the constant, spurious claim by leftists that the Church always opposes "liberation," as demonstrated by its reactions to the French and Russian Revolutions, and to the Spanish Civil War. In truth, it was astonishing how far the Church went to accommodate the French Revolution—even accepting elimination of the tithe and the seizure of all church property. Nevertheless, acting on their devotion to the atheism of the "Enlightenment," the radicals who took control of the French Revolution went on to declare the Church an enemy and attempted to eliminate it entirely. Is it credible to suggest that this left the Church a choice as to whether to continue to support the Revolution? In similar fashion, subsequent leftist regimes have denounced religion and attempted to wipe it out—as in such instances as the Russian Revolution and the Spanish Civil War. It seems absurd to suggest that opposition to these brutal attacks shows that the Church favors tyrants; one could as well claim it shows the Church as the enemy of tyrants.

Before pursuing these matters, it will be useful to more clearly distinguish the basic division of labor and outlook in the "Church."

Two Churches

Christianity began as an obscure Jewish sect that rapidly spread across the Roman world until by early in the fourth century a large number of Romans had been converted (especially in the city of Rome)[6] whereupon they were joined by the Emperor Constantine. That changed everything. What had once been a persecuted faith of outsiders, now became the object of imperial favor and largess.

Ironically, the immense favoritism that the Emperor Constantine showed towards Christianity did it substantial harm. When he elevated the clergy to high levels of wealth, power and status so that bishops "became grandees on a par with the wealthiest senators,"[7] not surprisingly "there was a stampede into the priesthood."[8] Soon Christian offices, and especially the higher positions, were dominated by the sons of the aristocracy—some of them gaining bishoprics even before being baptized. Subsequently, gaining a church position was mainly a matter of influence, commerce, and eventually of heredity. Simony became the rule—an extensive and expensive traffic in religious offices, not only involving the sale of high offices such as bishoprics but even of lowly parish placements. There quickly arose great clerical families whose sons followed their fathers, uncles, and grandfathers into holy offices. Even the papacy soon ran in families. Pope Innocent (401–17) was the son of his predecessor Pope Anastasias (399–401). Pope Silverius (536–37) was the son of Pope Hermisdas (514–23). Many other popes were the sons, grandsons, nephews, and brothers of bishops and cardinals. Worse yet, competing for high church offices eventually became so corrupt and intense that during the period 872 though 1012, a third of all popes died violent deaths, many of them having been murdered as a result of the constant intrigues among the Roman ecclesiastical families,[9] and at least one was killed by an irate husband.[10]

Of course, many who entered the religious life were neither careerists nor libertines; even some sons of the clerical families were deeply sincere. For, at the same time that there had begun a "stampede" into the priesthood by the sons of privilege, there was a rapid expansion of monasticism, which, perhaps surprisingly, also was dominated by the privileged—75 percent of ascetic medieval saints were sons and daughters of the nobility, including many sons and daughters of kings.[11] By the middle of the fourth century, there were thousands of monks and nuns, nearly all of them living in organized communities. As time passed, the number of monks and nuns continued to soar. Consequently, there arose what, in effect, became two parallel churches. These can usefully be identified as the *Church of Power* and the *Church of Piety*.

The Church of Power was the main body of the Church as it evolved in response to the immense status and wealth bestowed on the clergy by Constantine. It included the great majority of priests, bishops, cardinals, and popes who ruled the Church most of the time until the Counter-Reformation began during the sixteenth century. Most clergy of the Church of Power were sensible and temperate men, but they tended to be worldly in both senses of that term—practical and morally lax.

In contrast, the Church of Piety pressed for virtue over worldliness and constantly attempted to reform the Church of Power. Starting in 1046 came an interlude lasting for over a century, during which the Church of Piety had control of the papacy. Indeed, in 1073 a monk became pope (Gregory VII), and the next three popes also were monks, including Urban II, who launched the First Crusade. Even after the Church of Power recaptured the papacy, it was unable to silence the Church of Piety because it retained an unyielding base in monasticism, which, in turn, had very strong family ties to the ruling elites.

In practice, there was a division of labor between the two churches. The task of conversion, especially of pagan territories, was left to the Church of Piety, and so was the task of evangelism. It was monks who travelled from village to village, preaching in each. Education at all levels also was the province of the Church of Piety—including all the tutors of the nobility as well as their confessors. The Church of Piety founded and staffed all of the universities, and therefore, all the great theologians and scholars belonged to the Church of Piety—even those who rose to be bishops and cardinals (see chapter 7). On the other hand, most local parishes were staffed by the Church of Power as was the task of administering Christendom. Perhaps surprisingly, the two churches often were in accord when it came to dealing with the state—they claimed the right to sit in judgment on it.

On Worldly Rulers

Bernard Lewis, the distinguished Princeton authority on Islam, noted that the idea of the separation of church and state "is, in a profound sense, Christian."[12] In most other civilizations religion and state are one. Of course, it all began when Jesus stipulated: "Render therefore unto Caesar the things that are Caesar's; and unto God the things that are God's" (Matthew 22:20). In this spirit, the Church was generally content to leave political power to secular rulers while taking a rather skeptical view of their moral legitimacy. Indeed, although Saint Paul had argued that Christians must obey secular rulers, no matter how evil, unless they were ordered to violate a commandment, once the threat of persecution no longer hung over them, Christian theologians became increasingly critical of the moral authority of the state. In *The City of God*, Saint Augustine revealed that while the state was essential for an orderly society, it still was lacking in fundamental legitimacy:

> What are kingdoms but great robberies? For what are robberies themselves, but little kingdoms? The band itself is made up of men; it is ruled by the authority of a prince, it is knit tougher by the pact of the confederacy; the booty is divided by the law agreed on. If, by the admittance of abandoned men, this evil

increases to such a degree that it holds places, fixes abodes, takes possession of cities, and subdues people, it assumes more plainly the name of a kingdom, because reality is now manifestly conferred on it, not by removal of covetousness, but by the addition of impunity. Indeed, that was the apt and true reply which was given to Alexander the Great by a pirate who had been seized. For when the king has asked the man what he meant by keeping hostile possession of the sea, he answered with bold pride, "What thou meanest by seizing the whole earth; but because I do it in a petty ship, I am called a robber, whilst thou who dost it with a great fleet art styled emperor."[13]

This "shocking realism"[14] has often surprised and upset Augustine's readers. But given the immense authority of the writer, this view shaped Christian political sensibilities ever since. Christian writers have always felt free to make suggestions for improving the state, for making it more equitable, and even for dispensing with monarchies altogether. An extremely important step in that direction involved the vigorous condemnation of the notion of the "divine right of kings"—although such claims were sometimes asserted by kings (mainly Protestant monarchs), they were invariably rejected by the Church. Moreover, by insisting on the secularity of kingship, the Church made it possible to examine the basis of worldly power and the interplay of rights and rule. Late in the fourteenth century, John Wycliffe pointed out that if kings were chosen by God and rule with divine rights, then God must assist and approve the sins of tyrants—"a blasphemous conclusion."[15] Hence, it was not a sin to oppose tyrants.

This had already been admitted a century earlier by Thomas Aquinas, if a bit grudgingly. After having warned of the many perils of acting to remove a tyrant, including the fact that all too often an even worse tyranny results, Aquinas wrote in *On Kingship*: "If to provide itself with a king belongs to the right of a given multitude, it is not unjust that the king be deposed or have his power restricted by that same multitude if, becoming a tyrant, he abuses his royal power." However, Aquinas counseled that "a scheme should be carefully worked out which would prevent the multitude ruled by a king from falling into the hands of a tyrant."[16] And, in fact, that's what took place in many European domains, with the full support of the Church.

In England in 1215, a coalition of nobles and Church officials, including all of the bishops as well as the master of the Knights Templar, imposed the *Magna Carta* on King John, severely limiting royal powers. At that same time, a number of Italian city-states evolved republican forms of government, here too with the active participation of the Church hierarchy.[17]

Of course, most of Europe remained traditional kingdoms. And here the role of the Church to mitigate royal abuse and tyranny took the form of sanctions imposed on rulers, either by their confessors or by official church actions.

Some sense of the influence of confessors on the nobility was revealed in chapter 5 in the discussion of pilgrimages to the Holy Land. Many nobles journeyed to Jerusalem, some of them barefoot all the way, because their confessors required them to do so in order to gain absolution. Many of the sins involved were merely personal, such as murder of a wife or rival, but some of them involved abuse of their power. Of course, confessors usually were able to mitigate tyrannical impulses with far less severe penances than a pilgrimage to the Holy Land. Indeed, most often they served as a conscience whispering in the ear of rulers as to their responsibilities.

Much more dramatic were the actions by church officials, especially the pope, to limit royal power and misbehavior. Indeed, medieval popes claimed the right to depose kings. Sometimes their efforts to do so succeeded, and sometimes not, but the threat was real and most kings were leery of provoking the pope. The point being that the Church never was under royal control and did not assume a commonality of interests. Indeed, the Church was entirely comfortable with the Italian city-state republics. Unfortunately, the radicals who arose during the so-called Enlightenment and their revolutionary heirs failed to grasp this point—or dismissed it because of their intentions to destroy all forms of religion.

"Enlightenment" Philosophes and Leftist Anti-Religion

Voltaire (1694–1778) did not oppose the Catholic Church because it sided with tyrants—after all, he was a close friend of Frederick the Great. Voltaire opposed the Church because he loathed religion. Indeed, he and Frederick agreed that religion would disappear by about 1810.[18] However, many of the other *philosophes* of this era did regard church and state as one and hated them both. As Voltaire's associate Denis Diderot (1713–84) proclaimed, "Man will never be free until the last king is strangled with the entrails of the last priest." This was the perspective that eventually shaped the French Revolution and all subsequent leftist policies. But, even Voltaire's less extreme outlook shaped the bloody programs inaugurated by French revolutionaries when they attempted to fully "dechristianize" France.

Voltaire held that orthodox religion was the source of much evil "being the mother of fanaticism and civil discord; it is the enemy of mankind."[19] To be rid of fanaticism, Voltaire "proposed the suppression of ecclesiastical hierarchy . . . the abolition of clerical celibacy . . . and the closing of all monasteries."[20] To gauge how much Voltaire influenced the actual leaders of the French Revolution, it must be noted that Anacharsis Cloots, who was a foremost dechristianizer, led the campaign to have Voltaire "pantheonized"[21]—the revolutionary equivalent of being canonized. Thus, in 1791, with elaborate ceremony, a bust of Voltaire was placed in a former Parisian church that had been converted into the Panthéon.

Another famous philosophe, Jean-Jacques Rousseau (1712–78), had considerable impact on the French revolutionaries, especially on the infamous Maximilien Robespierre, who frequently eulogized him and was inspired by him to initiate the Cult of Reason to replace Christianity. And in 1794, Rousseau's remains were moved to the Panthéon in Paris.

But perhaps the greatest legacy of the Enlightenment figures to the French dechristianizers was the angry atheists: Jean Meslier, Claude Helvétius, and Denis Diderot. I noted the latter's position above. Helvétius too denounced religion as a sinister evil. As for Meslier, ironically he was a Catholic priest who wrote a last testament that was read only after his death. In it he revealed his angry atheism, denouncing Jesus as a "vile and wretched good-for-nothing, low-born, ignorant, untalented and awkward."[22] He also attacked Catholic priests as charlatans who duped the people out of their money. In 1793, the regime of the French Revolution erected a statue to Meslier.

Of particular significance is that the philosophes were not persecuted by the Catholic Church (although Rousseau was threatened by Protestants in Geneva). Their writings were widely available in inexpensive editions without any Church interference. And all of them died natural deaths. The critical point being that they were not reacting to attacks by Churchmen; rather, it was they who picked the fight and defined religion as the enemy.

French Revolutionaries and the Church (1789–99)

It is important to know that the Church—especially the higher clergy—supported very substantial pre-Revolutionary reforms. Then, after the fall of the Bastille in July 1789, the Church representatives in the National Assembly agreed to relinquish their principal source of revenue—the tithe. This consisted of a tax of 10 percent of income per year to be paid to the Church by everyone, from the nobility to the peasants. The elimination of the tithe was greeted by strong protests from local clergy who asked how they were supposed to finance their parishes without tithes—all schools as well as most hospitals and charities were provided by the Church. But the higher clergy did not relent.[23] Nor did they gain anything for the Church by their agreement.

On November 2, 1789, all the property of the Church was taken over by the Assembly, and the next month there began a massive sale of Church lands. Next, on February 13, 1790, the Assembly forced all the monasteries and convents to close and required the religious orders to dissolve. All monks and nuns were released from their vows by state edict and directed to disperse. Still, the Church members of the Assembly continued to participate.

Then, on July 12, 1790, ostensibly to deal with the fact that the local parishes were unfunded due to the loss of the tithe, the Assembly passed the Civil Constitution of the Clergy which made all clergy employees of the state and directed that they would devote themselves primarily to recording births, death, and marriages. The new law also required all clergy to swear an oath to support this constitution and affirm that they had no allegiance to the pope. Those who swore to the oath were known as juring priests, and they made up about 24 percent of the clergy.[24] This "secularization" of the clergy finally drove the Church into opposition. The pope pronounced excommunication on all juring priests who failed to recant their oaths to support the constitution within sixty days as well as all Catholics who continued to be faithful to those priests. The Assembly responded by criminalizing all clergy who failed to take the oath (known as nonjuring clergy), making them liable to ten years in prison.

Soon, matters grew much worse. The National Assembly was disbanded in September 1791 and replaced by the Legislative Assembly, in which the Church had no part, soon to be replaced by the Committee of Public Safety, a collection of bitterly antireligious tyrants who had aims far beyond controlling the Church and confiscating its wealth. They would settle for nothing less than putting an end to religion! And their efforts were brutal, extensive, tyrannical, and, eventually, absurd.

In September 1792, in what came to be called the September Massacres, an angry mob stirred up by revolutionary leaders drowned three bishops and more than two hundred priests in Paris. Many priests and nuns were executed in Lyons, and hundreds of priests were imprisoned in Rochefort.

Also in 1792, partly to gain public funds and partly to impede administration of the sacraments, the Committee "confiscated large quantities of metal plate, chalices, ciboria and candlesticks"[25] from the churches.

In January 1793, King Louis XVI was beheaded, soon to be followed to the guillotine by 16,594 victims in Paris and another 25,000 elsewhere in France. In addition to Queen Marie Antoinette and as many nobles as the revolutionaries could find, the dead included some bishops and nearly a thousand priests.[26]

On October 21, 1793, a law was passed making all nonjuring priests and all persons caught harboring them liable to death on sight.

In November 1793, a French Republican Calendar was introduced, with the aim of dechristianizing France. It abolished Sunday, and each month was made up of three ten-day weeks so as to make it difficult for the people to know when the old Sunday occurred. The tenth day was designated as a day of rest (unsuccessfully, as most people continued to rest on Sunday).[27] All saints' days were prohibited. The calendar also did away with the year of our Lord, setting 1789 as year 1. In addition, all street and place names with any religious references were to be changed—the town of St. Tropez was renamed Héraclée.[28] The Catholic practice of giving children saints' names also was opposed, and the use of revolutionary names such as "Fraternity" was urged. Very few parents did so, however.[29]

On September 29, 1795, an edict prohibited all public manifestations of religion. Priests could not wear clerical clothing in public nor could monks and nuns continue to appear in their robes and habits. All outdoor religious processions and worship were outlawed. (When Father Pierre-René Rogues was seen carrying the Eucharist through the streets of Vannes in Brittany on Christmas Eve, he was arrested and executed.)[30]

Church bells could not be rung. No religious statues or crosses could be visible to the general public; hence huge bonfires were set with piles of wooden crosses in many towns and cities.[31] The prohibition was extended to cemeteries and prompted an orgy of smashing tombstones that bore crosses or religious inscriptions. Church buildings, now belonging to the state, were usually kept locked, leaving most villages without a place of worship. No buildings could be purchased for religious purposes.

On October 25, 1795, a law was proclaimed reaffirming the death penalty for nonjuring priests and gave all priests who had clandestinely reentered France fifteen days to leave or be executed.

In addition, leading revolutionaries initiated new cults to replace religion. The most prominent of these was the Cult of Reason, which met in confiscated churches to worship statues of the Goddess Reason—in Paris the cult took over the Cathedral of Notre Dame in 1793. The Christian altar was replaced with one devoted to liberty, and the inscription "To Philosophy" was engraved in stone above the cathedral's doors.[32] During "services," girls clad in white robes pranced around a woman dressed up as the Goddess of Reason, wearing a provocative gown. Many claimed that scandalous things took place during cult celebrations.

In the spring of 1794, Robespierre denounced the Cult of Reason and sent its leaders—including his former revolutionary colleagues Hébert Momoro and Anacharsis Cloots—to the guillotine, replacing the Cult of Reason with his own Cult of the Supreme Being, which was formally inaugurated on May 7, 1794. This new cult was an effort by Robespierre to draw back from the complete atheism of the Revolution in favor of a weak deism. Then, of course, Robespierre himself went to the guillotine on July 28, 1794, and his cult died with him.[33]

However, eleven days prior to his death, Robespierre sent sixteen Carmelite nuns from Compiègne to the guillotine. In 1790, when the Assembly dissolved all the religious orders, the nuns had refused to leave their convent. But their building was confiscated and they were turned out into the street. Obeying the new law, the nuns adopted lay clothing, but they took lodgings together and continued their life of prayer. This was deemed criminal, and eventually they were arrested, taken to Paris, and condemned. The nuns wore their religious garb when taken to the guillotine, but after death they were stripped and thrown naked into a common grave. Subsequently, they were beatified by Pope Pius X in May 1906.[34]

Finally, Napoleon rose to power. The Revolution was over and with it efforts to dechristianize France or wipe out religion altogether. In 1801, Napoleon signed a concordat with Pope Pius VII that restored the Church's legal status, but not its property. Although the churches were returned, the tithe was not reinstated. The French state continued to pay salaries to the clergy, but allowed them to worship in public and to accept the pope's authority.

In light of these facts, it seems to me absurd to claim that the Church opposed the French Revolution, having stood still for the loss of the tithe and for the confiscation of its property. I think it far more accurate to claim that the revolutionaries bore full responsibility for initiating the conflict with the Church—and quite needlessly in terms of their initial aims.

Unfortunately, in the aftermath of the French Revolution, it has become an article of leftist faith that the Church is a bulwark in defense of tyranny. As Friedrich Engels proclaimed in 1844: "We want to sweep away everything that claims to be supernatural and superhuman. . . . For that reason, we have once and for all declared war on religion and religious ideas and care little about whether we are called atheists or anything else."[35] Then, despite the fact that the Church and religion played little or no role in the failure of the attempted revolutions in many European nations, in 1848, the left's angry focus on religion was undiminished. Representative of the prevailing leftist view was the official statement on socialism and religion, issued by the Executive Committee of the Socialist Party of Great Britain in January 1911: "Socialism is the natural enemy of religion. . . . The entry of Socialism is, consequently, the exodus of religion. No man can be consistently both a socialist and a Christian. . . . Socialism, both as a philosophy and as a form of society, is the antithesis of religion."[36]

In Pursuit of a Godless Russia

After Lenin and the Bolsheviks seized power in Russia in 1917, the horrors they inflicted on the clergy and dedicated laity made the French Revolution seem like a picnic. Here, too, there was no initial opposition to the Revolution by either the Russian Orthodox or by the Roman Catholic clergy (the latter being relatively small in number). Rather, Lenin condemned religion as "unutterable vileness," and from the earliest days, the Communist regime tried to destroy the churches. Even so, who could have predicted that the primary method of destruction would be sadistic murders?

By the early 1920s, even the Western press was aware that many bishops and priests had been executed, some of them tortured. At that time, the well-accepted statistics were that during their first five years in power, the Bolsheviks had executed twenty-eight Orthodox bishops and more than twelve hundred priests. This figure did not include the widespread executions of monks and nuns that took place during the forced closure of 579 monasteries and convents—thousands must have been killed. And, of course, many thousands more clergy, monks, and nuns were imprisoned, sent to labor camps, or shut up in mental hospitals.[37] In 1922, a concentration camp for clergy was established in a former Orthodox monastery on an island in the White Sea. Eight metropolitans, twenty archbishops, and forty-seven Orthodox bishops died there, "executed by firing squad."[38]

It turns out that these shocking events and statistics give but the slightest glimmer of the immensity of the horror that occurred. Following the collapse of the Soviet Union, a Presidential Commission, chaired by Alexander Yakovlev, gained access to the relevant archives and discovered that about two hundred thousand clergy (including many rabbis), monks, and nuns had been executed by the Soviet regime.[39] In his shocking report, Yakovlev (who was known as the "Father of Glasnost" for his role in liberal reforms) noted:

> The official term *execution* was often a euphemism for murder, fiendishly refined. For example, Metropolitan Vladimir of Kiev was mutilated, castrated, and shot, and his corpse was left naked for the public to desecrate. Metropolitan Veniamin of St. Petersburg, in line to succeed the patriarch, was turned into a pillar of ice: he was doused with cold water in the freezing cold. Bishop Germogen of Tobolsk . . . was strapped alive to the paddlewheel of a steamboat and mangled by the rotating blades. Archbishop Andronnik of Perm . . . was buried alive. Archbishop Vasily was crucified and burned.

The documents bear witness to the most savage atrocities against priests, monks, and nuns: they were crucified on the central doors of iconostases, thrown into cauldrons of boiling tar, scalped, strangled with priestly stoles, given Communion with melted lead, and drowned in holes in the ice.[40]

Nor was the mass slaughter limited to clergy, monks, and nuns. Millions of devout laity were slaughtered too. Keep in mind that the killings and imprisonment were not clustered in the first few years of the Revolution. Even in the 1960s and 1970s, the killings continued and tens of thousands were shipped off to the immense chain of prison camps known as the Gulag. All told, the total number of Russians executed because of their religion is now placed in excess of twenty million.[41]

It remains an astonishing fact that these statistics have received almost no coverage in the Western press. Worse yet, even as late as the 1960s, many very influential figures in Western Europe and the United

States denied all reports of mistreatment of clergy in the Soviet Union, condemning all such claims as misinformation spread by reactionaries and fascists.[42]

The Spanish Civil War

Perhaps nothing fostered the belief that the Catholic Church embraces tyrants more than the Spanish Civil War (1936–39) did. In part, this was because it occurred during the 1930s when infatuation with Soviet Communism was at its peak in Western Europe and the United States. The party line was that the Spanish Republicans stood for liberty and freedom while General Francisco Franco was a murderous fascist. Of course, the participation of Germany and Italy in supporting Franco

---

Box 9.1. Some leading historians whose work informed this chapter. Specific studies by each can be found in the bibliography.

NIGEL ASTON is reader in early modern history at the University of Leicester in Great Britain. After graduating from Durham University, he received his PhD from Oxford. He has written extensively on the leftist conflict with religion, including *Christianity in Revolutionary Europe, 1750–1830* and *The French Revolution 1789–1802*.

JOSE M. SANCHEZ is emeritus professor of history at Saint Louis University. He earned his PhD at the University of New Mexico and specialized in the connections between religion and radicalism in modern Europe, as is evident in his most famous work, *The Spanish Civil War as a Religious Tragedy* (1987).

with supplies and air support seemed proof that the Civil War pitted fascism versus freedom. Never mind that the Soviet Union not only was supplying the leftists but also was actually in control of the Republican government and the anti-Franco forces; the myth was sustained that the "loyalists" truly represented the people. Hitler's primary motive in supporting Franco was to prevent the Soviets from gaining control of Spain. As for Franco being an ally of Hitler, during World War II he refused to support Germany by seizing Gibraltar and closing the Mediterranean to allied shipping, despite severe pressure from Hitler to do so and with the German army in control of neighboring France. Instead, Spain remained neutral, allowing American and British representatives to travel freely. No doubt Franco was a dictator and no doubt his forces executed thousands of Republicans. However, Franco did not initiate

FRANK TALLETT is head of the School of Humanities at the University of Reading in Great Britain. A fellow of the Royal Historical Society, he has specialized in warfare in medieval and early modern Europe and has given special attention to the religious aspects of the French Revolution.

ALEXANDER YAKOVLEV (1923–2005) was not a historian, but a Soviet politician who ended up producing the most revealing history of religion and revolution of the twentieth century. Wounded at the siege of Leningrad during World War II, in 1958 he was an exchange student for one year at Columbia University. He subsequently spent a decade as the Soviet ambassador to Canada. When Mikhail Gorbachev became head of the Soviet Union, Yakovlev became a trusted advisor. With the dissolution of the Soviet Union, Yakovlev gained access to the government archives and wrote a series of carefully documented reports, one of which revealed the mass murders committed by the regime, which was published in the West as *A Century of Violence in Soviet Russia*.

conflict with the Republic; he intervened in response to extreme provocations, including ongoing episodes of radical-led violence that the government refused to control. The Republicans gave the Church no choice but to support Franco, if only because he offered protection to the clergy, monks, and nuns from Republican death squads.

In the United States, the Spanish Civil War caused a bitter conflict, with many Catholics supporting Franco, while the liberal left—from the Roosevelt Democrats to the Communist Party USA—was fiercely on the side of the Republic. Indeed, the Communist Party recruited several thousand young Americans to go to Spain and fight in the Abraham Lincoln Brigade. The Protestant establishment also lined up against Franco, as did the academic establishment and the whole intellectual community, often citing Catholic support for Franco as solid evidence that the Church was on the side of repression and thereby was anti-American as well. But things were not that simple.

The Spanish conflict began in April 1931, when a coalition of left-wing parties overthrew the monarchy and proclaimed the Second Republic. Many clergy initially welcomed the rise of the Republic, only to be confronted with vicious anticlericalism. Manuel Azaña, new president of the Republic, proclaimed that legislation was urgently needed to prohibit clergy and nuns from teaching children as a matter "of public health."[43] On May 11, 1931, mobs spurred by leftist agitators began burning churches and *conventos* (residences for priests, monks, or nuns) in Madrid, and the anti-Church arson spread down the coast. The government refused to use force to stop the destruction—President Manuel Azaña declared that "all the conventos in Spain are not worth the life of a single Republican."[44] Eventually, the attacks petered out. During the next two years, the Republican government called for the dissolution of all Catholic religious orders, nationalized nearly all Church property, and prohibited the clergy from teaching in any schools. Then, all religious processions were banned.

On February 20, 1932, the very influential Republican weekly *La Traca* "depicted a guillotine in the middle of a group of frightened priests, nuns, and pious people, with the caption: This [the guillotine] working for two hours a day for a month, would free Spain of all the evil rubbish which wants to make the Republic a failure."[45]

In 1934, miners went on strike in northern Spain and soon proclaimed the start of the Revolution, prompting the widespread burning of churches and the murder of thirty-four priests. The Spanish army, acting without the support of the Republican government, put down the revolt using Moroccan troops.

In 1936, the struggle between the Republican radicals and the conservatives (who controlled the Spanish army) came to a crisis, touching off an anti-Catholic massacre. Scholars now agree that beginning slightly prior to Franco's intervention in Spain and lasting for several months, Republicans murdered 13 bishops, 4,172 diocesan priests and seminarians, 2,364 monks and friars, and 283 nuns—a total of 6,832.[46] And, as in Russia, the deaths often involved bizarre brutality. Some "were hanged, drowned, suffocated, burned to death, or buried alive. On many occasions, victims were tortured . . . which could include forcing the victims to strip naked, beating, cutting, skinning and mutilation. In the cases of mutilation, there was a morbid fixation on genitalia. . . . Finally, irrespective of the type of death they had suffered, the corpses of clerics were likely to be dragged through the streets, exposed in public places or desecrated in many ways."[47]

There are other accounts: "Nor was the anticlericalism limited to killing. Thousands of churches were burned, religious objects were profaned, nuns' tombs were opened and the petrified mummies displayed to ridicule, and religious ceremonies were burlesqued. Indeed, practically any imaginable anticlerical act was not only possible but likely."[48]

In January 1937, a minister of the Republican government prepared an official report for his colleagues about antireligious activities that had occurred in the previous six months. In the area controlled by the Republic: "All statues, altars, and objects of worship had been destroyed; all churches had been closed to worship; most churches in Catalonia had been burned; [government] organizations had taken metallic objects of worship (bells, crucifixes, etc.) and melted them down for military use; church buildings had been turned into garages, offices, factories, and shops; all conventos had been emptied; police had been searching private homes for religious objects and destroying them; clergy had been arrested, imprisoned, and killed by the thousands; and there were hundreds of clerics still in prison."[49]

Is it really discreditable that the pope condemned the Republic and that committed Catholics rebelled against it?

But that was the view that prevailed among non-Catholic Americans. Consider the case of the superb film *For Whom the Bell Tolls* (1943), starring Gary Cooper and Ingrid Bergman. The movie was based on Ernest Hemingway's great 1940 novel of the same title. To prepare to write it, Hemingway spent time in Spain. The plot involves an American who has gone to Spain to fight for the Republicans and who, being assigned to blow up a bridge as part of a new offensive, teams up with a rebel band. He manages to down the bridge but is wounded, and the movie ends as he sacrifices himself by hunkering down behind a machine gun to cover the escape of the others. The movie was a hit and was nominated for nine Academy Awards, including Best Picture, Best Actor, and Best Actress. But, on Oscar night, only Katina Paxinou (Best Supporting Actress) won. It was generally conceded that Hollywood voters resented the rather two-sided view of Spanish politics taken by the film. Even though the hero fought for the Republic, the Soviet influence was acknowledged and the hero expressed communist opinions. And, in a remarkable flashback scene, the movie showed the leader of the rebel band participating in the murder of a number of priests. It might be significant that when the movie was shortened for rerelease, that scene was cut out.

Conclusion

It simply isn't true that the Church opposes freedom and democracy. Rather, it tends to oppose tyrants, especially those who attempt to destroy the Church.

The myth of the Protestant Ethic. Here we see Martin Luther nailing his 95 Theses to the door of the Castle Church and thereby initiating the Reformation. It has too long been the false belief among social scientists that it was the Reformation that brought about the rise of capitalism in Europe and with it, the modern era.

Protestant Modernity 10

I WAS RAISED ON the glories of the Reformation. Like all Luther-ans, each Sunday I was further enlightened about Catholic wickedness and about how Martin Luther had set us free to think for ourselves and to seek knowledge, thereby bringing about the modern world. Although I had outgrown much of this by the time I entered graduate school, once there I was instructed in depth and detail in the gospel of Max Weber (1864–1920): that Protestantism gave birth to a unique work ethic that spawned capitalism, and thus it is that moder-nity is a direct result of the Reformation.

That Weber's entire thesis was nonsense should have been obvious to all competent scholars from the start (and it was to economic historians). Yet, even now it lives on among sociologists, being recounted in detail in every introductory textbook on the market. I shall deal once and for all with Weber shortly. But first, let me dispatch all variations of the notion linking the Reformation to religious freedom.

Reformation and Freedoms

The fundamental tie between the Reformation and religious freedom is said to reside in Luther's theological conclusion that each person is responsible for her or his own salvation, and therefore, everyone must be free to believe according to their own convictions and to worship as they wish. But, Luther believed nothing of the sort. People may need to accomplish their own salvation, but what they were to believe and how they were to worship were firmly fixed—the Reformation merely replaced monopoly Catholic churches with monopoly Protestant churches. Indeed, a common measure by which scholars decide when (and if) any particular German city turned Protestant is the date when it passed a law making it a criminal offense to celebrate Mass. As for the English Reformation, the Anglicans were soon burning Lutherans as well as hanging any Catholic priests they could find. In Calvin's Geneva too, Lutherans and Catholics were prohibited, and citizens were free only to be Calvinists. Soon thereafter, Catholics, as well as Protestants of all varieties, were busy burning witches—except in Spain and Italy, where the Inquisition prevented such madness (chapter 6). To the extent that there is religious freedom in Europe today (and it falls far short of the American standard), it was evolved by political leaders faced with a diversity of faiths.

Nevertheless, it continues to be the accepted wisdom that by stressing individual responsibility for salvation, the Reformation resulted in a great religious revival—that free from the Catholic compulsion and provided with worship services in their own language, people flocked to church. Nonsense!

Extraordinary reports on the lack of popular religious participation are available for Lutheran Germany based on the regular visitations by higher church officials to local communities, beginning in 1525. These have been extracted by the distinguished American historian Gerald Strauss who noted, "I have selected only such instances as could be multiplied a hundredfold."[1]

In Saxony (1574): "You'll find more of them out fishing than at service. . . . Those who do come walk out as soon as the pastor begins his sermon."[2] In Seegrehna (1577): "A pastor testified that he often quits his church without preaching . . . because not a soul has turned up to hear him."[3] In Barum (1572): "It is the greatest and most widespread complaint of all pastors hereabouts that people do not go to church on Sundays. . . . Nothing helps; they will not come . . . so that pastors face near-empty churches."[4] In Braunschweig-Grubenhagen (1580s): "Many churches are empty on Sundays."[5] In Weilburg (1604): "Absenteeism from church on Sundays was so widespread that the synod debated whether the city gates should be barred on Sunday mornings to lock everyone inside. Evidence from elsewhere suggests that this expedient would not have helped."[6]

Nevertheless, it is not clear that having a large turnout at Sunday services would have been desirable. That's because when people did come to church so many of them misbehaved! In Nassau (1594): "Those who come to service are usually drunk . . . and sleep through the whole sermon, except sometimes they fall off the benches, making a great clatter, or women drop their babies on the floor."[7] In Wiesbaden (1619): "[During church] there is such snoring that I could not believe my ears when I heard it. The moment these people sit down, they put their heads on their arms and straight away they go to sleep."[8] In addition, many brought their dogs inside the church, "Barking and snarling so loudly that no one can hear the preacher."[9] In Hamburg (1581): "[People make] indecent gestures at members of the congregation who wish to join in singing the hymns, even bringing dogs to church so that due to the loud barking the service is disturbed."[10] In Leipzig (1579–80): "They play cards while the pastor preaches, and often mock or mimic him cruelly to his face; . . . cursing and blaspheming, hooliganism, and fighting are common. . . . They enter church when the service is half over, go at once to sleep, and run out again before the blessing is given. . . . Nobody joins in singing the hymn; it made my heart ache to hear the pastor and the sexton singing all by themselves."[11]

As Martin Luther himself put it in 1529: "Dear God help us. . . . The common man, especially in the villages, knows absolutely nothing about Christian doctrine; and indeed many pastors are in effect unfit and incompetent to teach. Yet they all are called Christians, are baptized, and enjoy the holy sacraments—even though they cannot recite either the Lord's Prayer, the Creed or the Commandments. They live just like animals."[12]

Some revival. One must doubt that things could have been any worse in Catholic parishes.

Weber and Capitalism

In 1904–05, Max Weber—a celebrated German sociologist—published *Die Protestantische Ethik Und Der Geist Des Kapitalismus*. It was well received by Protestant German scholars. Weber's work became known in the United States when several young Americans earned their PhDs in Germany and then took positions in leading American universities, especially Talcott Parsons at Harvard. In 1930, Parsons published an English translation of Weber's book, *The Protestant Ethic and the Spirit of Capitalism*. However, this translation was published only in England and attracted rather few American readers. The visibility of Weber's work in America increased when one of Parsons's students, Robert K. Merton, applied Weber's arguments to the "scientific revolution" (chapter 7). Then, in 1958, an American publisher brought out a paperback version of the Parson translation. It has sold several hundred thousand copies, most of them to American college students.

Weber's first sentence posed the matter to be addressed: "A glance at occupational statistics for any country of mixed religious composition brings to light with remarkable frequency . . . the fact that business leaders and owners of capital, as well as the higher grades of skilled labour, and even more the higher technically and commercially trained personnel of modern enterprises, are overwhelmingly Protestant." How could this be explained?

According to Weber, Protestants dominated the capitalist economy of the West because of all the world's religions, only Protestantism provided a moral vision that led people to restrain their material consumption while vigorously seeking wealth. Weber argued that prior to the Reformation, restraint on consumption was invariably linked to asceticism and, hence, to condemnations of commerce. Conversely, the pursuit of wealth was linked to profligate consumption. Either cultural pattern was inimical to capitalism. Weber claimed that the Protestant ethic shattered these traditional linkages, creating a culture of frugal entrepreneurs content to systematically reinvest profits in order to pursue ever greater wealth, and therein lies the key to capitalism and the path to modernity.

Perhaps because it was such an elegant thesis, it was so widely accepted despite the fact that it was so obviously wrong. In fact, the first sentence of the book was dead wrong. As a great deal of subsequent research has demonstrated, Protestants were not more likely to hold the high-status capitalist positions than were Catholics. Catholic areas of western Europe did not lag in their industrial development. And even more obvious at the time Weber wrote was that fully developed capitalism had appeared in Europe many centuries *before* the Reformation!

As the British historian Hugh Trevor-Roper (1914–2003) explained, "The idea that large-scale industrial capitalism was ideologically impossible before the Reformation is exploded by the simple fact that it existed."[13] The celebrated Fernand Braudel (1902–85) complained that "all historians have opposed this tenuous theory [the Protestant Ethic], although they have not managed to be rid of it once and for all. Yet it is clearly false. The northern countries took over the place that earlier had been so long and brilliantly been occupied by the old capitalist centers of the Mediterranean. They invented nothing, either in technology or business management."[14] Moreover, during their critical period of economic development, these northern centers of capitalism were Catholic, not Protestant—the Reformation still lay well into the future.

In fact, capitalism was a very Catholic invention: it first appeared in the great Catholic monastic estates, way back in the ninth century.

On Capitalism

Several thousand books have been written about capitalism, but very few authors explain what they mean by that term. This is not because no definition is needed;[15] it is because capitalism is very difficult to define, having originated not as an economic concept but as a pejorative term first used by nineteenth-century leftists to condemn wealth and privilege. To adapt the term for serious analysis is a bit like trying to make a social scientific concept out of "reactionary pig."[16] Fully aware that it might be good strategy to let readers supply their own meaning of capitalism, it seems irresponsible to base any analysis on an undefined term. Therefore, *capitalism* is an economic system wherein privately owned, relatively well-organized and stable firms pursue complex commercial

---

Box 10.1. Some leading historians whose work informed this chapter. Specific studies by each can be found in the bibliography.

FERNAND BRAUDEL (1902–85) is second only to Marc Bloch as the most influential French historian of the past century. He spent the early part of his career teaching in the French equivalent of high schools, some of them in Algeria (then a French colony). But, he was determined to write history and gathered material on the Mediterranean world, especially during the days of Spanish domination. He served in the French army during World War II and was captured by the Germans and interned in Germany. There, without his books or his notes, relying only on his prodigious memory, he drafted his great work, *The Mediterranean and the Mediterranean World in the Age of Philip II*. When it was published in 1949, it ensured his lasting fame. In 1947, he and Lucien Febvre (also a major historian) managed to obtain funding from the Rockefeller Foundation to found a section on economic and social sciences at the École Pratique des Hautes Études—one of France's most distinguished research and higher education institutions. There, he and Febvre cofounded the Annales School of Historical Studies, which soon dominated the field.

RANDALL COLLINS is the Dorothy Swaine Professor of Sociology at the University of Pennsylvania. He spent much of his childhood in Europe,

activities within a relatively free (unregulated) market, taking a systematic, long-term approach to investing and reinvesting wealth (directly or indirectly) in productive activities involving a hired workforce, guided by anticipated and actual returns.[17]

The phrase *complex commercial activities* implies the use of credit, some degree of diversification, and little reliance on direct producer-to-consumer transactions. The term *systematic* implies adequate accounting practices. *Indirect* investment in productive activities extends the

where his father served as a member of the US diplomatic corps. He graduated from Harvard University and received his PhD from the University of California, Berkeley (where he and I were fellow students). This chapter benefitted from his work debunking the Protestant Ethic, but he is most admired for his huge (1,098 pages) *The Sociology of Philosophies.*

LESTER LITTLE is the Dwight W. Morrow Professor of History, emeritus, at Smith College. He is a former director of the American Academy in Rome and an expert on the medieval economy. It was Little who demonstrated that capitalism originated in the early religious communities, especially in his book *Religious Poverty and the Profit Economy in Medieval Europe* (1978).

GERALD STRAUSS (1922–2006) was distinguished professor of history at the University of Indiana. Born in Germany, his family moved to the United States to escape Nazi persecution in 1939. He served in the US army during World War II and after the war attended Boston University. He then earned his PhD from Columbia University and began his academic career as an assistant professor at the University of Alabama in 1957, moving to Indiana two years later. He specialized in the Lutheran Reformation and wrote a series of fine books on the subject—*Luther's House of Learning* (1978) served me well. Strauss also was a fine cellist and played in amateur string quartets.

definition to include bankers and passive stockholders. The definition excludes profit-seeking ventures assembled for short-term activities, such as an elite-backed voyage by privateers or a "one-shot" trade caravan. It also excludes commerce conducted directly by the state or under extensive state control (or exclusive license), such as foreign trade in ancient China or tax farming in medieval Europe. Undertakings based on coerced labor, such as Roman slave-based industries, are excluded too. Most of all, this definition excludes "simple" commercial transactions—the buying and selling that has gone on among merchants, traders, and the producers of commodities through the centuries and around the world.

Consistent with this definition, everyone writing on capitalism (whether or not they actually define the term) accepts that it rests upon free markets, secure property rights, and free (uncoerced) labor.[18] Free markets are needed in order for firms to enter areas of opportunity, which is precluded when markets are closed or highly regulated by the state. Only if property rights are secure will people invest in pursuit of greater gains, rather than hide, hoard, or consume their wealth. Uncoerced labor is needed so firms can attract *motivated* workers or dismiss them in response to market conditions. Coerced labor not only lacks motivation, but it may be difficult to obtain and hard to get rid of. It is the capacity to motivate work and the systematic reinvestment of profits that account for the immense productivity of capitalism.

The Rise of "Religious Capitalism"

The Bible often condemns greed and wealth—"For the love of money is the root of all evil" (1 Tim. 6:10)—but it does not directly condemn commerce or merchants. However, many of the very early church fathers shared the views prevalent in the Greco-Roman world that commerce is a degrading activity and, at best, involves great moral risk—that it is very difficult to avoid sin in the course of buying and selling.[19] However, soon after the conversion of Constantine (312 CE), the Church ceased to be dominated by ascetics, and attitudes toward commerce began to mellow, leading Augustine to teach that wickedness was not inherent in commerce, but that, as with any occupation, it was up to the individual to live righteously.[20]

Augustine also ruled that price was not simply a function of the seller's costs, but also of the buyer's desire for the item sold. In this way, Augustine gave legitimacy not merely to merchants, but to the eventual deep involvement of the Church in the birth of capitalism,[21] when its earliest forms began to appear in about the ninth century in the great estates belonging to monastic orders. Because of the immense increases in agricultural productivity that resulted from such significant innovations, such as the switch to horses, the heavy moldboard plow, and the three-field system, the monastic estates were no longer limited to mere subsistence agriculture. Instead, they began to specialize in particular crops or products and to sell these at a profit, allowing them to purchase their other needs, which led them to initiate a cash economy. They also began to reinvest their profits to increase their productive capacity, and as their incomes continued to mount, this led many monasteries to became banks, lending to the nobility—as they did to so many Crusaders. As Randall Collins noted, this was not merely a sort of "proto" capitalism involving only the "institutional preconditions for capitalism, . . . but a version of the developed characteristics of capitalism itself."[22] Collins referred to this as "religious capitalism,"[23] adding that the "dynamism of the medieval economy was primarily that of the Church."[24]

Throughout the medieval era, the Church was by far the largest landowner in Europe, and its liquid assets and annual income not only far surpassed that of the wealthiest king, but probably that of all of Europe's nobility added together.[25] A substantial portion of this wealth flowed into the coffers of the religious orders, much of it in payments and endowments in return for liturgical services—Henry VII of England paid to have ten thousand masses said for his soul.[26] In addition to receiving many gifts of land, most orders reinvested wealth in buying or reclaiming more land, thus initiating an era of rapid growth that often resulted in extensive property holdings scattered over a large area. Although dwarfed by the huge monastic center at Cluny, which may have had a thousand priories by the eleventh century, many monastic orders had established fifty or more outposts.[27] In the twelfth century, under the leadership of Saint Bernard of Clairvaux, the Cistercians protested against the extravagance of Cluny, but being well-organized and frugal, they quickly amassed some of the largest estates in Europe— many Cistercian houses farmed one hundred thousand acres, and one in Hungary had fields totaling two hundred fifty thousand acres.[28] In addition to gifts, much of this growth was achieved by incorporating previously untilled tracts as well as by clearing forests and draining submerged areas. For example, monks at the monastery of Les Dunes recovered about twenty-five thousand acres of fertile fields from the marshes along the Flanders coast.[29]

This period of great expansion was motivated in part by population growth,[30] and in even greater part by increases in productivity. Until this era, the estates were largely self-sufficient—they produced their own food, drink, and fuel, they made their own cloth and tanned their own leather, they maintained a smithy and often even a pottery. But, with the great gains in productivity came *specialization* and *trade*. Some estates only produced wine, others grew only several grains, some only raised cattle or sheep—the Cistercians at Fossanova specialized in raising fine horses.[31] Meanwhile, the rapid increase in agricultural surpluses encouraged the founding and growth of towns and cities— indeed, many of the monastic centers themselves became cities. Writing about the great monastery of St. Gall in Switzerland in 820, Christopher Dawson (1889–1970) noted that it was "no longer the simple religious community envisaged by the old monastic rules, but a vast complex of buildings, churches, workshops, store-houses, offices, schools and alms-houses, housing a whole population of dependents, workers and servants like the temple cities of antiquity."[32]

When estates grew into small cities and sustained many scattered out-

hundred chickens can easily be disputed as to the value of the owed poultry: are these to be old hens, roosters, or pullets? But, the precise meaning of owing someone two ounces of gold is not in doubt. Not only did the great Church estates begin to extend one another monetary credit, as they became increasingly rich they also began to *lend money at interest*, and so did some bishops. During the eleventh and twelfth centuries, Cluny lent large sums at interest to various Burgundian nobles,[35] while in 1071 the bishop of Liège lent the incredible sum of 100 pounds of gold and 175 marks of silver to the countess of Flanders and subsequently lent 1,300 marks of silver and 3 marks of gold to the duke of Lower Lorraine. In 1044, the bishop of Worms lent twenty pounds of gold and a large (unspecified) amount of silver to Emperor Henry III. There were many similar instances—according to surviving records, in this era bishops and monasteries were the usual source of loans to the nobility.[36] By the thirteenth century, monastic lending often took the form of a *mort-gage* (literally, "dead pledge"), wherein the borrower pledged land as security, and the lender collected all income from that land during the term of the loan and did not deduct this income from the amount owed. This practice often resulted in additions to the monastery's lands because the monks were not hesitant to foreclose.[37]

But the monks did more than invest in land or lend from their bursting treasuries. They began to leave their fields, vines, and barns and retire into liturgical "work," conducting endless paid masses for souls in purgatory and for living benefactors who wished to improve their fates in the next world. Monks now enjoyed leisure and luxury. The monks at Cluny "were given plentiful and choice foods. Their wardrobe was renewed annually. The manual labor prescribed by the rule [of Saint Benedict] was reduced to entirely symbolic tasks about the kitchen. The monks lived like lords."[38] It was the same in the other great houses. And all of this was possible because the great monasteries began to utilize a *hired labor force*, who not only were more productive than the monks had been,[39] but also more productive than tenants required to provide periods of compulsory labor. Indeed, these tenants had long since been satisfying their labor obligations by money payments.[40] Thus, as "religious capitalism" unfolded, monks still faithfully performed their duties, but aside from those engaged in liturgy, the rest now "worked" as executives and foremen. In this way, the medieval monasteries came to resemble remarkably "modern" firms—well administered and quick to adopt the latest technological advances.[41]

The Virtues of Work and Frugality

Traditional societies celebrate consumption while holding work in contempt. This is true not only of the privileged elite, but even of those whose days are spent in toil. Notions such as the "dignity" of labor or the idea that work is a virtuous activity were incomprehensible in ancient Rome or in any other precapitalist society. Rather, just as spending is the purpose of wealth, the preferred approach to work is to have someone else do it and, failing that, to do as little as possible. In China, the Mandarins grew their fingernails as long as they could (even wearing silver sheaths to protect them from breaking) in order to make it evident that they did no labor. Consequently, capitalism seems to require and to encourage a remarkably different attitude toward work—to see it as intrinsically virtuous and also to recognize the virtue of restricting one's consumption. Of course, Max Weber identified this as the Protestant Ethic, so-called because he believed it to be absent from Catholic culture. But Weber was wrong.

Belief in the virtues of work and of simple living did accompany the rise of capitalism, but this was centuries before Martin Luther was born.[42] Despite the fact that many, perhaps even most, monks and nuns were from the nobility and wealthiest families,[43] they honored work not only in theological terms, but also by actually doing it. In Randall Collins words, they "had the Protestant ethic without Protestantism."[44]

The virtue of work was made evident in the sixth century by Saint Benedict, who wrote in his famous *Rule*: "Idleness is the enemy of the soul. Therefore the brothers should have specified periods for manual labor as well as prayerful reading. . . . When they live by the labor of their hands, as our fathers and the apostles did, then they are really monks."[45] Or, as Walter Hilton, the English Augustinian, put it in the fourteenth century, "By the discipline of the physical life we are enabled for spiritual effort."[46] It is this commitment to manual labor that so distinguishes Christian asceticism from that found in the other great religious cultures, where piety is associated with rejection of the world and its activities. In contrast with Eastern holy men, for example, who specialize in meditation and live by charity, medieval Christian monastics lived by their own labor, sustaining highly productive estates. This not only prevented "ascetic zeal from becoming petrified in world flight,"[47] but it sustained a healthy concern with economic affairs. Although the "Protestant Ethic" thesis is wrong, it is entirely legitimate to link capitalism to a "Christian Ethic."

Thus it was that, beginning in about the ninth century, the growing monastic estates came to resemble "well-organized and stable firms," that "pursued complex commercial activities within a relatively free market," "investing in productive activities involving a hired workforce," "guided by anticipated and actual returns." If this was not capitalism in all its glory, it was certainly close enough. Moreover, these economic activities of the great religious orders made Christian theologians think anew about their doctrines concerning profits and interest. Granted that Augustine had approved profits. But were there no moral limits to profit margins? As for usury, the Bible condemned it; but if interest was forbidden, how could one buy on credit or borrow needed funds?

Capitalism and Theological Progress

Christian theology has never crystallized. If God intended that scripture would be more adequately grasped as humans gained greater knowledge and experience, this warranted continuing reappraisal of doctrines and interpretations. And so it was.

INITIAL CHRISTIAN OPPOSITION TO INTEREST AND PROFITS

During the twelfth and thirteenth centuries, Catholic theologians, including Thomas Aquinas, declared that profits were morally legitimate and, while giving lip service to the long tradition of opposition to "usury," these same theologians justified interest charges. In this way, the Catholic Church made its peace with early capitalism many centuries before there even were any Protestants.

Christianity inherited opposition to interest (usury) from the Jews. Deuteronomy 23:19–20 admonishes: "You shall not charge interest on loans to another Israelite, interest on money, interest on provisions, interest on anything that is lent. On loans to a foreigner you may charge interest, but on loans to another Israelite you may not charge interest."

That interest could be charged to foreigners explains the role of Jews as money lenders in Christian societies, a role sometimes imposed on them by Christians in need of funds. (It also had the consequence, usually ignored by historians, that medieval Christians with money to lend often masqueraded as Jews.)[48]

Of course, the prohibition in Deuteronomy did not necessarily bar Christians from charging interest since they were not Israelites. But, the words of Jesus in Luke 6:34 were taken to prohibit interest: "If you lend to those from whom you hope to receive, what credit is that to you? Even sinners lend to sinners, to receive as much again. But love your enemies, do good, and lend, expecting nothing in return."

Interest on loans was thus defined as the "sin of usury," and widely condemned in principle while pretty much ignored in actual practice. In fact, as already noted, by late in the ninth century, some of the great religious houses ventured into banking, and bishops were second only to the nobility in their reliance on borrowed money. In addition to borrowing from monastic orders, many bishops secured loans from private Italian banks that enjoyed the full approval of the Vatican. Hence, in 1229, when the bishop of Limerick failed to fully repay a loan to a Roman bank, he was excommunicated by the pope until he had negotiated a new agreement under which he ended up repaying 50 percent interest over the course of eight years.[49] The need for loans often was so great and so widespread that Italian banks opened branches all across the continent. Although many bishops, monastic orders, and even the Roman hierarchy ignored the ban on usury, opposition to interest lingered. As late as the Second Lateran Council in 1139, the Church "declared the unrepentant usurer condemned by the Old and New Testaments alike and, therefore, unworthy of ecclesiastical consolations and Christian burial."[50] Nevertheless, documents prove "that in 1215 there were usurers at the Papal Court from which a needy prelate could obtain a loan."[51]

As many of the great Christian monastic orders continued to maximize profits and to lend money at whatever rate of interest the market would bear, they were increasingly subjected to a barrage of condemnations from more traditional clergy who accused them of the sin of avarice. What was to be done?

THEOLOGY OF THE "JUST PRICE" AND OF LEGITIMATE INTEREST

Obviously, people couldn't be expected to simply give away the products of their labor. But, was there no limit to what they should charge? How could one be sure that an asking price was not sinfully high?

Writing in the thirteenth century, Saint Albertus Magnus proposed the "just price" was simply what "goods are worth according to the estimation of the market at the time of sale."[52] That is, a price was just if that's what uncoerced buyers were willing to pay. Adam Smith could not have found fault with this definition. Echoing his teacher, but using many more words, Saint Thomas Aquinas began his analysis of just prices by posing the question, "Whether a man may lawfully sell a thing for more than it is worth?"[53] He answered by first quoting Augustine that it was natural and lawful for "you wish to buy cheap, and sell dear." Next, Aquinas excluded fraud from legitimate transactions. Finally, he recognized that worth was not really an objective value—"the just price of things is not absolutely definite"—but was a function of the buyer's desire for the thing purchased and the seller's willingness or reluctance to sell, so long as the buyer was not misled, or under duress. To be just, a price had to be the same for all potential buyers at a given moment, thus barring price discrimination. Aquinas's respect for market forces was best revealed by his story about a merchant who brought grain to a country suffering a famine and who knew that other merchants soon would bring much more grain to this area. Was it sinful for him to sell at the prevailing, high market price, or should he have informed the buyers that soon more grain would arrive, thus causing the price to decline? Aquinas concluded that this merchant could, in good conscience, keep quiet and sell at the current high price.

As to interest on loans, Aquinas was unusually confusing. In some writings he condemned all interest as the sin of usury, in other passages he accepted that lenders deserved compensation, although he was fuzzy as to how much and why.[54] However, prompted by the realities of a rapidly expanding commercial economy, many of Aquinas's contemporaries, especially the Canonists, were not so cautious, but began "discovering" many exceptions wherein interest charges were not usurious.[55] For example, if a productive property, such as an estate, was given as security for a loan, the lender could take all of the production during the period of the loan and not deduct it from the amount owed.[56] Many other exclusions involved the "costs" to the lender of not having the money available for other commercial opportunities, such as buying goods for resale or acquiring new fields. Since these alternative opportunities for profit were entirely licit, it was licit to compensate a lender for having to forgo them.[57] In this same spirit, it was deemed proper to charge interest for goods bought on credit.[58] As for banks, aside from the exemptions noted above, they did not make straight loans at a fixed rate of interest since these would have been deemed usurious on grounds that there was no "adventure of the principal." The notion was that interest was legitimate only if the amount yielded was uncertain in advance, being subject to "adventure." But it took very little finesse for bankers to evade this prohibition by trading notes, bills of exchange, or even currencies in ways that seemed adventuresome, but which in fact had entirely predictable returns and thus constituted loans and produced the equivalent of interest.[59] Thus, while the "sin of usury" remained on the books, so to speak, "usury" had become essentially an empty term.

Thus, by no later than the thirteenth century, the leading Christian theologians had fully debated the primary aspects of emerging capitalism—profits, property rights, credit, lending, and the like. As Lester K. Little summed up: "In each case they came up with generally favorable, approving views, in sharp contrast to the attitudes that had prevailed for six or seven centuries right up to the previous generation."[60] Capitalism was fully and finally freed from all fetters of faith.[61]

It was a remarkable shift. These were, after all, theologians who had separated themselves from the world. Most of them had taken vows of poverty. Most of their predecessors had held merchants and commercial activities in contempt. Had asceticism truly prevailed in the religious orders, it seems most unlikely that Christian disdain for and opposition to commerce would have mellowed, let alone have been radically transformed. This theological revolution was the result of direct experience with worldly imperatives. For all their genuine acts of charity, monastic administrators were not about to give all their wealth to the poor or to sell their products at cost. It was the active participation of the great houses in free markets that caused monastic theologians to reconsider the morality of commerce, which was abetted by the marked worldliness of the Church hierarchy.

Unlike those in the religious orders, few holding higher Church positions had taken vows of poverty, and many displayed a decided taste for profligate living. Bishops and cardinals were among the very best clients of "usurers." That is not surprising since nearly everyone holding an elite Church position had purchased his office as an investment, anticipating a substantial return from Church revenues. Indeed, as noted in chapter 9, men often were able to buy appointments as bishops or even cardinals without having held any prior Church positions, sometimes before they were ordained or even baptized![62] This aspect of the medieval Church was an endless source of scandal and conflict, spawning many heretical mass sect movements, and culminating in the Reformation. But these worldly aspects of the Church paid serious dividends in the development of capitalism. The Church didn't stand in the way—rather it both justified and took an active role in the Commercial Revolution of the twelfth and thirteenth centuries.[63]

Capitalist City-States

Although capitalism developed in the great monastic estates, it soon found a very receptive setting in the newly democratic Italian city-states. In the tenth century, they rapidly began to emerge as the banking and trading centers of Europe, exporting a stream of goods purchased from suppliers in northern Europe, especially in Flanders, Holland, and England, their primary customers being Byzantium and the Islamic states, especially those along the coast of north Africa. Subsequently, the Italian city-states industrialized and soon were producing a large volume of manufactured goods not only for export across the Mediterranean, but they also began shipping a great many products back to northern Europe and the British Isles. For example, eyeglasses (not only for nearsightedness, but for farsightedness as well) were mass-produced by plants in both Florence and Venice, and tens of thousands of pairs were exported annually.

Perhaps the most striking aspect of Italian capitalism was the rapid perfection of banking. The Italian bankers quickly developed and adopted double-entry bookkeeping. To facilitate long-distance trade, Italian banks invented bills of exchange, making it possible to transfer funds on paper rather than undertake the difficult and very dangerous practice of transporting coins or precious metal from a bank in Florence to one in Genoa, let alone from a trading company in Venice to a woolens dealer in England. Italian bankers also initiated insurance to guard against loss of long-distance shipments by land or sea. Perhaps the most important of all the Italian banking innovations was the perfection of modern arithmetic, based on the adoption of Hindu-Arabic numerals and the concept of zero. Even addition and subtraction were daunting chores for Romans, given their cumbersome numeral system. The new system was revolutionary in terms of its ease and accuracy, and arithmetic schools soon sprang up in all the leading northern Italian city-states, eventually even enrolling students sent from northern Europe. With easy and accurate arithmetic available, business practices were transformed.[64] All of this accompanied the proliferation of banks in the Italian city-states. By the thirteenth century, there were 38 independent banks in Florence, 34 in Pisa, 27 in Genoa, 18 in Venice—a combined total of 173 in the leading Italian city-states.[65] Moreover, most of these Italian banks had foreign branches. In 1231, there were 69 Italian banking houses operating branches in England and nearly as many in Ireland. In fact, until well into the fifteenth century, every bank in western Europe was either in Italy or was a branch of an Italian bank.[66]

The proximate cause of the rise of Italian capitalism was freedom from the rapacious rulers who repressed and consumed economic progress in most of the world, including most of Europe. Although their political life often was turbulent, these city-states were true republics able to sustain the freedom required by capitalism. Second, centuries of technological progress had laid the necessary foundations for the rise of capitalism, especially the agricultural surpluses needed to sustain cities and to permit specialization. In addition, Christian theology encouraged extremely optimistic views about the future, which justified long-term investment strategies, and by this time theology also provided moral justifications for the business practices fundamental to capitalism.

Conclusion

Now for a remarkable irony. Quite possibly the most profound and lasting consequence of the Protestant Reformation was that it prompted the Catholic Reformation or Counter-Reformation. At the Council of Trent (1551–52, 1562–63), the Catholic Church ended simony (the sale of church offices), enforced priestly celibacy, and made available official, inexpensive Bibles in local languages (vulgates). In short, the Church of Piety permanently replaced the Church of Power. At Trent, the Church also decided to establish a network of seminaries to train men for the local priesthood. Hence, by the eighteenth century, in most places the Church was staffed by literate men well versed in theology and whose vocations had been shaped and tested in a formal, institutional setting. Thus, the Church did confront the modern world.

Postscript

~~~~~~

I T IS GENERALLY assumed that the days of rampant anti-Catholic
bigotry are long past, having been put to rest with the election
of John F. Kennedy in 1960. True enough, popular comedians
no longer tell scurrilous jokes about priests or the pope, nor do many
Protestant preachers still thunder on about the sins of the Vatican. But,
a quiet kind of anti-Catholicism remains widespread precisely because
any sensible person would resent any organization that was guilty of
even some of the charges examined in the previous chapters. Thus, it is
vital that these anti-Catholic falsehoods be purged from the historical
record.

To that end, it probably is important that this book was not written
by a Catholic or by anyone associated with a Catholic university. Had
it been, it would be all too easy to dismiss it as a work of special plead-
ing. As it happens, this book was written by someone affiliated with
Baylor, the world's largest Baptist university. Not so very long ago,
Baylor was a hotbed of militant anti-Catholicism. Every viciously anti-
Catholic work, from the *Awful Disclosures of Maria Monk* (1850) to Paul
Blanshard's *American Freedom and Catholic Power* (1949), is to be found in
the Baylor library. These books were not purchased as examples of hate
literature. At the time they were acquired, these volumes were thought
to be appropriate reading for undergraduates.

Those days are over. I am not a Baptist, nor are scores of Baylor faculty.
In fact, some of Baylor's most distinguished scholars are Roman Catholics, as are a fifth of the faculty overall. I am codirector of the Institute

for Studies of Religion (ISR) at Baylor, and among our affiliated scholars there are not only Catholics, but Jews, Buddhists, and a Muslim. Moreover, ISR has entered into a formal agreement with the Berkley Center at Georgetown University (a Catholic institution) to sustain a joint venture, the Religious Freedom Project. This undertaking was announced during a Papal Audience involving both Baylor and Georgetown scholars on December 14, 2013—something that would have been inconceivable only a few years ago.

Notes

INTRODUCTION
1. Russell, 1997.
2. See Ira Gershwin's lyrics from *They All Laughed*: "They all laughed at Christopher Columbus, when he said the world was round, they all laughed when Edison recorded sound."
3. Russell, 1997.
4. Ibid.
5. Bernhard, 2014.
6. Russell, 2003, 30.
7. Maltby, 1971, 4.
8. See Dawkins, 2006; Sagan, 1996.
9. Stark, 2001, 2003, 2005, and 2014.
10. Stark, 1996, 2006, and 2011.
11. Mattingly, 1959, 375.
12. Russell, 1997.

CHAPTER 1
1. Glock and Stark, 1966, xv.
2. September 26, 1964, page 1.
3. Stark, 2001, chapter 3.
4. Gager, 1983; Isaac, 1971, 1974; Osborn, 1985; Ruether, 1974.
5. Ruether, 1974, 184.
6. Isaac, 1971, 508.
7. Osborn, 1985, 341.
8. Gager, 1983, 88.
9. Ibid.
10. Quoted in Augustine, *City of God* 6:11.
11. Cicero, *Pro Flacco* 28:69.
12. Tacitus, *The Histories* 5:1–13 (The Jews).
13. Smallwood, 1981, 129.
14. Tacitus, *Annales* 2:85.
15. Suetonius, *Tiberius* 36.
16. Cassius Dio, *Historia Romana* 67:14.
17. The entire paragraph is based on Schäfer, 1997.
18. Smallwood, 1999, 169.
19. Stark, 2007, chapter 3.

20. All biblical quotations are from the New Revised Standard Version.
21. Sanders, 1987.
22. Evans, 1993, 17.
23. Stark, 2006.
24. Ibid., 67.
25. Meeks, 1983.
26. Frend, 1965; Hare, [1967] 2005; Parkes, 1934.
27. Katz, 1999, 265.
28. Hare, [1967] 2005, 3.
29. Oberman, 1992, 293.
30. Schäfer, 2007, 146.
31. The definitive work was thought to be Johann Maier's study published in Germany in 1978, which claimed to prove that there were no references to Jesus in the Talmud. Unfortunately, Maier was only concerned to discover passages that added reliable historical knowledge of Jesus, and he dismissed the many references to Jesus as fanciful, ignoring their immense interest as the "missing side" of an authentic polemical battle.
32. Seaver, 1952; Williams, 1935.
33. Seaver, 1952, 7.
34. Schäfer, 2007, 9.
35. Stark, 2001.
36. Graetz, 1894, 37–39.
37. Kedar, 1984.
38. Gidal, 1988, 30.
39. Chazan, 1986, 29.
40. Poliakov, 1965, 35–36.
41. Lambert, 1992; Moore, 1976, 1985; Russell, 1971.
42. Stark, 2001, 121.
43. Ibid., 123.
44. Ibid., chapter 3.
45. Tyerman, 2006.
46. Asbridge, 2004, 82.

47. Grosser and Halperin (1983) are not very critical about sources, but even they only accuse Peter the Hermit's followers of pressing Jewish communities for financial donations. Nor does Runciman (1951) attribute any attacks on Jews to the People's Crusade.
48. Baron, 1957; Chazan, 1980; Graetz, 1998; Grosser and Halperin, 1983; Flannery, 1965; Poliakov, 1965; Runciman, 1951; Stark, 2001.
49. Poliakov, 1965, 45.
50. Madden, 1999, 20.
51. Runciman, 1951; 1:141.
52. In Poliakov, 1965, 48.
53. Stark, 2001, chapter 3.
54. In Chazen, 1980, 107–8.
55. Magnus, 1997, 18.
56. Stark, 2001, chapter 3.
57. Ziegler, 1971.
58. Cohen, 1996; Goiten, 1964.
59. In Fletcher, 1992, 172.
60. Graetz, 1894, 214.
61. Kayser, 1949, 50.
62. In Fletcher, 1992, 171.
63. Mann, 1992, xi.
64. Alroy, 1975, 185.
65. Fletcher, 1992, 173.
66. Hodgson, 1974: 1:268.
67. Payne, [1959] 1995, 105.
68. Hodgson, 1974; Payne, [1959] 1995.
69. Stark, 2001, chapter 3.
70. Stark, 2007, chapter 8.
71. Chazan, 1986, 29.
72. Browe, in Katz, 1994, 317.
73. Augustine, *Reply to Faustus*.
74. Katz, 1994, 317.
75. Doino, 2004, 159.
76. Shirer, [1960] 1990, 234–35.
77. In Dalin, 2005, 100.
78. Marchione, 2002, 50.
79. Ibid., 117.
80. As quoted on the cover of the 1997 Johns Hopkins University Press paperback edition of *The Deputy*: "Outstanding," *New Yorker*; "Extraordinary," *San Francisco Chronicle*; "Quite possibly the most important Christian document to develop from the abysmal tragedy of World War II," *Los Angeles Times*.
81. Sontag 1964, reprinted in Sontag, 2001, 128.
82. Duffy, 1997, 264.
83. In Dalin, 2005, 11.
84. These scholars include: Robert Louis Wilken, Owen Chadwick, Michael Novack, John Lukas, Michael Burleigh, Heinz Hürten, Joseph Bottum, Russell Hittinger, Thomas

Brechenmacher, William D. Rubinstein, Michal Marrus, Eamon Duffy, and many others.
85. Doino, 204, 169.
86. Rychlak, 2000.
87. Ibid., epilogue.
88. Dalin, 2005, 2–3.
89. Carroll, 2001, 22.
90. Wilken, 2001, 22.
91. Zuccotti, 2001, 301.
92. Dalin, 2005, 17.
93. Dalin, 2004, 18.
94. Kurzman, 2007.
95. National Archives and Records Administration, College Park, MD, CIA Selected Documents, 1941–47, box 4; as quoted in Doino, 2004, 162.

CHAPTER 2
1. Evangelical Protestant groups condemn them as well.
2. Meyer, 2005, 2.
3. Jenkins, 2001, 41.
4. Meyer, 2005, 1.
5. Remarks made on a TV special and quoted in Jenkins, 2001, 5.
6. Pagels, 1979, 150.
7. Ruether, 1998, 51.
8. Quoted in Allen, 1996, 67.
9. Quoted in Jenkins, 2001, 167.
10. Baigent et al., 1983.
11. Ehrman, 2003, 2006; King, 2003a, 2003b; Leloup, 2002; Meyer, 2005, Pagels, 1979, 2005.
12. Translation by Layton, 1987.
13. Perkins, 1990, 371.
14. Funk et al., 1993, 4.
15. Jenkins, 2001, 103.
16. King, 2003b, 3–4.
17. Layton, 1987.
18. King, 2003b, 3–6, 13–14.
19. Leloup, 2002, 11–12.
20. Ehrman, 2006, 82.
21. Ibid., 173.
22. Both are quoted in the April 6, 2006, edition of the *New York Times* in the story on the *Gospel of Judas*.
23. Jenkins, 2001, 29.
24. Meyer, 2005, 2.
25. Quoted in Jenkins, 2001, 110.
26. Quoted in Williams, 1996, 8.
27. Layton, 1987, 24.
28. All quotes from *The Secret Book According to John* are from Layton's (1987) version.
29. Williams, 1996, 10.
30. Ibid., 11.
31. Ibid.

32. Perkins, 1980, 16.
33. Remarkably, in celebrating the greater enlightenment of the Gnostics, Elaine Pagels and Karen King (2007) avoid discussing sex. Indeed, in her 1979 book on the Gnostic gospels Pagels's very brief mentions of sex are limited to conventional Christianity.
34. Douglas M. Parrott's translation.
35. Nock, 1933, 252.
36. Perkins, 1980, 10.
37. Layton, 1987, 273–74.
38. I have presented quantitative data on the link between Gnostics and pagans in Stark, 2006.
39. Rudolph, 1987, 367.
40. In Wright, 2006, 98.
41. Irenaeus, *Against Heresies* 1:31.1.

CHAPTER 3
1. Stark, 1996, 2006, 2007.
2. Calculated with the same formula used in Stark 1996, 2006, 2007.
3. Gibbon [1776–88] 1994, 1:15.447.
4. Gibbon [1776–88] 1994, 1:2.57.
5. In Voltaire, *A Treatise on Toleration and Other Essays.*
6. Gibbon [1776–88] 1994, 1:16.539.
7. Kirsch, 2004, 18.
8. Bowersock, 1990, 6.
9. Gibbon [1776–88] 1994, 1:20.750.
10. Brown, 1998, 633.
11. Ibid., 641.
12. Among them are Peter Brown, Jean Delumeau, H. A. Drake, and Ramsay MacMullen.
13. In Brown, 1998, 641.
14. Brown, 1998; MacMullen, 1997.
15. Harl, 1990, 14.
16. MacMullen, 1997, 28.
17. Stark, 2006, chapter 3.
18. Even one of the strongest current proponents of the traditional view that Constantine quickly destroyed paganism has admitted that there is no evidence of pagan protests: "The opposition to Christianity can [only] be guessed rather than demonstrated" in Momigliano, 1963, 94.
19. Winkelman, 1961 in Drake, 2000, 246.
20. Geffcken, [1920] 1978, 120.
21. Both quotes from Bradbury, 1994, 123.
22. Drake, 2000, 247.
23. Drake, 1996, 29.
24. Brown, 1995; Drake, 2000.
25. Drake, 2000, 244.
26. Quoted in Drake, 2000, 244–87.
27. Ibid., 247.

28. Ibid., 249.
29. Salzman, 1990.
30. Both quotations from Brown, 1995, 12.
31. Brown, 1995, 15.
32. Ibid., 18.
33. For a summary, see Stark, 2004, chapter 3.
34. Bowersock, 1978, 18.
35. Gibbon [1776–88] 1994, 2:28.864.
36. Levenson, 1990, 510.
37. Bowersock, 1978, 79–93, 16.
38. Geffcken, [1920] 1978, 139.
39. Levenson, 1990, 510.
40. Bowersock, 1978, 18.
41. Gibbon, [1776–88] 1994, 2:28.866–67.
42. Chuvin, 1990, 44.
43. Geffcken, [1920] 1978, 144.
44. Athanassiadi, 1993, 13.
45. Drake, 2000, 434.
46. Ibid., 435.
47. Ibid., 434.
48. Ibid., 436.
49. *Oratio*, xviii, quoted in Drake, 1996, 34.
50. Wilken, 1983, 128.
51. Bloch, 1963, 195.
52. Harl, 1990, 7.
53. Ibid.
54. Lactantius, *Divine Institutes* 5.23.
55. Harl, 1990, 27.
56. Ibid., 14.
57. MacMullen, 1997.
58. Bradbury, 1994, 134.
59. In ibid., 133.
60. Brown, 1992, 23.
61. Bradbury, 1994, 133.
62. In Brown, 1995, 42.
63. Ibid.
64. Bradbury, 1994, 135–36.
65. Brown, 1998, 632.
66. Ibid., 642.
67. Gibbon, [1776–88] 1994, 3:28.71, 77.
68. Beugnot, 1835; Bloch, 1963.
69. Stark, 1996.
70. Brown, 1992, 136.
71. For a summary, see ibid.
72. MacMullen, 1997, 159.
73. Fletcher, 1997, 236.
74. Brøndsted, 1965, 306.
75. *Ecclesiastical History* 1.30.
76. Thomas, 1971, 48.
77. MacMullen, 1997, 123–24.
78. Ibid., 108.
79. Ibid., 115.
80. Thomas, 1971, 48.
81. Delumeau, 1977, 176.
82. Seznec, 1972, 3.
83. In Brown, 1998, 634.

84. Dodds, 1965, 132.
85. Brown, 1998, 633.

CHAPTER 4
1. Boorstin, 1983, 100.
2. Bury, 1914, 31.
3. Manchester, 1993, 3, 5.
4. Mommsen, 1942, 237.
5. Voltaire, *Works* XII.
6. Quoted in Gay, 1966.
7. Gibbon, [1776–88] 1994, 2:1443.
8. Russell, 1959, 142.
9. Burckhardt, [1860] 1990, 19; Stark, 2005.
10. Russell, 1959, 232.
11. Bouwsma, 1979, 4.
12. Hollister, 1992, 7.
13. Wells, 2008, 143–44.
14. Gimpel, 1976, viii, 1.
15. White, 1940, 151.
16. Stark, 2006.
17. Chandler, 1987.
18. Lopez, 1976, 43.
19. Gimpel, 1976, 16.
20. Gies and Gies, 1994, 113.
21. Stark, 2005, chapter 5.
22. Gies and Gies, 1994, 117.
23. Gimpel, 1976, 25–27.
24. Stark, 2005, chapter 5.
25. Landes, 1998, 46.
26. Montgomery, 1968; White, 1962.
27. Lane, [1934] 1992, 35–53.
28. Barclay and Schofield, 1981, 488.
29. Needham, 1980.
30. Stark, 2003a, chapter 4.
31. Bonnassie, 1991, 30.
32. Bloch, 1975, 14.
33. In Bonnassie, 1991, 54.
34. Bloch, 1975, 11.
35. Ibid., 30.
36. Daniel, 1981, 705.
37. Gardner and Crosby, 1959, 236.
38. De la Croix and Tansey, 1975, 353.
39. Johnson, 2003, 190.
40. Lopez, 1967, 198.
41. Colish, 1997, 266.
42. Manchester, 1993, 103–4.
43. Cohen, 1985; Gingerich, 1975; Jaki, 2000; Rosen, 1971.
44. Hollister, 1992, 8.
45. Grant, 1996, 23.
46. Pernoud, 2000, 24.
47. Ferguson, 1939, 8.
48. Stark, 2003a, chapter 2.
49. Stark, 2007, chapter 1.
50. Stark, 2014.
51. Rahner, 1975, 1687.

52. Tertullian, *On Repentance* 1.
53. Clement, *Recognitions of Clement* II:LXIX.
54. In Lindberg and Numbers, 1986, 27–28.
55. Southern, 1970a, 49.
56. In Lindberg, 1986, 27.
57. Augustine, *City of God* 22:24.
58. In Gimpel, 1961, 165.
59. Ibid., 149.
60. In Hartwell, 1971, 691.
61. Baillie, 1951; Nisbet, 1980.
62. Macmurray, 1938, 113.

CHAPTER 5
1. Prawer, 1972. Nowhere in the book does Prawer define colonialism, and even he admits that the flow of wealth was from Europe into the Kingdom of Jerusalem.
2. Ekelund et al., 1996.
3. Quotes from Madden, 2002b.
4. Curry, 2002, 36.
5. June 20, 1999, section 4, p. 15.
6. "Christian Apology for the Crusades: The Reconciliation Walk," Ontario Consultants on Religious Tolerance, last modified November 4, 2005, www.religioustolerance. org/chr_cru1.htm.
7. Quoted in Richard, 1999, 475.
8. Hume, *The History of England*, 1761, 1:209.
9. Quoted in Richard, 1999, 475.
10. Riley-Smith, 2003, 154.
11. Gibbon [1776–88] 1994, 6:58.
12. Duby, 1977; France, 1997; Mayer, 1972.
13. Mayer, 1972, 22—25.
14. Ekelund et al., 1996. This is one of the most inept and uninformed efforts at trying to apply economic principles by analogy that I have ever encountered.
15. In Riley-Smith, 2003, 159.
16. Spielvogel, 2000, 259.
17. Armstrong, [1991] 2001, xii.
18. Including Alfred J. Andrea, Peter Edbury, Benjamin Z. Kedar, Thomas F. Madden, Edward M. Peters, Jean Richard, Jonathan Riley-Smith, and Christopher Tyerman.
19. Runciman, 1951, 1:49.
20. Ibid., 1:47.
21. Ibid., 1:79.
22. Payne, 1984, 18–19.
23. Ibid., 28–29.
24. Five major versions of the speech exist, each being incomplete, and there are several translations of each into English. I have selected excerpts from several versions.
25. Carroll, 2001, 241.
26. Edbury, 1999, 95.
27. Ibid.; Reed, 1999.

28. Edbury, 1999, 95.
29. Gillingham, 1999, 59.
30. Madden, 1999, 12.
31. Riley-Smith, 1997.
32. Ibid.
33. Ibid., 49.
34. Ibid., 29–30.
35. Ibid., 28.
36. Erdoes, 1988, 26.
37. Riley-Smith, 1997, 28.
38. Quoted in Riley-Smith, 1997, 72.
39. Runciman, 1951, 1:339–40.
40. Hillenbrand, 1999, 54.
41. Hamilton, 2000; LaMonte, 1932; Phillips, 1995; Prawer, 1972; Riley-Smith, 1973; Runciman, 1951; Tyerman, 2006.
42. In Hillenbrand, 1999, 77.
43. Tyerman, 2006, 178.
44. Madden, 1999, 49.
45. Tyerman, 2006, 179.
46. Riley-Smith, 1997, 17.
47. Issawi, 1957, 272.
48. Phillips, 1995, 112.
49. Madden, 2002b, 3.
50. Kedar, 1984.
51. Ibid.
52. Runciman, 1951, 3:480.
53. Madden, 2002a; also Tyerman, 2006, xv.
54. Irwin, 2006, 213.
55. Tyerman, 2006, 351.
56. Siberry, 1995, 368.
57. In ibid., 115.
58. Quoted in Madden, 1999, 78.
59. Madden, 1999, 181.
60. Ibid.
61. Ibid., 181–82.
62. Armstrong, [1991] 2001, 448.
63. In Hillenbrand, 1999, 230.
64. Armstrong, [1991] 2001, xiv.
65. Riley-Smith, 2003, 160–61.
66. Peters, 2003, 6.
67. Hillenbrand, 1999, 4–5.
68. In ibid., 45.
69. There was no Arabic term for "Crusades."
70. Knobler, 2006, 310.
71. Ibid.
72. Ibid.
73. Lewis, 2002, 3.
74. Peters, 2003; Riley-Smith, 2003.
75. Andrea, 2003, 2.
76. Sivan, 1973, 12.
77. Knobler, 2006, 320.
78. Various Muslims quoted by Riley-Smith, 2003, 162.

CHAPTER 6
1. Maltby, 1971, 35.
2. Peters, 1989, 133–34.
3. *The Columbia Encyclopedia*, 6th ed., s.v. "Inquisition."
4. Durant, 1950, 784.
5. Paris, 1961, 4.
6. Llorente, [1823] 1967.
7. Whitechapel, 2002.
8. Robertson, 1902, 290.
9. Hunt, 1994, 79.
10. Whitechapel, 2002, 5.
11. Rawlings, 2006, 1.
12. Peters, 1989, 134.
13. Contreras and Henningsen, 1986; Given, 1997; Haliczer, 1990; Henningsen, 1980; Henningsen and Tedeschi, 1986; Kamen, 1993, 1997; Levack, 1995; Monter, 1990; Rawlings, 2006.
14. See Henningsen and Tedeschi, 1986.
15. Rawlings, 2006, 37.
16. Monter, 1990.
17. Contreras and Henningsen, 1986.
18. Holinshed ([1587] 1965) claims 72,000 were executed by Henry.
19. Gatrell, 1994, 7.
20. Dowling [1845] 2002, 16.
21. Kamen, 1997, 190; Madden, 2003, 30.
22. Rawlings, 2006, 33.
23. Peters, 1989, 93.
24. Madden, 2003, 30.
25. Ibid., 29.
26. Daly, 1978; Davies, 1996, 567; Dworkin, 1974; Hughes, 1952.
27. Burr, 1987, 1.
28. Trethowan, 1963, 343.
29. Burckhardt [1885] 1990; Lecky [1865] 1903.
30. Hobbes, [1651] 1956, 21.
31. Trevor-Roper, [1969] 2001, 112.
32. Briggs, 1998.
33. Hyslop, 1925, 4
34. Ewen, 1929; Levack, 1995; Thomas, 1971.
35. Briggs, 1998; Katz, 1994; Levack, 1995.
36. Monter, 1990.
37. See Stark, 2003a, 258.
38. Lea, 1906–7, 4, 206.
39. Contreras and Henningsen, 1996, 103.
40. O'Neil, 1987, 11.
41. For a full treatment of these matters see Stark, 2003a, chapter 3.
42. Ibid.
43. O'Neil, 1987, 90.
44. Kamen, 1993, 238.
45. Ibid., 197.
46. Ibid., 274.
47. Ibid.

48. Robbins, 1959, 45.
49. Roth, 2002, xi.
50. Decter, 2007.
51. Stark, 2001, chapter 4.
52. Gerber, 1994, 117.
53. For example, "Most of the above-mentioned converts were forced," Netanyahu, 2001, xvi. See also Perez, 2005.
54. Perez, 2005, 10.
55. Roth, 2002, 320.
56. Calculated by the author from Contreras and Henningsen, 1986, and Monter, 1990.
57. Roth, [1964] 1996, 132.
58. Chejne, 1983.
59. Perez, 2005, 45.
60. Bainton [1952] 1985, 131.
61. Peters, 1989, 122.
62. Fernandez, 1997, 483.
63. Kamen, 1997, 268.
64. Ibid.
65. Fernandez, 1997, 483.
66. Stark, 2003a, 258.
67. Goodish, 1976.
68. Kamen, 1997, 268.
69. Fernandez, 1997, 494.
70. Kamen, 1997, 134.
71. Monter and Tedeschi, 1986.
72. Findlen, 1993; Hyde, 1964.
73. Ellerbe, 1995; Kirsch, 2008, MacCulloch, 2010.
74. Ellerbe, 1995, 1.
75. Kirsch, 2008.

Chapter 7

1. All efforts to trace the source of this quote attributed to the pope have failed. It simply appears in some late-nineteenth-century histories without attribution. See Keefe, 1986.
2. Godkin, 1879, xiv.
3. Quoted in Finocchiaro, 2009, 68.
4. Gribbin, 2005, xiv.
5. Feuerbach, 1986, 5.
6. Locke, *Essay Concerning Human Understanding* 3.9.
7. Quoted in Dales, [1973] 1994, 170.
8. Augustine, *City of God* 5:1.
9. *On Repentance* 1.
10. Clement, *Recognitions of Clement* II:LXIX.
11. Southern, 1970a, 49.
12. Grant, 1996, 182.
13. Ibid., 183.
14. Ibid., 184.
15. Haskins, [1923] 2002, 3.
16. Colish, 1997, 266.
17. Grant, 1996; Porter, 1998.
18. Porter, 1998, 56.
19. Mason, 1962.
20. Porter, 1998.
21. Grant, 1996, 205.
22. Schachner, 1938, 3.
23. Quoted in Grant, 2007, 148–49.
24. I have written on this at length on this in Stark, 2003a, chapter 2.
25. Crombie, 1953; Dales, [1973] 1994.
26. Dales, [1973] 1994, 83–86.
27. Ibid., 64.
28. Crombie, 1953; Grant, 1996.
29. Lindberg, 1992, 230.
30. Clegg, 2004; Easton, 1952.
31. Clegg, 2004, 99.
32. Quoted in Fisher and Unguru, 1971, 358.
33. Bridges, 1914, 162.
34. Adams, 1987; Panaccio, 2004.
35. Clagett, 1968; Grant, 1971.
36. Bellitto, 2004; Yamaki, 2001.
37. Danielson, 2000, 98; Mason, 1962, 120–21.
38. Cohen, 1985; Jaki, 2000.
39. Crosby, 1997, 104.
40. Cohen, 1985, 107.
41. Jaki, 2000; Rosen, 1971.
42. Shapin, 1996, 1.
43. For the list, see Stark, 2014, 307–8.
44. Russell, 1959, 232.
45. Kearney, 1964, especially 95.
46. Ibid.; Rabb, 1965.
47. Shapiro, 1968, 288.
48. Kocher, 1953, 4.
49. Ozment, 1980, 191.
50. Rashdall, [1936] 1977, 3:408.
51. Kearney, 1964, 100.
52. Stone, 1964.
53. Stone, 1972, 75.
54. McCloskey, 2010, 403.
55. Whitehead [1925] 1967, 13.
56. Ibid., 12.
57. Descartes, *Oeuvres* 8:61.
58. In Crosby, 1997, 83.
59. Whitehead [1925] 1967, 13.
60. Needham, 1954–84, 581.
61. Lindberg, 1992, 54.
62. Jaki, 1986, 105.
63. I have written extensively on this in Stark, 2003a, chapter 2.
64. In Bradley, 2001, 160.
65. In Merton, 1938, 447.
66. Einstein, *Letters to Solovine*, 131.
67. Quoted in Finocchiaro, 2009, 68.
68. Quoted in ibid.
69. Drake and O'Malley, 1960.
70. Brooke and Cantor, 1998, 20.

71. Ibid., 110.
72. Published by University of California Press.
73. Shea, 1986, 132.
74. Dawkins, 2006, 98.

CHAPTER 8
1. Maxwell, 1975, 10.
2. For example, Hurbon, 1992; Noonan, 1993.
3. Brett, 1994, 57, 58.
4. Aquinas, *Summa* q.3, a.3.
5. Ibid. q.92, a.1–2.
6. In Panzer, 1996, 8.
7. Cantor, 1993, 38.
8. Auping, 1994; Panzer, 1996.
9. Panzer, 1996, 19–21. Italics mine.
10. Ibid., 22.
11. Ibid., 33.
12. Latourette, 1975, 944.
13. Delumeau, 1977; Genovese, 1974.
14. Gay, 1969, 411.
15. Davis, 196, 258.
16. Goveia, 1969, 132.
17. Schafer, 1994, 2–3.
18. Tannenbaum, [1946] 1992.
19. Klein, 1969, 145.
20. Klein, 1967; Meltzer, 1993; Thomas, 1997; Turley, 2000.
21. Beckles, 1989; Dunn, 1973; Goveia, 1969; Sheridan, 1974; Watson, 1989.
22. Fogel, 1989, 36.
23. Mathieson, 1926, 38–40.
24. Johnson, 1910, 89.
25. Harris, 1963, 1964.
26. Davis, 1966, 228–29.
27. Ibid., 243.
28. Abou, 1997; Boxer, 1962; Caraman, 1975; Furneaux, 1969; Graham, 1901; Mörner, 1965.
29. The word "reductions" was used here as in cooking—as to reduce a sauce—based on the fact that the Jesuits had concentrated the Guarani into far denser settlements than those they had inhabited before.
30. Abou, 1997, 65.
31. Garay, [1900] 1965; Madariaga, [1948] 1965. For an excellent summary, see Caraman, 1975.
32. Hanke, 1951.

Chapter 9
1. Unlike too many academics, I respect Wikipedia, consult it almost daily, and support it financially. Its critics seem unaware of the many howling errors that can be found in any edition of *Britannica*.
2. Niebuhr, 1944 in McGreevy, 1997, 98.

3. Dewey, 1949 in McGreevy, 1997, 98.
4. Hook, 1940 in McGreevy, 1997, 128.
5. Parsons, 1940.
6. Stark, 2011.
7. Duffy, 1997, 27.
8. Fletcher, 1997, 38.
9. Cheetham, 1983; Duffy, 1997.
10. Cheetham, 1983; McBrien, 2000.
11. Stark, 2004, 56.
12. Lewis, 2002, 96.
13. Augustine, *City of God* 4:4.
14. Deane, 1973, 423.
15. In O'Donovan and O'Donovan, 1999, 492.
16. Aquinas, *On Kingship* 1:6.
17. Stark, 2005, 83–94.
18. Redman, 1949, 26.
19. Gliozzo, 1971, 274.
20. Ibid., 275.
21. Ibid., 75.
22. Quoted in Gliozzo, 1971, 280.
23. Aston, 2000, 126.
24. Kennedy, 1989, 151.
25. Tallett, 1991, 6.
26. Greer, 1935.
27. Tallett, 1991, 4.
28. Wikipedia, "Dechristianization of France."
29. Tallett, 1991, 5.
30. Aston, 2000, 281.
31. Tallett, 1991, 6.
32. Kennedy, 1989, 343.
33. Doyle, 1989; Kennedy, 1989.
34. Wikipedia, "Martyrs of Compiègne."
35. In Peris, 1998, 47.
36. In Vaughan, 1912, 170–74.
37. Pospielovsky, 1987.
38. Wikipedia, "Persecution of Christians in the Soviet Union."
39. Fletcher, 1995.
40. Yakovlev, 2002, 156.
41. Barrett and Johnson, 2001.
42. Hollander, 1998.
43. Sánchez, 1987, 6.
44. Ibid., 7–8.
45. de la Cueva, 1998, 368.
46. Ibid., 355.
47. Ibid., 356.
48. Sánchez, 1987, 11.
49. Ibid., 12.

CHAPTER 10
1. Strauss, 1975, 49.
2. Ibid.
3. Ibid.
4. Strauss, 1978, 278.

5. Ibid., 278–79.
6. Ibid., 283.
7. Ibid., 284.
8. Strauss, 1975, 56–57.
9. Strauss, 1978, 284.
10. Strauss, 1975, 59.
11. Strauss, 1978, 273.
12. Quoted in Parker, 1992, 45.
13. Trevor-Roper [1969] 2001, 20–21.
14. Braudel, 1977, 66–67.
15. Although some authors actually remark that "everyone knows" what capitalism is; cf. Rosenberg and Birdzell, 1986, vi.
16. The orthodox Marxist definition is plain and simple: Capitalism exists where the actual producers are wage laborers who do not own their tools, and these, as well as the raw materials and finished products, are owned by their employer (see Sombart, 1902, as well as Hilton, 1952). Taken seriously, this definition would make capitalists out of all owners of small craft shops, such as potteries and metal smithies in ancient times. That seems especially odd since Marxists cling to their belief that capitalism first appeared during (and caused) the Industrial Revolution, a necessary assumption for those who accept Marx's theory of social change wherein all history rests on changes in modes of production. Thus, Marxists condemn all "talk about capitalism before the end of the eighteenth century" (Braudel, 1979, 2:238), equating capitalism with "the modern industrial system" (Gerschenron, 1970, 4). But, for those of us who associate capitalism with particular kinds of firms and markets, the Marxist definition is not useful.
17. Stark, 2005, 56.
18. For all of his fulminating about "wage slavery," Marx opened his study Pre-Capitalist Economic Formations with the statement that "one of the historic conditions for capital is free labour."
19. Little, 1978, 38.
20. Baldwin, 1959, 15.
21. Mumford, 1966, 266.
22. Collins, 1986, 47.
23. Ibid., 55.
24. Ibid., 52.
25. Hayes, 1917; Herlihy, 1961; Ozmont, 1975.
26. Dickens, 1991.
27. Little, 1978, 62.
28. Johnson, 2003, 144.
29. Gimpel, 1976, 47.
30. Gilchrist, 1969; Russell, 1958, 1972.
31. Little, 1978, 93.
32. Dawson, 1957, 63.
33. Duby, 1974, 218.
34. Little, 1978, 65.
35. Ibid.
36. Fryde, 1963, 441–43.
37. de Roover, 1948, 9.
38. Duby, 1974, 216.
39. Ibid., 91.
40. Ibid.
41. Gimpel, 1976, 47.
42. Mumford, 1967, 1:272.
43. Dawson, 1957; Hickey, 1987; King, 1999; Mayr-Harting, 1993; Stark, 2003b.
44. Collins, 1986, 54.
45. Benedict, Rule chapter 40, "The Daily Manual Labor."
46. Hilton, 1985, 3.
47. Friedrich Prinz, as translated by Kaelber, 1998, 66.
48. In Nelson, 1969, 11; also Little, 1978, 56–57.
49. Gilchrist, 1969, 107.
50. Nelson, 1969, 9.
51. Olsen, 1969, 53.
52. In his Commentary on the Sentences of Peter Lombard, quoted in de Roover, 1958, 422.
53. I have relied on the translations of Aquinas's Summa Theologica provided by Monroe, 1975.
54. Little, 1978, 181.
55. Gilchrist, 1969; Little, 1978; Raftus, 1958.
56. Gilchrist, 1969, 67.
57. Hunt and Murray, 1999, 73.
58. Dempsey, 1943, 155, 160.
59. de Roover, 1946, 154.
60. Little, 1978, 181.
61. Southern, 1970b, 40.
62. For a summary, see Stark 2003a.
63. Lopez, 1952, 289, 1976.
64. Gies and Gies, 1969.
65. de Roover, 1963, 75–76.
66. de Roover, 1963; Hunt, 1994; Lloyd, 1982.

Bibliography and Recommended Reading

Abou, Sèlim. 1997. *The Jesuit "Republic" of the Guaranis (1609–1768)*. New York: Crossroad Publishing Co.

Adams, Marilyn. 1987. *William of Ockham*. New York: Mariner Books.

Allen Charlotte. 1996. "The Search for the No-Frills Jesus: Q." *Atlantic Monthly*, December: 51–68.

———. 1998. *The Human Christ: The Search for the Historical Jesus*. New York: The Free Press.

Alroy, Gil Carl. 1975. *Behind the Middle East Conflict: The Real Impasse between Arabs and Jews*. New York: G. P. Putnam's Sons.

Andrea, A. J. 2003. "The Crusades in Perspective: The Crusades in Modern Islamic Perspective." *History Compass* 1: 1–4.

Armstrong, Karen. [1991] 2001. *Holy War: The Crusades and Their Impact on Today's World*. 2nd ed. New York: Random House.

Asbridge, Thomas. 2004. *The First Crusade: A New History*. Oxford: Oxford University Press.

Ashworth, John. 1992. "The Relationship between Capitalism and Humanitarianism." In *The Antislavery Debate: Capitalism and Abolitionism as a Problem of Historical Interpretation*, edited by Thomas Bender, 180–99. Berkeley: University of California Press.

Aston, Nigel. 2000. *Religion and Revolution in France, 1780–1804*. Washington, DC: Catholic University of America Press.

———. 2002. *Christianity and Revolutionary Europe, 1750–1830*. Cambridge: Cambridge University Press.

Athanassiadi, Polymnia. 1993. "Persecution and Response in Late Paganism: The Evidence of Damascius." *The Journal of Hellenic Studies* 113: 1–29.

Auping, John A. 1994. *Religion and Social Justice: The Case of Christianity and the Abolition of Slavery in America*. Mexico City: Universidad Iberoamericana.

Baillie, John. 1951. *The Belief in Progress*. New York: Charles Scribner's Sons.

Bainton, Roland. [1952] 1985. *The Reformation of the Sixteenth Century*. Boston: Beacon.

Baldwin, John W. 1959. *The Medieval Theories of the Just Price*. Philadelphia: The American Philosophical Society.

Barclay, Cycil Nelson, and Vice Adm. Brian Betham Schofield. 1981. "Gunnery." In *Encyclopaedia Britannica*, 488–98. Chicago: University of Chicago Press.

Barnes, Timothy D. 1995. "Statistics and the Conversion of the Roman Aristocracy." *Journal of Roman Studies* 85: 135–147.

Baron, Salo Wittmayer. 1957. *A Social and Religious History of the Jews*. Vols. 3, 4, and 5. New York: Columbia University Press.

Barrett, David B., and Todd M. Johnson. 2001. *World Christian Trends, AD 30–AD 2200*. Pasadena, CA: William Carey Library.

Beckles, Hilary. 1989. *White Servitude and Black Slavery in Barbados, 1627–1715.* Knoxville: University of Tennessee Press.

Beevor, Antony. 2006. *The Battle for Spain.* London: Penguin Books.

Bellitto, Christopher. 2004. *Introducing Nicholas of Cusa.* Mahwah, NJ: Paulist Press.

Bernhard, Roland. 2014. "Kolumbus end die Erdkugel." ["Columbus and the Globe"]. *Damals* 46: 45–46.

Beugnot, Arthur Auguste. 1835. *Histoire de la destruction du paganisme en Occident.* 2 vols. Paris: Firmin Didot Freres.

Blackburn, Robin. 1998. *The Making of New World Slavery.* London: Verso.

Blanshard, Paul. 1949. *American Freedom and Catholic Power.* Boston: Beacon Press.

Bloch, Herbert. 1963. "The Pagan Revival in the West at the End of the Fourth Century." In *The Conflict between Paganism and Christianity in the Fourth Century*, edited by Arnaldo Momigliano, 193–218. Oxford: Clarendon Press.

Bloch, Marc. 1975. *Slavery and Serfdom in the Middle Ages.* Berkeley: University of California Press.

Bock, Darrell L. 2006. *The Missing Gospels: Unearthing the Truth behind Alternative Christianities.* Nashville: Thomas Nelson.

Bolenius, Emma Miller. 1919. *The Boys' and Girls' Reader: Fifth Reader.* Boston: Houghton Mifflin.

Bonnassie, Pierre. 1991. *From Slavery to Feudalism in South-Western Europe.* Cambridge: Cambridge University Press.

Boorstin, Daniel J. 1983. *The Discoverers.* New York: Random House.

Bouwsma, William J. 1979. "The Renaissance and the Drama of Western History." *The American Historical Review* 84: 1–15.

Bowersock, Glen W. 1990. *Hellenism in Late Antiquity.* Ann Arbor: University of Michigan Press.

Boxer, Charles R. 1962. *The Golden Age of Brazil, 1695–1750.* Berkeley: University of California Press.

Bradbury, Scott. 1994. "Constantine and the Problem of Anti-Pagan Legislation in the Fourth Century." *Classical Philology* 89: 120–39.

Bradley, Walter I. 2001. "The 'Just So' Universe: The Fine-Tuning of Constants and Conditions in the Cosmos." In *Signs of Intelligence: Understanding Intelligent Design*, edited by William A. Demski and James M. Kushiner, 157–70. Grand Rapids: Brazos Press.

Braudel, Fernand. 1977. *Afterthoughts on Material Civilization and Capitalism.* Baltimore: Johns Hopkins University Press.

Brett, Stephen F. 1994. *Slavery and the Catholic Tradition.* New York: Peter Lang.

Bridges, John Henry. 1914. *The Life & Work of Roger Bacon.* London: Williams and Norgate.

Briggs, Robin. 1998. *Witches and Neighbors.* New York: Penguin Books.

Brøndsted, Johannes. 1965. *The Vikings.* Baltimore: Penguin Books.

Brooke, John, and Geoffrey Cantor. 1998. *Restructuring Nature.* Oxford: Oxford University Press.

Brown, Peter. 1992. *Power and Persuasion in Late Antiquity: Towards a Christian Empire.* Madison: University of Wisconsin Press.

————. 1995. *Authority and the Sacred: Aspects of the Christianization of the Roman World.* Cambridge: Cambridge University Press.

————. 1998. "Christianization and Religious Conflict." *Cambridge Ancient History* 13: 632–64.

Burckhardt, Jacob. [1860] 1990. *The Civilization of the Renaissance in Italy.* New York: Penguin.

Bury, J. B. 1914. *A History of Freedom of Thought.* London: Williams and Norgate.

Cantor, Norman F. 1993. *The Civilization of the Middle Ages.* Rev. ed. New York: HarperCollins.

Caraman, Philip. 1975. *The Lost Paradise: The Jesuit Republic in South America.* New York: Dorest Press.

Carroll, James. 2001. *Constantine's Sword: The Church and the Jews—A History.* Boston: Mariner Books.

———. 2004. *Crusade: Chronicles of an Unjust War*. New York: Metropolitan Books.

Chandler, Tertius. 1987. *Four Thousand Years of Urban Growth: An Historical Census*. Lewiston, NY: The Edward Mellen Press.

Chazan, Robert, ed. 1980. *Church, State, and Jew in the Middle Ages*. West Orange, NJ: Behrman House.

———. 1986. *European Jewry and the First Crusade*. Berkeley: University of California Press.

Cheetham, Nicholas. 1983. *Keeper of the Keys: A History of Popes from St. Peter to John Paul II*. New York: Scribner's.

Chejne, Anwar G. 1983. *Islam and the West: The Moriscos*. Albany: State University of New York Press.

Chuvin, Pierre. 1990. *A Chronicle of the Last Pagans*. Cambridge, MA: Harvard University Press.

Clegg, Brian. 2004. *The First Scientist: A Life of Roger Bacon*. Cambridge, MA: Da Capo Press.

Clough, Bradley S. 1997. "Buddhism." In *God*, edited by Jacob Neusner, 56–84. Cleveland: Pilgrim Press.

Cohen, I. Bernard. 1985. *Revolution in Science*. Cambridge, MA: Belknap Press.

Cohen, Mark. 1996. "Islam and the Jews: Myth, Counter-Myth, History." In *Jews among Muslims: Communities in the Precolonial Middle East*, edited by Shlomo Deshen and Walter P. Zenner, 50–63. London: Macmillan.

Colish, Marica L. 1997. *Medieval Foundations of the Western Intellectual Tradition, 400–1400*. New Haven, CT: Yale University Press.

Collins, Randall. 1986. *Weberian Sociological Theory*. Cambridge: Cambridge University Press.

Contreras, Jaime, and Gustave Henningsen. 1986. "Forty-four Thousand Cases of the Spanish Inquisition (1540–1700): Analysis of a Historical Data Bank." In *The Inquisition in Early Modern Europe: Studies on Sources and Methods*, edited by Gustav Henningsen and John Tedeschi, 100–129. DeKalb: Northern Illinois University Press.

Cornwell, John. 1999. *Hitler's Pope: The Secret History of Pius XII*. New York: Viking.

Coulton, C. G. [1938] 1959. *Inquisition and Liberty*. Boston: Beacon Hill.

Crombie, A. C. 1953. *Robert Grosseteste and the Origins of Experimental Science*. Oxford, England: Clarendon Press.

Crosby, Alfred W. 1997. *The Measure of Reality*. Cambridge: Cambridge University Press.

Curry, Andrew. 2002. "The Crusades, the First Holy War." *US News & World Report* 8 (April): 36.

Dales, Richard C. [1973] 1994. *The Scientific Achievement of the Middle Ages*. Philadelphia: University of Pennsylvania Press.

Dalin, David G. 2004. "Pius XII and the Jews." In *The Pius War*, edited by Joseph Bottum and David G. Dalin, 13–24. Lanham, MD: Lexington Books.

———. 2005. *The Myth of Hitler's Pope: How Pope Pius XII Rescued Jews from the Nazis*. Washington, DC: Regnery Publishing.

Daly, Mary. 1978. *Gyn/Ecology: The Metaethics of Feminism*. Boston: Beacon.

Daniel, Ralph Thomas. 1981. "Music, Western." In *Encyclopaedia Britannica*, 15: 704–15. Chicago: University of Chicago Press.

Danielson, Dennis. 2000. *The Book of the Cosmos*. Cambridge, MA: Perseus.

Davies, Norman. 1996. *Europe: A History*. Oxford: Oxford University Press.

Davis, David Brion. 1966. *The Problem of Slavery in Western Culture*. Ithaca, NY: Cornell University Press.

Dawkins, Richard. 2006. *The God Delusion*. Boston: Houghton Mifflin.

Dawson, J. M. 1957. *Separate Church & State Now*. New York: R. R. Smith.

Deane, Herbert A. 1973. "Classical and Christian Political Thought." *Political Theory* 1: 415–26.

Decter, Jonathan P. 2007. *Iberian Jewish Literature: Between al-Andalus and Christian Europe*. Bloomington: University of Indiana Press.

De la Croix, Horst, and Richard G. Tansey. 1975. *Gardiner's Art through the Ages* (6th ed.). New York: Harcourt Brace Jovanovich.

De la Cueva, Julio. 1998. "Religious Persecution, Anticlerical Tradition and Revolution: On Atrocities against the Clergy During the Spanish Civil War." *Journal of Contemporary History* 33: 355–69.

Delumeau, Jean. 1977. *Catholicism between Luther and Voltaire*. London: Burns & Oates.

Dempsey, Bernard W. 1943. *Interest and Usury*. Washington DC: American Council on Public Affairs.

De Roover, Raymond. 1948. *Money, Banking and Credit in Bruges*. Cambridge, MA: Medieval Academy of America.

———. 1958. "The Concept of the Just Price." *Journal of Economic History* 18: 418–34.

Dickens, A. G. 1991. *The English Reformation*. University Park: Pennsylvania State University Press

Doino, William, Jr. 2004. "An Annotated Bibliography of Works on Pius XII, the Second World War, and the Holocaust." In *The Pius War*, edited by Joseph Bottum and David G. Dalin, 97–280. Lanham, MD: Lexington Books.

Dowling, John. [1845] 2002. *The History of Romanism*. Lincolnshire, IL: Vance.

Doyle, William. 1989. *The Oxford History of the French Revolution*. Oxford: Oxford University Press.

Drake, H. A. 2000. *Constantine and the Bishops: The Politics of Intolerance*. Baltimore, MD: Johns Hopkins University Press.

Drake, Stillman, and C. D. O'Malley. 1960. *The Controversy of the Comets of 1618*. Philadelphia: University of Pennsylvania Press.

Drescher, Seymour, and Stanley L. Engerman, eds. 1998. *A Historical Guide to World Slavery*. New York: Oxford University Press.

Duby, Georges. 1974. *The Chivalrous Society*. Berkeley: University of California Press.

Duffy, Eamon. 1997. *Saints and Sinners: A History of Popes*. New Haven, CT: Yale University Press.

Dunn, Richard S. 1973. *Sugar and Slaves*. Chapel Hill: University of North Carolina Press.

Durant, Will. 1950. *The Age of Faith. The Story of Civilization: Part IV*. New York: Simon and Schuster.

Dworkin, Andrea. 1974. *Woman Hating: A Radical Look at Sexuality*. New York: Dutton.

Easton, Stewart C. 1952. *Roger Bacon and the Search for a Universal Science*. New York: Columbia University Press.

Edbury, Peter. 1999. "Warfare in the Latin East." In *Medieval Warfare: A History*, edited by Maurice Keen, 89–112. Oxford: Oxford University Press.

Ehrman, Bart D. 2003. *Lost Christianities: The Battles for Scripture and the Faiths We Never Knew*. Oxford: Oxford University Press.

———. 2006. *The Lost Gospel of Judas Iscariot: A New Look at Betrayer and Betrayed*. Oxford: Oxford University Press.

Einstein, Albert. 1987. *Letters to Solovine*. New York: Philosophical Library.

Ekeland, Robert B., Robert F. Hèbert, Robert Tollison, Gary M. Anderson, and Audrey B. Davidson. 1999. *Sacred Trust: The Medieval Church as an Economic Firm*. New York: Oxford University Press.

Elkins, Stanley M. [1959] 1976. *Slavery: A Problem in American Institutional and Intellectual Life*. Rev. 3rd ed. Chicago: University of Chicago Press.

Ellerbe, Helen. 1995. *The Dark Side of Christian History*. Windermere, FL: Morningstar and Lark.

Erdoes, Richard. 1988. *AD 1000: Living on the Brink of the Apocalypse*. New York: Harper and Row.

Evans, Craig A. 1993. "Faith and Polemic: The New Testament and First-Century Judaism." In *Anti-Semitism and Early Christianity*, edited by Craig A. Evans and Donald A. Hagner, 1–17. Minneapolis: Fortress Press.

Ewen, C. L'Estrange. 1929. *Witch Hunting and Witch Trials*. London: Kegan, Paul, Trench, Trübner.

Ferguson, Wallace K. 1939. "Humanist Views of the Renaissance." *American Historical Review* 45:1–28.

Fernandez, André. 1997. "The Repression of Sexual Behavior by the Aragonese Inquisition between 1560 and 1700." *Journal of the History of Sexuality* 7: 469–501.

Feuerbach, Ludwig. [1843] 1986. *Principles of the Philosophy of the Future*. Indianapolis: Hackett Publishing Co.

Findlen, Paul. 1993. "Humanism, Politics and Pornography in Renaissance Italy." In *The Invention of Pornography*, edited by Lynn Hunt, 49–108. Cambridge, MA: MIT. Press.

Finocchiaro, Maurice A. 2009. "Myth 8: That Galileo Was Imprisoned and Tortured for Advocating Copernicanism." In *Galileo Goes to Jail: And Other Myths About Science and Religion*, edited by Ronald L. Numbers, 68–78. Cambridge, MA: Harvard University Press.

Flannery, Edward H. 1985. *The Anguish of the Jews: Twenty-Three Centuries of Anti-Semitism*. Rev. ed. Mahwah, NJ: Paulist Press.

Fletcher, Philippa. 1995. "Inquiry Reveals Lenin Unleashed Systematic Murder of 200,000 Clergy." *Reuters*, November 29.

Fletcher, Richard. 1992. *Moorish Spain*. Berkeley: University of California Press.

———. 1997. *The Barbarian Conversion: From Paganism to Christianity*. New York: Henry Holt and Company.

Fogel, Robert William. 1989. *Without Consent or Contract: The Rise and Fall of American Slavery*. New York: W. W. Norton.

France, John. 1997. *Victory in the East*. Cambridge: Cambridge University Press.

Frend, W. H. C. 1965. *Martyrdom and Persecution in the Early Church*. Oxford: Basil Blackwell.

Fryde, E. B. 1963. "Chapter VII." In *The Cambridge Economic History of Europe*. Vol. 3: 430–553. Cambridge: Cambridge University Press.

Fisher, N. W., and Sabetai Unguru. 1971. "Experimental Science and Mathematics in Roger Bacon's Thought." *Traditio* 27: 353–78.

Funk, Robert W., Roy W. Hoover, and the Jesus Seminar. 1993. *The Five Gospels: The Search for the Authentic Words of Jesus*. New York: Macmillan.

Furneaux, Robin. 1969. *The Amazon: The Story of a Great River*. London: Hamilton.

Gager, John G. 1983. *The Origins of Anti-Semitism: Attitudes towards Judaism in Pagan and Christian Antiquity*. New York: Oxford University Press.

Galilei, Galileo. [1632] 1953. *Dialogue Concerning the Two Chief World Systems*. Berkeley: University of California Press.

Garay, Blas. [1900] 1965. "The Guarani Missions—A Ruthless Exploitation of the Indians." In *The Expulsion of the Jesuits from Latin America*, edited by Magnus Mörner, 63–78. New York: Knopf.

Gardner, Helen, and Sumner McK. Crosby. 1959. *Helen Gardner's Art through the Ages*. New York: Harcourt, Brace, & World.

Gatrell, V. A. C. 1994. *The Hanging Tree: Execution and the English People, 1770–1868*. Oxford: Oxford University Press.

Gay, Peter. 1966. *The Enlightenment: The Rise of Modern Paganism*. New York: W. W. Norton & Co.

———. 1969. *The Enlightenment: An Interpretation*. New York: W. W. Norton & Co.

Geffcken, Johannes. [1920] 1978. *The Last Days of Greco-Roman Paganism*. Amsterdam: North-Holland Publishing Co.

Genovese, Eugene D. 1974. *Roll, Jordan, Roll: The World the Slaves Made*. New York: Pantheon Books.

Gerber, Jane S. 1994. *The Jews of Spain*. New York: Free Press.

Gerschenkron, Alexander. 1970. *Europe in the Russian Mirror*. Cambridge: Cambridge University Press.

Gibbon, Edward. [1776–88] 1994. *The History of the Decline and Fall of the Roman Empire*. 3 Vols. London: Allen Lane.

Gidal, Nachum T. 1988. *Jews in Germany: From Roman Times to the Weimar Republic*. Cologne, Germany: Könemann.

Gies, Frances, and Joseph Gies. 1994. *Cathedral, Forge, and Waterwheel: Technology and Invention in the Middle Ages*. New York: HarperCollins.

Gilchrist, John. 1969. *The Church and Economic Activity in the Middle Ages*. New York: St. Martin's Press.

Gillingham, John. 1999. "An Age of Expansion: c. 1020–1204." In *Medieval Warfare: A History*, edited by Maurice Keen, 59–88. Oxford: Oxford University Press.

Gimpel, Jean. 1976. *The Medieval Machine: The Industrial Revolution of the Middle Ages*. New York: Penguin Books.

Gingerich, Owen. 1975. "'Crisis' Versus Aesthetic in the Copernican Revolution." *Vistas in Astronomy* 17: 85–93.

Given, James B. 1997. *Inquisition and Medieval Society: Power, Discipline, and Resistance in Languedoc*. Ithaca, NY: Cornell University Press.

Gliozzo, Charles A. 1971. "The Philosophes and Religion: Intellectual Origins of the Dechristianization Movement in the French Revolution." *Church History* 40: 273–83.

Glock, Charles Y., and Rodney Stark. 1966. *Christian Beliefs and Anti-Semitism*. New York: Harper & Row.

Godkin, Georgina Sarah. 1878. *Life of Victor Emmanuel II*. Vol. 1. London: Macmillan and Company.

Goiten, S. D. 1964. *Jews and Arabs: Their Contact through the Ages*. New York: Schocken Books.

Goldhagen, Daniel Jonah. 2002. *A Moral Reckoning: The Role of the Catholic Church in the Holocaust and Its Unfulfilled Duty to Repair*. New York: Knopf.

Goodish, Michael. 1976. "Sodomy in Medieval Secular Law." *Journal of Homosexuality* 1: 295–302.

Goodspeed, Edgar. 1931. *Strange New Gospels*. Chicago: University of Chicago Press.

Goveia, Elsa V. 1969. "The West Indian Slave Law of the Eighteenth Century." In *Slavery in the New World: A Reader in Comparative History*, edited by Laura Foner and Eugene D. Genovese, 113–37. Englewood Cliffs, NJ: Prentice-Hall.

Graetz, Heinrich Hirsh. 1894. *History of the Jews*. Vol. 3. Philadelphia: The Jewish Publication Society of America.

Graham, R. B. Cunninghame. 1901. *A Vanished Arcadia: Being Some Account of the Jesuits in Paraguay, 1607–1776*. London: Heinemann.

Grant, Edward. 1971. *Nicole Oresme and the Kinematics of Circular Motion*. Madison: University of Wisconsin Press.

———. 1996. *The Foundations of Modern Science in the Middle Ages: Their Religious, Institutional, and Intellectual Contexts*. Cambridge: Cambridge University Press.

———. 2007. *A History of Natural Philosophy: From the Ancient World to the Nineteenth Century*. Cambridge: Cambridge University Press.

Greeley, Andrew M. 1977. *An Ugly Little Secret: Anti-Catholicism in North America*. Kansas City, MO: Sheed, Andrews, and McMeel.

Greer, Donald. 1935. *The Incidence of the Terror during the French Revolution: A Statistical Interpretation*. Cambridge, MA: Harvard University Press.

Gribbin, John. 2005. *The Fellowship: Gilbert, Bacon, Harvey, Wren, Newton, and the Story of a Scientific Revolution*. New York: Overlook Press.

Grosser, Paul E., and Edwin G. Halperin. 1983. *Anti-Semitism: Causes and Effects. An Analysis and Chronology of Nineteen Hundred Years of Anti-Semitic Attitudes and Practices*. New York: Philosophical Library.

Haliczer, Stephen. 1990. *Inquisition and Society in the Kingdom of Valencia, 1487–1834*. Berkeley: University of California Press.

Hamilton, Bernard. 2000. *The Leper King & His Heirs*. Cambridge: Cambridge University Press.

Hanke, Lewis. 1951. *Bartolomé de las Casas: An Interpretation of His Life and Writings*. The Hague, Netherlands: M. Nijhoff.

Hare, Douglas R. A. [1967] 2005. *The Theme of Jewish Persecution of Christians in the Gospel According to Matthew*. Cambridge: Cambridge University Press.

Harl, K. W. 1990. "Sacrifice and Pagan Belief in Fifth- and Sixth-Century Byzantium." *Past and Present* 128: 7–27.

Harris, Marvin. 1963. *The Nature of Cultural Things*. New York: Random House.

———. 1964. *Patterns of Race in the Americas*. New York: Walker & Co.

Hartwell, Robert. 1971. "Historical Analogism, Public Policy, and Social Science in Eleventh- and Twelfth-Century China." *American Historical Review* 76: 690–727.

Haskins, Charles Homer. [1923] 2002. *The Rise of Universities*. New Brunswick, NJ: Transaction.

Hayes, Carlton J. 1917. *Political and Social History of Modern Europe*. 2 vols. New York: Macmillan.

Henningsen, Gustav. 1980. *The Witches Advocate: Basque Witchcraft and the Spanish Inquisition (1609–1614)*. Reno: University of Nevada Press.

Henningsen, Gustav, and John Tedeschi. 1986. *The Inquisition in Early Modern Europe: Studies on Sources and Methods*. DeKalb: Northern Illinois University Press.

Herlihy, David. 1957. "Church Property on the European Continent. 701–1200." *Speculum* 18: 89–113.

Hickey, Anne Ewing. 1987. *Women of the Roman Aristocracy in Christian Monastics*. Ann Arbor, MI: UMI Research Press.

Hillenbrand, Carole. 1999. *The Crusades: Islamic Perspectives*. Edinburgh: Edinburgh University Press.

Hilton, R. H. 1952. "Capitalism—What's in a Name?" *Past and Present*, 1: 32–43.

Hilton, Walter. 1985. *Toward a Perfect Love*. Portland, OR: Multnomah Press.

Hobbes, Thomas. [1651] 1956. *Leviathan*. Vol. 1. Chicago: Henry Regnery Company.

Hodgson, Marshall G. S. 1974. *The Venture of Islam: Conscience and History in a World Civilization*. 3 vols. Chicago: University of Chicago Press.

Holinshed, Raphael. [1587] 1965. *Holinshed's Chronicles*. New York: AMS.

Hollander, Paul. 1998. *Political Pilgrims*. 4th ed. New Brunswick, NJ: Transaction Publishers.

Hollister, C. Warren. 1992. "The Phases of European History and the Nonexistence of the Middle Ages." *Pacific Historical Review* 61: 1–22.

Hughes, Pennethorne. 1952. *Witchcraft*. London: Longmans, Green.

Hunt, Dave. 1994. *A Woman Rides the Beast: The Roman Catholic Church and the Last Days*. Eugene, OR: Harvest House.

Hurbon, Laennec. 1992. "The Church and Afro-American Slavery." In *The Church in Latin America*, edited by Enrique Dussel. Maryknoll, NY: Orbis Books.

Hyde, H. Montgomery. 1964. *A History of Pornography*. New York: Dell.

Hyslop, Theo B. 1925. *The Great Abnormals*. New York: Doran.

Irwin, Robert. 2006. *Dangerous Knowledge: Orientalism and Its Discontents*. Woodstock: Overlook Press.

Isaac, Jules. 1971. *Jesus and Israel*. New York: Holt, Rinehart, and Winston.

———. 1974. *The Teaching of Contempt: Christian Roots of Anti-Semitism*. New York: Holt, Rinehart, and Winston.

Issawi, Charles. 1957. "Crusades and Current Crisis in the Near East: A Historical Parallel." *International Affairs* 33: 269–79.

Jaki, Stanley L. 1986. *Science and Creation*. Edinburgh: Scottish Academic Press.

———. 2000. *The Savior of Science*. Grand Rapids: Eerdmans.

Jenkins, Philip. 2001. *Hidden Gospels: How the Search for Jesus Lost Its Way*. Oxford: Oxford University Press.

———. 2003. *The New Anti-Catholicism: The Last Acceptable Prejudice*. Oxford: Oxford University Press.

Johnson, Harry Hamilton. 1910. *The Negro in the New World*. London: Methuen & Co.

Johnson, Paul. 2003. *Art: A New History*. New York: HarperCollins.

Kaelber, Lutz. 1998. *Schools of Asceticism*. University Park: Pennsylvania State University Press.

Kamen, Henry. 1993. *The Spanish Inquisition: A Historical Revision*. London: Weidenfeld & Nicholson.

———. 1997. *The Phoenix and the Flame: Catalonia and the Counter Reformation*. New Haven, CT: Yale University Press.

Katz, Steven T. 1994. *The Holocaust in Historical Context*. Vol. 1. New York: Oxford University Press.

———. 1999. "The Rabbinic Response to Christianity." In *The Cambridge History of Judaism*, vol. 4., edited by Steven T. Katz, 259–98. Cambridge: Cambridge University Press.

Kayser, Rudolf. 1949. *The Life and Times of Jehudah Halevi*. New York: Philosophical Library.

Kearney, H. F. 1964. "Puritanism, Capitalism, and the Scientific Revolution." *Past & Present* 28: 81–101.

Kedar, Benjamin Z. 1984. *Crusade and Mission: European Approaches toward the Muslims*. Princeton, NJ: Princeton University Press.

Keefe, Donald J. 1986."Tracking a Footnote." *Catholic Scholars' Newsletter* 9: 4.

Kennedy, Emmet. 1989. *A Cultural History of the French Revolution*. New Haven, CT: Yale University Press.

King, Karen L. 2003a. *What Is Gnosticism?* Cambridge, MA: Belknap Press.

King, Peter. 1999. *Western Monasticism*. Kalamazoo, MI: Cistercian Publications.

———. 2003b. *The Gospel of Mary of Magdala: Jesus and the First Woman Apostle*. Santa Rosa, CA: Polebridge Press.

Kirsch, Jonathan. 2004. *The Grand Inquisitor's Manual*. San Francisco: HarperOne.

———. 2008. *God against the Gods*. New York: Viking.

Klein, Herbert S. 1967. *Slavery in the Americas: A Comparative Study of Virginia and Cuba*. Chicago: University of Chicago Press.

———. 1969. "Anglicanism, Catholicism, and the Negro Slave." In *Slavery in the New World: A Reader in Comparative History*, edited by Laura Foner and Eugene D. Genovese, 138–69. Englewood Cliffs, NJ: Prentice-Hall.

———. 1986. *African Slavery in Latin America and the Caribbean*. New York: Oxford University Press.

Knight, Margaret. 1974. *Honest to Man: Christian Ethics Re-examined*. Buffalo, NY: Prometheus Books.

Knobler, Adam. 2006. "Holy Wars, Empires, and the Portability of the Past: The Modern Uses of the Medieval Crusade." *Comparative Studies in Society and History* 48: 293–325.

Kocher, Paul H. 1953. *Science and Religion in Elizabethan England*. San Marino, CA: The Huntington Library.

Komoszewski, J., M. James Sawyer, and Daniel B. Wallace, eds. 2006. *Reinventing Jesus*. Grand Rapids: Kregel.

Kurzman, Dab. 2007. *A Special Mission: Hitler's Secret Plot to Seize the Vatican and Kidnap Pius the XII*. New York: Perseus Books.

Landes, David S. 1998. *The Wealth and Poverty of Nations*. New York: W. W. Norton & Company.

Lambert, Malcolm. 1992. *Medieval Heresy*. Oxford: Basil Blackwell.

LaMonte, John L. 1932. *Feudal Monarchy in the Latin Kingdom of Jerusalem, 1100–1291*. Cambridge, MA: Harvard University Press.

Lane, Frederic Chapin. [1934] 1992. *Venetian Ships and Shipbuilders of the Renaissance*. Baltimore, MD: Johns Hopkins University Press.

Latourette, Kenneth Scott. 1975. *A History of Christianity*. Vol. 2. Rev. ed. San Francisco: HarperSanFrancisco.

Layton, Bentley. 1987. *The Gnostic Scriptures*. Garden City, NY: Doubleday.

Lea, Henry C. 1906–7. *A History of the Inquisition in Spain*. 4 vols. New York: Macmillan.

Lecky, W. E. H. [1865] 1903. *History of the Rise and Influence of the Spirit of Rationalism in Europe*. New York: Appleton.

Leloup, Jean-Yves. 2002. *The Gospel of Mary Magdalene*. Rochester, VT: Inner Traditions.

Levack, Brian P. 1995. *The Witch-Hunt in Early Modern Europe*. 2nd ed. London: Longman.

Levenson, David B. 1990. "Julian." In *Encyclopedia of Early Christianity*, edited by Everett Ferguson, 510–11. New York: Garland.

Lewis, Bernard. 2002. *What Went Wrong?* Oxford: Oxford University Press.

Lindberg, David C. 1978. *Science in the Middle Ages*. Chicago: University of Chicago Press.

———. 1986. "Science and the Early Church." In *God and Nature: Historical Essays on the Encounter between Christianity and Science*, edited by David C. Lindberg and Ronald L. Numbers, 19–48. Berkeley: University of California Press.

———. 1992. *The Beginnings of Western Science*. Chicago: University of Chicago Press.

Lindberg, David C., and Ronald L. Numbers, eds. 1986. *God and Nature: Historical Essays on the Encounter between Christianity and Science*. Berkeley: University of California Press.

Little, Lester K. 1978. *Religious Poverty and the Profit Economy in Medieval Europe*. Ithaca, NY: Cornell University Press.

Llorente, Juan Antonio. [1823] 1967. *A Critical History of the Inquisition of Spain*. Williams-town, MA: John Lilburne.

Lopez, Robert S. 1967. *The Birth of Europe*. New York: M. Evans and Company.

———. 1976. *The Commercial Revolution of the Middle Ages, 950–1350*. Cambridge: Cambridge University Press.

———. 1977. "The Practical Transmission of Medieval Culture." In *By Things Seen: Reference and Recognition in Medieval Thought*, edited by David Lyle Jeffrey, 125–42. Ottawa: University of Ottawa Press.

MacCulloch, Diarmaid. 2010. "Evil Is Just." *London Review of Books* 32 (May 13): 23–24.

Mack, Burton. 1993. *The Lost Gospel: The Book of Q and Christian Origins*. New York: HarperCollins.

MacMullen, Ramsay. 1997. *Christianity and Paganism in the Fourth to Eighth Centuries*. New Haven, CT: Yale University Press.

Macmurray, John. 1938. *The Clue to History*. London: Student Christian Movement.

Madariaga, Salvador [1948] 1965. "The Fall of the Jesuits—The Triumph of the Philosophers." In *The Expulsion of the Jesuits from Latin America*, edited by Magnus Mörner, 33–52. New York: Knopf.

Madden, Thomas F. 1999. *A Concise History of the Crusades*. Lanham, MD: Rowman & Littlefield.

———. 2002a. "The Crusades in the Checkout Aisle." *Crisis Magazine* (April 12).

———. 2002b. "The Real History of the Crusades." *Crisis Magazine* (April 1).

———. 2003. "The Truth about the Spanish Inquisition." *Crisis Magazine* (October): 24–30.

Magnus, Shulamit S. 1997. *Jewish Emancipation in a German City, Cologne, 1798–1871*. Stanford, CA: Stanford University Press.

Maltby, William S. 1971. *The Black Legend in England: The Development of Anti-Spanish Sentiment, 1558–1660*. Durham, NC: Duke University Press.

Manchester, William. 1993. *World Lit Only by Fire: The Medieval Mind and the Renaissance*. New York: Little, Brown and Company.

Mann, Vivian B. 1992. "Preface." In *Convivencia: Jews, Muslims, and Christians in Medieval Spain*, edited by Vivian B. Mann, Thomas G. Glock, and Jerrilyn D. Dodds. New York: George Braziller.

Marchione, Margherita. 2002. *Consensus and Controversy: Defending Pope Pius XII*. New York: Paulist Press.

Marty, Martin E. 1993. "Churches as Winners, Losers." *Christian Century* 110, no. 3 (January 27): 88.

Mason, Stephen F. 1962. *A History of the Sciences*. Rev. ed. New York: Macmillan.

Massa, Mark S. 2003. *Anti-Catholicism in America: The Last Acceptable Prejudice*. New York: Crossroad.

Mathieson, William Law. 1926. *British Slavery and Its Abolition*. London: Longmans, Green & Co.

Mattingly, Garrett. 1959. *The Armada*. Boston: HoughtonMifflin.

Maxwell, John Francis. 1975. *The History of the Catholic Teaching Concerning the Moral Legitimacy of the Institution of Slavery*. London: Barry Rose Publishers.

Mayer, Hans Eberhard. 1972. *The Crusades*. Oxford: Oxford University Press.

Mayr-Harting, Henry. 1993. "The West: The Age of Conversion (700–1050). In John Mac-Manners, ed., *The Oxford History of Christianity*, 101–29. Oxford: Oxford University Press.

McCloskey, Deirdre N. 2010. *Bourgeois Dignity: Why Economics Can't Explain the Modern World*. Chicago: University of Chicago Press.

McBrien, Richard P. 2000. *Lives of Popes*. San Francisco: HarperSanFrancisco.

McGreevy, John T. 1997. "Thinking in One's Own: Catholicism in the American Imagination, 1928–1960." *Journal of American History* 84: 97–131.

Meeks, Wayne. 1983. *The First Urban Christians*. New Haven, CT: Yale University Press.

Meltzer, Milton. 1993. *Slavery: A World History*. New York: Da Capo Press.

Merton, Robert K. 1938. "Science, Technology and Society in Seventeenth-Century England." *Osiris* 4 (part 2): 360–632.

Meyer, Marvin. 2005. *The Gnostic Discoveries*. San Francisco: HarperSanFrancisco.

Momigliano, Arnoldo, ed. 1963. *The Conflict between Paganism and Christianity in the Fourth Century*. Oxford: Clarendon Press.

Mommsen, Theodore E. 1942. "Petrarch's Conception of the 'Dark Ages.'" *Speculum* 17: 226–42.

Monter, E. William. 1990. *Frontiers of Heresy: The Spanish Inquisition from the Basque Lands to Sicily*. Cambridge: Cambridge University Press.

Monter, E. William, and John Tedeschi. 1986. "Towards a Statistical Profile of Italian Inquisitions, Sixteenth to Eighteenth Centuries." In *The Inquisition in Early Modern Europe: Studies on Sources and Methods*, edited by Gustav Henningsen and John Tedeschi, 130–57. DeKalb: Northern Illinois University Press.

Montgomery, Field-Marshall Viscount (Bernard). 1968. *A History of Warfare*. New York: World.

Moore, R. I. 1976. *The Birth of Popular Heresy*. New York: St. Martin's Press.

———. 1985. *The Origins of European Dissent*. Oxford: Basil Blackwell.

Mörner, Magnus. 1965. *The Expulsion of the Jesuits from Latin America*. New York: Knopf.

Mumford, Lewis. 1966. *The Myth of the Machine*. New York: Harcourt Brace.

Needham, Joseph. 1954–84. *Science and Civilization in China*. 6 vols. Cambridge: Cambridge University Press.

———. 1980. "The Guns of Khaifeng-fu." *Times Literary Supplement* (January 11).

Nelson, Benjamin. 1969. *The Idea of Usury*. 2nd ed. Chicago: University of Chicago Press.

Netanyahu, B. 2001. *The Origins of the Inquisition in Fifteenth-Century Spain*. 2nd ed. New York: New York Review of Books.

Nisbet, Robert. 1980. *History of the Idea of Progress*. New York: Basic Books.

Nock, A. D. 1933. *Conversion: The Old and New in Religion from Alexander to the Great Augustine of Hippo*. Oxford: Clarendon Press.

Noonan, John T., Jr. 1993. "The Development of Moral Doctrine." *Theological Studies* 54: 666–77.

Nordstrom, Justin. 2006. *Danger on the Doorstep: Anti-Catholicism and American Print Culture in the Progressive Era*. Notre Dame, IN: University of Notre Dame Press.

Oberman, Heiko A. 1992. *Luther: Man between God and the Devil*. New York: Doubleday.

O'Donovan, Oliver, and Joan Lockwood O'Donovan, eds. 1999. *A Sourcebook in Christian Political Thought*. Grand Rapids: Eerdmans.

O'Neil, Mary R. 1987. "Magical Healing, Love Magic and the Inquisition in Late-Sixteenth-Century Modena." In *Inquisition and Society in Early Modern Europe*, edited by Stephen Haliczer, 88–114. London: Croom Helm.

Orti, Vincente Cárcel. 2008. *Pio XI entre la República y Franco*. Barcelona: Biblioteca Autoores Christianos.

Osborn, Robert T. 1985. "The Christian Blasphemy." *Journal of the American Academy of Religion* 53: 339–63.

Ozment, Steven. 1975. *The Reformation in the Cities*. New Haven, CT: Yale University Press.

———. 1980. *The Age of Reform 1250–1550: An Intellectual and Religious History of Late Medieval and Reformation Europe*. New Haven, CT: Yale University Press.

Pagels, Elaine. 1979. *The Gnostic Gospels*. New York: Random House.

———. 2003. *Beyond Belief: The Secret Gospel of Thomas*. New York: Random House.

Pagels, Elaine, and Karen L. King. 2007. *Reading Judas: The Gospel of Judas and the Shaping of Christianity*. New York: Viking.

Panaccio, Claude. 2004. *Ockham on Concepts*. Aldershot, England: Ashgate.

Panzer, Joel S. 1996. *The Popes and Slavery*. New York: Alba House.

Paris, Edmond. 1961. *Genocide in Satellite Croatia, 1941–1954*. Chicago: American Institute for Balkan Affairs.

Parker, Goffrey. 1992. "Success and Failure during the First Century of the Reformation." *Past and Present* 136: 43–82.

Parkes, James. 1934. *The Conflict of the Church and the Synagogue*. London: Soncino Press.

Parsons, Talcott. 1940, "Memorandum for the Council on Democracy," Box 2, Parsons Papers.

Payne, Robert. [1959] 1995. *The History of Islam*. New York: Barnes & Noble.

———. 1984. *The Dream and the Tomb: A History of the Crusades*. New York: Stein & Day.

Perez, Joseph. 2005. *The Spanish Inquisition: A History*. New Haven, CT: Yale University Press.

Peris, Daniel. 1998. *Storming the Heavens: The Soviet League of the Militant Godless*. Ithaca, NY: Cornell University Press.

Perkins, Pheme. 1980. *The Gnostic Dialogue*. New York: Paulist Press.

———. 1990. "Gnosticism." In *Encyclopedia of Early Christianity*, edited by Everett Ferhuson, 317–76. New York: Garland.

Pernoud, Régine. 2000. *Those Terrible Middle Ages: Debunking the Myths*. San Francisco: Ignatius Press.

Peters, Edward. 1989. *Inquisition*. Berkeley: University of California Press.

———. 1995. "Jewish History and Gentile Memory: The Expulsion of 1492." *Jewish History* 8: 9–34.

———. 2003 "The *Firanj* Are Coming—Again." *Orbis* (Winter): 3–17.

Phillips, Jonathan. 1995. "The Latin East 1098–1291." In *The Oxford Illustrated History of the Crusades*, edited by Jonathan Riley-Smith, 112–40. Oxford: Oxford University Press.

Poewe, Karla. 2005. *New Religions and the Nazis*. New York: Routledge.

Poliakov, Léon. 1965. *The History of Anti-Semitism: From the Time of Christ to the Court Jews*. Vol. 1. New York: Vanguard Press.

Porter, Roy. 1998. *The Greatest Benefit to Mankind: A Medical History of Humanity*. New York: W. W. Norton.

Pospielovsky, Dimitry V. 1987. *A History of Soviet Atheism in Theory, and Practice, and the Believer*. New York: St. Martin's Press.

Prawer, Joshua. 1972. *The Crusaders' Kingdom: European Colonialism in the Middle Ages*. New York: Praeger.

Preston, Paul. 2013. *The Spanish Holocaust*. New York: W. W. Norton.

Purkiss, Diane. 1996. *The Witch in History*. London: Routledge.

Rabb, Theodore K. 1965. "Religion and the Rise of Modern Science." *Past and Present* 31: 111–26.

Raftus, J. A. 1958. "The Concept of the Just Price." *Journal of Economic History* 18: 435–37.

Rahner, Karl. 1975. *Encyclopedia of Theology*. New York: Seabury Press.
Rashdall, Hastings. [1936] 1977. *The Universities of Europe in the Middle Ages*. 3 vols. Oxford: Oxford University Press.
Rawlings, Helen. 2006. *The Spanish Inquisition*. Oxford: Blackwell.
Read, Piers Paul. 1999. *The Templars*. New York: St. Martin's Press.
Redman, Ben Ray. 1949. *The Portable Voltaire*. New York: Penguin Books.
Richard, Jean. 1999. *The Crusades, c. 1071–c. 1291*. Cambridge: Cambridge University Press.
Riley-Smith, Jonathan. 1973. *The Feudal Nobility and the Kingdom of Jerusalem, 1174–1277*. New York: Macmillan.
———. 1986. *The First Crusade and the Idea of Crusading*. Philadelphia: University of Pennsylvania Press.
———. 1997. *The First Crusaders, 1095–1131*. Cambridge, England: Cambridge University Press.
———. 2003. "Islam and the Crusades in History and Imagination, 8 November 1898–11 September 2001." *Crusades* 2: 151–67.
———, ed. 1995. *The Oxford Illustrated History of the Crusades*. Oxford: Oxford University Press.
Robbins, Rossell Hope. 1959. *The Encyclopedia of Witchcraft and Demonology*. New York: Crown.
Robertson, John M. 1902. *A Short History of Christianity*. London: Watts & Co.
Rosen, Edward. 1971. *Three Copernican Treatises*. 3rd ed. New York: Octagon Books.
Rosenberg, Nathan, and L. E. Birdzell Jr. 1986. *How the West Grew Rich*. New York: Basic Books.
Roth, Cecil. [1964] 1996. *The Spanish Inquisition*. New York: Norton.
Roth, Norman. 2002. *Conversos, Inquisition, and the Expulsion of the Jews from Spain*. Madison: University of Wisconsin Press.
Rudolph, Kurt. 1987. *Gnosis: The Nature and History of Gnosticism*. San Francisco: HarperSanFrancisco.
Ruether, Rosemary Radford. 1974. *Faith and Fratricide: The Theological Roots of Anti-Semitism*. New York: Seabury Press.
———. 1998. *Women and Redemption*. Minneapolis: Fortress Press.
Runciman, Steven. 1951. *A History of the Crusades*. 3 vols. Cambridge: Cambridge University Press.
Russell, Bertrand. 1959. *Wisdom of the West*. New York: Doubleday.
Russell, Jeffrey Burton. 1965. *Dissent and Reform in the Early Middle Ages*. Berkeley: University of California Press.
———. 1971. *Religious Dissent in the Middle Ages*. New York: Wiley.
———. 1997. *Inventing the Flat Earth: Columbus and Modern Historians*. Westport, CT: Praeger.
Russell, Josiah Cox. 1958. *Late Ancient and Medieval Populations*. Transactions of the American Philosophical Society 48:3: 3–152.
———. 1972. *Medieval Regions and Their Cities*. Newton Abbot (UK): David & Charles.
Rychlak, Ronald J. 2000. *Hitler, the War, and the Pope*. Huntington, IN: Our Sunday Visitor.
Sagan, Carl. 1996. *The Demon-Haunted World*. New York: Ballantine Books.
Salzman, Michael. 1990. *On Roman Time: The Codex-Calendar of 354*. Berkeley: University of California Press.
Sampson, Philip J. 2001. *6 Modern Myths about Christianity & Western Civilization*. Downers Grove, IL: InterVarsity Press.
Sánchez, José. 1987. *The Spanish Civil War as a Religious Tragedy*. Notre Dame, IN: University of Notre Dame Press.
Sanders, J. T. 1987. *The Jews in Luke-Acts*. Philadelphia: Fortress Press.
Scarano, Francisco A. 1998. "Spanish Caribbean." In Dresher and Engerman, 137–42.
Schachner, Nathan. 1938. *The Medieval Universities*. New York: Frederick A. Stokes.

Schafer, Judith Kelleher. 1994. *Slavery, the Civil Laws, and the Supreme Court of Louisiana.* Baton Rouge: Louisiana State University Press.

Schäfer, Peter. 1997. *Judeophobia: Attitudes towards the Jews in the Ancient World.* Cambridge, MA: Harvard University Press.

———. 2007. *Jesus in the Talmud.* Princeton, NJ: Princeton University Press.

Seaver, James Everett. 1952. *Persecution of the Jews in the Roman Empire (300–428).* Lawrence: University of Kansas Press.

Seznec, Jean. 1972. *The Survival of the Pagan Gods.* Princeton, NJ: Princeton University Press.

Shapin, Steven. 1996. *The Scientific Revolution.* Chicago: University of Chicago Press.

Shapiro, Barbara J. 1968. "Latitudinarism and Science in Seventeenth-Century England." *Past and Present* 40: 16–41.

Shea, William R. 1986. "Galileo and the Church." In *God and Nature: Historical Essays on the Encounter between Christianity and Science,* edited by David C. Lindberg and Ronald L. Numbers, 114–35. Berkeley: University of California Press.

Sheridan, Richard B. 1974. *Sugar and Slavery: An Economic History of the British West Indies, 1623–1775.* Aylesbury, England: Ginn and Company.

Shirer, William L. [1960] 1990. *The Rise and Fall of the Third Reich.* New York: Simon and Schuster.

Siberry, Elizabeth. 1995. "Images of the Crusades in the Nineteenth and Twentieth Centuries." In *The Oxford Illustrated History of the Crusades,* edited by Jonathan Riley-Smith, 365–85. Oxford: Oxford University Press.

Sivan, Emmanuel. 1973. *Modern Arab Historiography of the Crusades.* Tel Aviv: Tel Aviv University, Shiloah Center for Middle Eastern and African Studies.

Smallwood, E. Mary. 1981. *The Jews under Roman Rule: From Pompey to Diocletian.* Reprint with corrections. Leiden: E. J. Brill.

———. 1999. "The Diaspora in the Roman Period before CE 70." In *The Cambridge History of Judaism,* vol. 3, edited by William Horbury, W. D. Davies, and John Sturdy, 168–91. Cambridge: Cambridge University Press.

Sombart, Werner. 1902. *Der modern Kapitalismas.* Leipzig: Duncker & Humblot.

Sontag, Susan. 1964. *Against Interpretation.* New York: Farrar, Straus, Giroux.

Southern, R. W. 1970a. *Medieval Humanism and Other Studies.* New York: Harper Torchbooks.

———. 1970b. *Western Society and the Church in the Middle Ages.* London: Penguin Books.

Spielvogel, Jackson J. 2000. *Western Civilization.* 4th ed. Belmont, CA: Wadsworth.

Stark, Rodney. 1996. *The Rise of Christianity.* Princeton, NJ; Princeton University Press.

———. 2001. *One True God: Historical Consequences of Monotheism.* Princeton, NJ: Princeton University Press.

———. 2003a. *For the Glory of God: How Monotheism Led to Reformations, Science, Witch-Hunts, and the End of Slavery.* Princeton, NJ: Princeton University Press.

———. 2003b. "Upper-Class Asceticism: Social Origins of Ascetic Movements and Medieval Saints." *Review of Religious Research* 45: 5–19.

———. 2004. *Exploring the Religious Life.* Baltimore, MD: Johns Hopkins University Press.

———. 2005. *The Victory of Reason: How Christianity Led to Freedom, Capitalism, and Western Success.* New York: Random House.

———. 2006. *Cities of God.* San Francisco: HarperSanFrancisco.

———. 2007. *Discovering God: A New Look at the Origins of the Great Religions and the Evolution of Belief.* San Francisco: HarperOne.

Stone, Lawrence. 1964. "The Educational Revolution in England, 1560–1640." *Past & Present* 28: 41–80.

———. 1972. *The Causes of the English Revolution.* New York: Harper & Row.

Strauss, Gerald. 1975. "Success and Failure in the German Reformation." *Past and Present* 67: 30–63.

———. 1978. *Luther's House of Learning.* Baltimore, MD: Johns Hopkins University Press.

Sweet, William Warren. 1939. *Religion on the American Frontier, 1783–1850: The Congregationalists*. Chicago: University of Chicago Press.

Tallett, Frank. 1991. "Dechristianizing France: The Year II and the Revolutionary Experience." In *Religion, Society and Politics in France Since 1789*, edited by Frank Tallett and Nicholas Atkin, 1–28. London: Hambledon Press.

Tannenbaum, Frank. [1946] 1992. *Slave and Citizen*. Boston: Beacon Press.

Thomas, Hugh. 1977. *The Spanish Civil War*. Rev. ed. New York: Harper & Row.

———. 1997. *The Slave Trade*. New York: Simon and Schuster.

Thomas, Keith. 1971. *Religion and the Decline of Magic*. New York: Charles Scribner's Sons.

Trethowan, W. H. 1963. "The Demonopathology of Impotence." *British Journal of Psychiatry* 109: 341–47.

Trevor-Roper, H. R. [1969] 2001. *The Crisis of the Seventeenth Century: Religion, the Reformation, and Social Change*. Indianapolis, IN: Liberty Fund.

Turley, David. 2000. *Slavery*. Oxford: Blackwell.

Tyerman, Christopher. 2006. *God's War: A New History of the Crusades*. Cambridge, MA: Belknap Press.

Watson, Alan. 1989. *Slave Law in the Americas*. Athens: University of Georgia Press.

Weber, Max. 1904–05. *The Protestant Ethic and the Spirit of Capitalism*. New York: Scribner.

Wells, Peter S. 2008. *Barbarians to Angels: The Dark Ages Reconsidered*. New York: W. W. Norton.

White, Lynn, Jr. 1940. "Technology and Invention in the Middle Ages." *Speculum* 15: 141–56.

———. 1962. *Medieval Technology and Social Change*. Oxford: Oxford University Press.

Whitechapel, Simon. 2002. *Flesh Inferno: Atrocities of Torquemada and the Spanish Inquisition*. New York: Creation Books.

Whitehead, Alfred North. [1925] 1967. *Science and the Modern World*. New York: Free Press.

———. [1929] 1979. *Process and Reality*. New York: Free Press.

Wilken, Robert L. 1983. *John Chrysostom and the Jews: Rhetoric and Reality in the Late Fourth Century*. Berkeley: University of California Press.

Williams, Arthur Lukyn. 1935. *Adversus Judaeos*. Cambridge: Cambridge University Press.

Williams, Michael Allen. 1996. *Rethinking "Gnosticism": An Argument for Dismantling a Dubious Category*. Princeton, NJ: Princeton University Press.

Witherington, Ben, III. 2006. *What Have They Done with Jesus?* San Francisco: Harper SanFrancisco.

Wright, N. T. 2003. *The Resurrection of the Son of God*. Minneapolis: Fortress Press.

———. 2006. *Judas and the Gospel of Jesus*. Grand Rapids: Baker Books.

Yakovlev, Alexander N. 2002. *A Century of Violence in Soviet Russia*. New Haven, CT: Yale University Press.

Yamaki, Kazuhiko. 2001. *Nicholas of Cusa: A Medieval Thinker for a Modern Age*. New York: Routledge.

Ziegler, Philip. 1971. *The Black Death*. New York: Harper Torchbooks.

Zuccotti, Susan. 2002. *Under His Very Windows: The Vatican and the Holocaust in Italy*. New Haven, CT: Yale University Press.

.

Illustration Creditss

Introduction—Credit: *Spanish Hunting Indians* / British Library, London, UK / © British Library Board. All Rights Reserved / Bridgeman Images.

Chapter 1—Credit: Adolf Hitler 1889–1945. German politician and the leader of the Nazi Party with the Vatican ambassador / Universal History Archive / UIG / Bridgeman Images.

Chapter 2—Credit: *Beginning of the Gospel of Thomas*, Nag Hammadi Codex II, c. 350 AD (ink on papyrus), Egyptian (4th century AD) / Coptic Museum, Cairo, Egypt / Photo © Zev Radovan / Bridgeman Images.

Chapter 3—Credit: Giovanni d'Alemagna, *Saint Apollonia Destroys a Pagan Idol*, c. 1442/1445, Tempera on panel, 59.4 x 34.7 cm (23 3/8 x 13 11/16 in.). National Gallery of Art, Washington, DC, Samuel H. Kress Collection / Image courtesy of the Board of Trustees, National Gallery of Art.

Chapter 4—Credit: *Monks in Prayer*, detail from Transit of St Nicholas, scene from *Stories of St Nicholas of Tolentino*, 1320–1325, by unknown artist, fresco, Chapel of St Nicholas, Basilica of Saint Nicolas of Tolentino, Tolentino. Italy, 14th century. / De Agostini Picture Library / A. Dagli Orti / Bridgeman Images.

Chapter 5—Credit: *The Four Leaders of the First Crusade* (engraving), French School (19th century) / Private Collection / © Look and Learn / Bridgeman Images.

Chapter 6—Credit: *Third Degree of Torture of the Inquisition*, engraved by L. C. Stadler, pub. by Cadell & Davies, London, c. 1813 (coloured engraving), English School (19th century) / Private Collection / Stapleton Collection / Bridgeman Images.

Chapter 7—Credit: *Italian Astronomer, Philosopher and Physicist Galileo Galilei in Prison for His Scientific Creed*, circa 1620. Original Publication: People Disc–HD0131. (Photo by Hulton Archive / Getty Images)

Chapter 8—Credit: *Priest with a Spanish Servant Boy and Slave* (coloured engraving), French School (16th century) / Bibliotheque Nationale, Paris, France / Bridgeman Images.

Chapter 9—Credit: *Generalissimo Franco (L) Paying a Formal Visit to Papal Legate Tedeschini.* Photo by Dmitri Kessel / LIFE Picture Collection / Getty Images.

Chapter 10—Credit: *Luther Nailing his 'Theses' to the Door of the Schloss-Kirk at Wittemberg*, illustration from 'The History of Protestantism' by James Aitken Wylie (1808–90), pub. 1878 (engraving), English School (19th century) / Private Collection / Stapleton Collection / Bridgeman Images.

Index

~~~~~~

Cicero, Marcus Tullius, 12
City of God (Augustine), 191–92
Clement IV (pope), 23, 145
Clement of Alexandria, 89
Clermont (southern Gaul), 18
Cloots, Anacharsis, 194, 198
Clovis II (king), 82
Code Noir
  misrepresentation modern historians
    by, 174–76, 178
  slave conditions moderation of, 174–80
  slave protections in, 175–76
Code of Justinian, 55
Código Negro Español
  as more humane than *Code Noir*, 176
  slave conditions moderation of, 174,
    176–80
  slave protections and rights in, 174,
    176–77
Cohen, I. Bernard, 151
Colbert, Jean-Baptiste, 175
Collins, Randall, 214–15, 217, 221
Cologne, 21
Columbus, Christopher, 233n2
  biography of, 2
  myth about voyage of, 2, 6
  opposition to, 1–2
  voyage of, 1
Comnenus, Alexius (emperor of
  Byzantium), 99
Constantine (emperor)
  Christianity rapid growth under, 53
  Christianity support of, 57, 73
  Christo-pagan culture under, 60, 66
  Edict to the Eastern Provincials by, 59
  Edict to the Palestinians by, 59
  no pagan protest against, 57, 235n18
  pagans appointed to political office by,
    57, 58
  peaceful pluralism emphasized by, 59
  tolerance during reign of, 55
*Constantine's Sword: The Church and the
  Jews–A History* (Carroll), 32–33
Constantinius (emperor), 66, 67
conversion. *See* baptism
Copernicus, Nicholaus
  on heliocentric model, 150–51
  *On the Revolutions of the Heavenly
    Spheres* by, 151
  on sun as center of solar system, 144–
    45, 150–51
Córdoba, 25
Corinthians, First, 7, 48

Cornwell, John
  as alienated Catholic, 3
  *Hitler's Pope: The Secret History of Pius
    XII* by, 31–32
Council of Trent, 228
Counter Reformation. *See* Catholic
  Reformation
Creation story, 45–46
the Crucifixion, 9
crusader kingdoms, 105–9
Crusader "War Crimes," 109–12
Crusades, 95
  anti-Semitic violence during, 19–23
  Christian holy places destroyed before,
    97–98
  Christian pilgrims violence against,
    97–98
  as conquests for colonies, 96, 236n1
  crusader kingdoms, 105–8
  as defensive response by Europe, 97
  as enormous monetary cost to nobil-
    ity, 101
  ethnic cleansing compared to, 94
  first, 19–22
  historians refuting negative claims
    about, 96
  historical misconceptions summary of,
    114–15
  Hitler compared to, 94
  Jerusalem pilgrimage common before,
    98, 104
  knights need for penance during, 102–4
  massacres by Christians and Muslims
    during, 109–12
  modern Christian apologies for, 93–94,
    236n6
  motives for, 102–5
  Muslim anger about, 114
  Muslim interest beginning in, 113
  pope speech inspiration for, 99–100
  religious threats perceived during,
    19–20
  as roots of modern Muslim hostility,
    93–94
  second, 22–23
  tolerance for pilgrims ending before,
    97–98

The Da Vinci Code, 51
Dalin, David G. (rabbi), 28, 32
Dampier, William, 136
the Dark Ages
  Age of Faith known as, 73

the Dark Ages (*continued*)
Age of Reason began during, 88–91
agricultural progress during, 77, 80
causes of progress during, 88–91
Christianization of slaves during, 82
commercial development during, 77
as concept to discredit Christianity, 153
after the fall of Rome, 4
high culture progress during, 83–86
intermarriage with slaves during, 82
manufacturing developments during, 76, 77
military development of, 77, 80–81
moral progress during, 81–83
myth of, 73–91
progress in many fields during, 77–85
reasons for myth of, 76–77
slavery abolished during, 81–83
technology development during, 77–81
theology, reason, and progress in, 88–91
transportation progress during, 77
vast trade networks during, 76
Western history as second era of, 75
Davis, David Brion
on "political correctness" sensitivity, 178
The Problem of Slavery in Western Culture by, 174
slavery conditions no distinctions with, 176–79
Dawkins, Richard, 167
Dawson, Christopher, 218
democracy, 187
The Deputy (Hochhuth), 30–31
Descartes, Rene
on natural laws, 160
as recognizing Scholastic roots, 91
Deuteronomy, 23:19-20, 223
Dewey, John, 187
dhimmis, Muslim discrimination of, 26
Dialogue Concerning the Two Chief World Systems (Galileo), 165
Diderot, Denis, 95, 194
Didymus Jude Thomas. *See also The Secret Gospel of Thomas*
as twin brother of Jesus, 39, 49
Dio, Cassius, 13
The Discoverers (Boorstin), 73
A Discovery and Plaine Declaration of Sundry Subtill Practices of the Holy Inquisition of Spain (Montanus), 117–18

discrimination, 34
against Catholics in college, 2
against Jews, 24, 26
dissection public, 142–43
distinguished bigots, 3
distortions, 174–80
of Catholic Church history, 5
divine right, of kings, 5, 187, 188, 192
Dodds, E. R., 71
Domesday Book, 78
Domitian (emperor), 12–13
d'Oresme, Nichole
on discovering natural laws of God, 160
earth rotation on axis by, 149
Dostoyevesky, Fyodor, 118
Dowling, John, 122
Drake, H. A., 55, 62, 63, 64
Drescher, Seymour, 174
Duby, George, 219
Duffy, Eamon, 31
Durant, Will, 118

early Christians
beliefs viewed as heretical by Jews, 15–16
conflicts with Jews, 14–16
conversion of Jews by, 15
Jewish attempts to punish, for heresy, 16
as minority, 15
original questions debated by, 38
earth, 1–2
Edbury, Peter, 101
Edison, Thomas, 233n2
Egypt, 13
Ehrman, Bart D., 42
Einstein, Albert, 165
on comprehensibility of the universe, 162
Eleusinian mysteries, 61
Eleventh Christian Commandment. *See The Eleventh Commandment*
The Eleventh Commandment, 27, 29
Elkins, Stanley M., 174
Ellerbe, Helen, 133
Emich of Leisingen, 20–21, 109
empiricism
medieval universities dominant force of, 142
as observation basis of science, 146
The Encyclopedia of Religious Freedom, 118

Encyclopedia of Science and Technology
(Asimov), 152
Engels, Friederich, 199
Engerman, Stanley L., 174
England, 24, 156, 158
the Enlightenment
anti-Catholic falsehoods during, 3
myth of, 83, 87–88
philosophes condemnation of religion
by, 194–95
religion, atheists and, 3, 195
after the Renaissance, 4, 74
science main advances in, 87–88
scientists religious faith important to,
87–88
Western History as third era of, 75
Ephraim of Bonn, 22–23
Eugene IV (pope), 170–71
Eusebius, 16, 50, 54, 57, 61
expulsion, 13
of Jews, 24–25

faith, 73, 89
act of, 121–22
science and, 87–88, 156
Feuerbach, Ludwig, 136
Flavius Claudius Julianus. *See* Julian
(emperor)
Flavius Clemens, 12
Fletcher, Richard, 26
*For the Glory of God: How Monotheism Led
to Reformation, Science, Witch-Hunts
and the End of Slavery* (Stark), 179
Foxe, John, 117
France, 24
Franco, Francisco (general), 202–4
French Revolution
on attempt to end religion, 196
Church declared enemy of, 188, 195–99
Church property taken by, 196
Church support of reforms before, 195
clergy executed during, 197
Committee of Public Safety, 196
Cult of Reason during, 195, 198
dechristianizing France goal of, 197
juring clergy oath of support to, 196
Napoleon concordat with Pius VII, 197
non-juring clergy criminalization of,
196–97
tithe relinquished by Church during,
195–96
Fulk III, count of Anjou, 104
Funk, Robert, 38, 40

Galileo
*Dialogue Concerning the Two Chief World
Systems* by, 165
in historical context, 164–66
as martyr to blind faith false, 135, 136,
163
religious despite Church conflict with,
166
Garden of Eden, 46
Gay, Peter, 175
Genovese, Eugene, 182
Gibbon, Edward
on Christian anti-paganism, 53
Christianization of Rome causes
of, 54
Crusades comments by, 95
Dark Ages myth perpetrator of, 76, 83
on the fall of Rome, 74
on "final destruction of Paganism," 67
*The History of the Decline and Fall of the
Roman Empire* by, 3
Julian praise of, 61
Gidal, Nachum T., 19, 28
Gies, Frances and Joseph, 78
Gimpel, Jean, 76, 79
Ginzburg, Carlo, 120
Giordano, Fra, 90
Gnostic Gospels. *See The Gospel of Judas;
The Gospel of Mary;* lost gospels; *The
Secret Book of John; The Secret Gospel
of Thomas*
God Against the Gods (Kirsch), 54
The God Delusion (Dawkins), 167
Godfrey of Bouillon, 93–94, 106–7
Golden Age, in Muslim Spain, 24–25
Goldhagen, Daniel Jonah, 33
The Gospel of Judas
discovery, 37, 42
Judas as most trusted apostle of, 42
mysteries of kingdom in, 42
The Gospel of Mary
among best-selling Gnostic texts, 37
discovery of, 38
female Church leadership and author-
ity of, 41
Mary Magdalene author of, 40
Mary Magdalene most important dis-
ciple of, 41
Mary Magdalene view of, 41
as radical interpretation of Jesus, 40
unreality of sin in, 41
The Gospel of Mary Magdalene (Leloup),
41–42